Eyewitness Accounts of the Restoration

Eyewitness Accounts of the Restoration

Milton V. Backman, Jr.

Deseret Book Company
Salt Lake City, Utah

© 1983 Milton V. Backman, Jr.
© 1986 Deseret Book Company

All rights reserved. No part of this book may be reproduced
in any form or by any means without permission in writing
from the publisher, Deseret Book Company, P.O. Box 30178,
Salt Lake City, Utah 84130.

Deseret Book is a registered trademark of Deseret Book Company.

First published by Grandin Book Company in 1983
First printed by Deseret Book Company July 1986

Library of Congress Catalog Card Number 86-71255

ISBN 0-87579-027-5

Printed in the United States of America

10   9   8   7   6   5   4   3   2

CONTENTS

PREFACE

In 1830, Parley P. Pratt, a young traveling preacher from Ohio, proclaimed to the inhabitants of western New York that God's authority was not upon the earth and that there was a need to restore the primitive purity of the New Testament Church. As he unfolded his message of concern, an old Baptist deacon told him that a "very strange book" had recently been published. This book, he added, is "purported to have been originally written on plates either of gold or brass, by a branch of the tribes of Israel; and to have been discovered and translated by a young man who lived near Palmyra, New York."

"How or where may I obtain this book?" Parley enquired.

"If you return tomorrow," the Baptist responded in essence, "I shall have a copy available."

The next morning, Parley P. Pratt returned to the deacon's home where he was given a book entitled, "The Book of Mormon." "I opened it with eagerness," Parley recalled, "and read its title page. I then read the testimony of several witnesses in relation to the manner of its being found and translated. After this I commenced its contents by course. I read all day; eating was a burden, I had no desire for food; sleep was a burden when the night came, for I preferred reading to sleep.

"As I read, the spirit of the Lord was upon me, and I knew and comprehended that the book was true, as plainly . . . as a man comprehends and knows that he exists. My joy was now full."

After receiving a witness that this book contained "the fulness of the gospel of a crucified and risen Redeemer," Parley P. Pratt traveled to Palmyra to seek more information about the coming forth of this ancient record. From there, he was directed to a farm located in Manchester, a few miles south of Palmyra, where Parley met Hyrum Smith, brother of Joseph Smith the latter-day prophet. Hyrum told him the particulars of the discovery of the record, its translation, the restoration of God's authority, and the organization of Christ's church in the latter-days.

"After duly weighing the whole matter in mind," Parley declared, "I saw clearly that these things were true." Believing in the reality of the restoration and in the authenticity of a book that was a new witness for Christ, the itinerant from Ohio sought baptism and joined the restored Church which had recently been organized.

The strange book that had been given to Parley P. Pratt by a Baptist deacon changed the life of this restorationist. "This discovery," he testified, greatly enlarged "his heart and filled his soul with joy and gladness." He declared that the information contained in the Book of Mormon was more precious than all the riches of the world. "Yes," he concluded, "I would not at that time have exchanged the knowledge I then possessed, for a legal title to all the beautiful farms, houses, villages and property which passed in review before me, on my journey through one of the most flourishing settlements of western New York."[1]

— — —

The story of the restoration of the everlasting gospel is one of the most remarkable histories in the annals of mankind. Joseph Smith, the young prophet-leader, and the men who followed him witnessed many remarkable events during the decade of the 1820s preparatory to the formal organization on April 6, 1830 of The Church of Jesus Christ of Latter-day Saints (referred to in this work as the Church or restored Church). All six men who participated in the organization of the Church were special witnesses of the restoration. Some learned through an angelic visitation and a voice from heaven that the Book of Mormon had been translated by the gift and power of God. All these men and others examined carefully the ancient record from which the translation had been made. One of these six men, Oliver Cowdery, not only viewed the ancient record and handled the plates, but, through the laying on of hands by messengers sent from God, received with Joseph Smith the authority to act in the name of God. The testimonies of these men are invaluable in understanding and appreciating these experiences.

Events leading to the organization of the Church have been related by many, both friend and foe, but no single compilation has been made of many of the unusual and powerful histories of this period which were recorded by the participants themselves shortly after the events transpired.

In 1951, Francis W. Kirkham published an exceptional collection of primary sources of the "evidence of divine power in the coming forth of the Book of Mormon" (*A New Witness for Christ in America*, 2 vols., 1951.) Since that work was published, many new records have been located and many specialized studies have been written that relate to the theme of

---

[1]Parley P. Pratt, *Autobiography of Parley Parker Pratt*, ed. Parley P. Pratt (Salt Lake City: Deseret Book Co., 1976), pp. 36-39.

Kirkham's history. Many sources cited by Francis W. Kirkham (along with many other primary and secondary accounts) have been incorporated into this volume but in a form very different from that employed by that scholar.

The purpose of this work is to reproduce the testimonies (descriptions of that which they saw and learned) of the participants in the restoration movement as they were initially recorded or published. Included in this publication are selections from all of Joseph Smith's major accounts of the rise of the Church. Two of these accounts were first published in 1842, and two were not published until 1969.

This volume begins with Joseph Smith's descriptions of his birth in Vermont in 1805, certain episodes in New England, and the Smith family's move to New York in 1816. To these accounts by Joseph have been added selected writings covering the same two decades recorded by his mother, Lucy Mack Smith. Descriptions of Joseph Smith's First Vision and the early appearances of Moroni have also been reproduced as initially recorded or published. Moreover, this volume contains early historical accounts of the restoration of the lesser and higher priesthoods, testimonies of the witnesses to the Book of Mormon, accounts of the publication of that record, and descriptions of the organization of the Church.

While many selections included in this work have been reproduced from the earliest recordings or publications of events, in a few instances secondary sources have been cited. The secondary sources have been selected from the writings of contemporaries who, according to the compiler, generally wrote reliable accounts, based on what they learned from the participants of the restoration.

The chapters in this work, therefore, contain the writings of Joseph Smith regarding a certain aspect of his experiences plus accounts recorded by his contemporaries. Joseph's writings have been integrated so that, in most instances, four different histories prepared by Joseph have been combined into one account. In these integrated narratives, the compiler has attempted to preserve the flavor of Joseph Smith's histories by reproducing almost verbatim that which the Prophet wrote. For the convenience of the reader (for the sake of clarity and standardization of different types of sources, published and unpublished), editorial changes have been made in spelling, capitialization, punctuation, and grammar so that the writings reflect current English usage. A few transitional words (inserted in brackets) have also been added so that the integrated accounts flow as one continuous narrative.

Included in the writings of Joseph Smith are all histories which were written or dictated by the Prophet or prepared and published under his supervision. Joseph Smith, for example, commenced writing a history of the Church in April 1838. On occasions, he was probably assisted in this activity by Sidney Rigdon, First Counselor in the Presidency of the Church.[2] This project was interrupted in October 1838 by the illegal imprisonment of the Prophet and the expulsion of the Saints from Missouri. Following Joseph's flight from Missouri in the spring of 1839, and his settlement in Commerce (renamed Nauvoo), Illinois, the Prophet resumed work on this history. In June of that year, aided by his scribe, James Mulholland, Joseph Smith dictated (with possible editorial changes and polishing) the history he had written in Missouri and then continued the work.[3] Between June and October 1839, Joseph supervised the preparation of a fifty-nine page manuscript history of the Church covering the period from 1805 to September 1830. Although this work was again temporarily interrupted by the untimely death of Mulholland and Joseph Smith's trip to the national capital to secure redress for crimes committed against the Saints in Missouri, Joseph, with the assistance of various scribes and historians continued to record this history until his martyrdom in 1844.

The first portion of the history of the Church (the manuscript that is in Mulholland's handwriting) was published in the *Times and Seasons* (a Mormon periodical printed in Nauvoo) between March 15, 1842, and March 1, 1843. When the publication began in serial form under the heading, "History of Joseph Smith," the Mormon Prophet was editor of that periodical. This account of the birth of Mormonism was introduced by the statement: "In the last number I gave a brief history of the rise and progress of the Church, I now enter more particularly into that history, and extract from my journal. (Joseph Smith)"[4] The initial printing of the early history of the Church written by Joseph with the assistance of Mulholland was a faithful rendition of the manuscript. Only minor editorial changes appeared in the printed work.

This work, then, is primarily a compilation of eyewitness accounts of some of the extraordinary events that led to the publication of the Book of

---

[2]Joseph Smith, *History of the Church of Jesus Christ of Latter-day Saints*, ed. B. H. Roberts, 7 vols. (Salt Lake City: The Church of Jesus Christ of Latter-day Saints, 1932-51), 3:35-36; 1:2, 18-19 (hereafter cited as *HC*).

[3]*HC* 3:375; Joseph Smith, Diary, June 10-14, 1839, Archives of The Church of Jesus Christ of Latter-day Saints (hereafter cited as Church Archives); Journal of James Mulholland, June 10-24, 1839, Church Archives.

[4]*Times and Seasons* 3 (March 15, 1842):726 (hereafter cited as *T&S*).

Mormon and the reestablishment of Christ's Church upon the earth. These events have important consequences for each of us, as well as for those who experienced them. This is their story—their testimonies in their own words. These testimonies of the authenticity of a sacred record and the reliability of the writings of a Prophet and his contemporaries are a powerful, modern witness of the reality of the restoration of the everlasting gospel.

ACKNOWLEDGMENTS

Although it is impossible to thank adequately all who have shared historical notes and references, read portions of the manuscript, offered suggestions, and assisted in other respects in the preparation of this work, a special note of appreciation is extended to Reid E. Bankhead for his constant encouragement and timely suggestions and to my father, Milton V. Backman, for his keen legalistic comments. Special appreciation is also extended to many of my colleagues who shared their insights and knowledge, including Richard L. Anderson, Larry Porter, J. Donl Peterson, Monte S. Nyman, and Lyndon W. Cook.

This work also could not have been completed without the cooperation of the staffs of many libraries and the assistance of many students enrolled at Brigham Young University. Librarians serving in the Archives of The Church of Jesus Christ of Latter-day Saints and the Reorganized Church of Jesus Christ of Latter Day Saints; the Special Collections libraries at Brigham Young University, Oberlin College, and Bowling Green State University; the Palmyra Kings Daughters Free Public Library (New York); the Ontario County Historians Office (Lyons); Waterloo and Seneca Falls historical societies; Western Reserve (Cleveland, Ohio) and Lake County historical societies; Library of Congress; Missouri Historical Society (St. Louis); State Historical Society of Missouri (Columbia); and Kansas City Public Library were especially helpful. Many students also assisted by typing, proofreading, and searching for information relating to the birth of Mormonism.

Appreciation is further extended to the Archives of The Church of Jesus Christ of Latter-day Saints for granting permission to quote from the 1832 manuscript of the life of Joseph Smith, the Prophet's 1835 diary, and other similar manuscripts and to Brent F. Ashworth, Provo, Utah, for extending to the writer permission to quote from the Lucy Smith letter dated January 23, 1829, and the Martin Harris letter dated January 13, 1873. Grateful acknowledgment is further extended to my wife, Kathleen McLatchy Backman, for her continual assistance and frequent suggestions.

CHAPTER ONE

Boyhood of a Prophet

I was born in the year of our Lord one thousand eight hundred and five, on the twenty-third day of December, in the town of Sharon, Windsor County, state of Vermont...My father, Joseph Smith, Sr., left the state of Vermont and moved to Palmyra, Ontario (now Wayne) County, in the state of New York, when I was in my tenth year, or thereabout [s][1] (Joseph Smith)

As Joseph Smith commenced dictating a history of the restoration movement in 1838, he discussed the earliest events in his life, including his birth in Vermont and his move to New York. Since this history included an account of the appearance of God, the Father, and His son, Jesus Christ, to a nineteenth-century prophet, the appearance of angels to

---

[1]"Joseph Smith-History," The Pearl of Great Price (Salt Lake City: The Church of Jesus Christ of Latter-day Saints, 1981), 1:3 (hereafter cited as JS-H; T&S 3 (March 15, 1842):727; and HC 1:2.) As explained in the Preface, the spelling, punctuation, capitalization, and grammar in this and other quotations from the writings of Joseph Smith have been edited to harmonize with current English usage. Although a few words have been rearranged for the sake of clarity, the ideas recorded by Joseph Smith and his scribes have not been changed. Generally, the words appear in this work as initially published in the *Times and Seasons* and the orthography generally harmonizes with the account published in The Pearl of Great Price.

1

this prophet and his close associates, and of the coming forth of a book that was a modern witness for Christ, inquirers might ask, "Was Joseph Smith a trustworthy individual?" "Was he a reliable historian?" and "How accurate are the historical writings which he (with the assistance of scribes) produced?" As this volume unfolds, these questions will be considered from different avenues of investigation. The initial approach will be to consider the reliability of Joseph Smith's writings concerning the earliest events in his life, events that transpired before his First Vision of 1820.

Most of the information available concerning the boyhood of Joseph Smith is located in the writings of the Prophet and his mother, Lucy Mack Smith. On four different occasions Joseph Smith wrote or dictated to scribes accounts of his religious experiences of the 1820's, and in three of these histories the Prophet briefly described events in his life that occurred before his First Vision in the spring of 1820. The first of these three accounts was an autobiography which was partly written by the Prophet and partly dictated to Frederick G. Williams in the fall of 1832. Although this autobiography was never completed, it included a few details not found elsewhere concerning his early activities in New England, and his move to New York. Another history (mentioned in the Preface) was commenced by the Prophet in 1838 and was initially published in Nauvoo in the *Times and Seasons* in serial form beginning in March 1842. Included at the end of this history (as Note A) is a description of Joseph's leg operation which occurred while the Smiths were living in New Hampshire. Another brief history was prepared by the Prophet (with the probable assistance of others) at the request of John Wentworth, editor of the *Chicago Democrat*, and this account was also initially published in the *Times and Seasons* in 1842. Although the Wentworth Letter was the last known history written by the Prophet, this account was the first of the Prophet's histories to be published. Primary sources relating to Joseph Smith's First Vision (plus other contemporary accounts) have previously been published in Milton V. Backman, Jr.'s *Joseph Smith's First Vision* (Salt Lake City: Bookcraft, 1980).

Some information, not found in any other primary source, relating to the boyhood of Joseph Smith was included in a family history prepared by Lucy Mack Smith. During the winter following the martyrdom of Joseph Smith, Lucy commenced dictating this history (which included a biography of her son, Joseph) to Martha Jane Knowlton Coray, a school teacher who had married Howard Coray, one of the scribes who had assisted Joseph in writing his history.[2] In an attempt to obtain increased accuracy in her work, Lucy directed Martha and Howard Coray to assist in rewriting her history.[3] A copy of the revised edition of Lucy's manuscript was obtained by her son, William. Eventually a copy of the document was secured by Isaac Sheen, a member of the Church living in Michigan. While Orson Pratt, a member of the Quorum of the Twelve Apostles, was traveling to England on a mission, he was shown the manuscript copy and purchased it from Sheen. This work was subsequently published in England under the title *Biographical Sketches of Joseph Smith, the Prophet, and his Progenitors for many Generations* (Liverpool: published for Orson Pratt and S. W. Richards, 1853). Selections from Lucy's history cited in this work are based upon the first published edition. A comparison has been made of Lucy's manuscript histories with the initial publication of her work and when a printing error occurred or when there was an omission of information that relates to the subject being discussed, words appearing in Lucy's manuscripts are quoted, with a footnote identifying the change.

---

[2]Joseph F. Smith, "History of the Prophet Joseph, by His Mother, Lucy Smith," *Improvement Era* 5 (November 1901):1; Lucy Smith's manuscript history (preliminary manuscript) p. 1, Church Archives; and Martha Jane Coray to Brigham Young, June 13, 1865, Church Archives. A copy of this letter has been reprinted in Howard Clair Searle, "Early Mormon Historiography: Writing the History of the Mormons, 1830-1858" (Ph.D. diss., University of California, Los Angeles, 1979), Appendix C.

[3]Autobiography of Howard Coray, p. 16, Church Archives. Howard Coray wrote that during the winter of 1844-45, Mother Smith requested his wife to assist her in writing the "history of Joseph; to act in the matter, only as her, Mother Smith's, amanuensis. This, my wife was persuaded to do; and so dropped the school. Not long had she worked in this direction, before I was requested also to drop the school and turn it over to Bro. William and Woolley, and help her in the matter of this history. After consulting Prest. Young, who advised me to do so, I consented; and immediately set to with my might. We labored together until the work was accomplished, which took us till near the close of 1845." Since Mother Smith did not die until May 3, 1856, she was in a position to review and approve the revisions made by the Corays. (Searle, "Early Mormon Historiography," pp. 384-85.)

A Selection from Joseph Smith's Diary for November 9, 1835 (in the handwriting of Warren Cowdery)

Selection from Joseph Smith's "1832 History"
The first half of the page is in the handwriting of Frederick G. Williams and the last half (the portion following the long dash) is in the handwriting of Joseph Smith.

Orson Pratt

Joseph Smith

Of particular significance in Joseph and Lucy's writings is the description of Joseph Smith's leg operation. Joseph's account was not published until after Lucy's death and was probably never examined by his mother. Therefore, the two independent descriptions of this event are now available for comparison. According to one contemporary, Lucy's account reads like a modern day medical report and includes many details that add credibility to this as well as her other writings.[4] Joseph, meanwhile, wrote his account from the perspective of the patient, yet the harmony in the two accounts is striking, and it provides evidence that Joseph and Lucy were reliable, trustworthy historians who had a capacity to describe accurately events which they witnessed.

******

Selections from the Writings of Joseph and Lucy Smith
Concerning his Boyhood Years

Joseph Smith

I was born in the year of our Lord one thousand eight hundred and five, on the twenty-third day of December, in the town of Sharon, Windsor County, . . . Vermont.[5]

Lucy Smith

After selling the farm at Tunbridge, we moved only a short distance, to the town of Royalton. Here we resided a few months, then moved again to Sharon, Windsor county, Vermont. In the latter place, my husband rented a farm of my father, which he cultivated in the summer, teaching school in the winter. In this way my husband continued labouring for a few years, during which time our circumstances gradually improved, until we found ourselves quite comfortable again.

---

[4]LeRoy S. Wirthlin, "Nathan Smith (1762-1828) Surgical Consultant to Joseph Smith," *BYU Studies* 17 (Spring 1977):319-337 and LeRoy S. Wirthlin, "Joseph Smith's Boyhood Operation: An 1813 Surgical Success," *BYU Studies* 21 (Spring 1981):131-54.

[5]JS-H 1:3 and *T&S* 3 (March 15, 1842):727.

In the meantime we had a son, whom we called Joseph, after the name of his father; he was born December 23, 1805. I shall speak of him more particularly by and by.

We moved thence to Tunbridge. Here we had another son, whom we named Samuel Harrison, born March 13, 1808. We lived in this place a short time, then moved to Royalton, where Ephraim was born, March 13, 1810. We continued here until we had another son, born March 13, 1811, whom we called William . . . .

In 1811, we moved from Royalton, Vermont, to the town of Lebanon, New Hampshire . . . .

As our children had, in a great measure, been debarred from the privilege of schools, we began to make every arrangement to attend to this important duty. We established our second son Hyrum in an academy at Hanover; and the rest, that were of sufficient age, we were sending to a common school that was quite convenient. Meanwhile, myself and companion were doing all that our abilities would admit of for the future welfare and advantage of the family, and were greatly blessed in our labours.

But this state of things did not long continue. The typhus fever came into Lebanon, and raged tremendously.[6]

Accounts of Joseph's Leg Operation

Joseph Smith

When I was five years old or thereabouts, I was attacked with the typhus fever, and at one time, during my sickness, my father despaired of my life. The doctor broke the fever, after which it settled under my shoulder. Dr. Parker called it a sprained shoulder and anointed it with bone ointment and freely applied the hot shovel when it proved to be a swelling under the arm. After it was opened, it discharged freely. Later the disease descended into my left leg and ankle and terminated in a fever sore of the worst kind. I endured the most acute suffering for a long time under the care of doctors [Nathan] Smith, Stone and [Cyrus] Perkins of

---

[6]Lucy Mack Smith, *Biographical Sketches of Joseph Smith, the Prophet and his Progenitors for Many Generations* (Liverpool: published for Orson Pratt and S. W. Richards, 1853), pp. 56-60 (hereafter cited as Lucy Smith, *Biographical Sketches*).

Hanover.[7] At one time eleven doctors came from Dartmouth Medical College, at Hanover, New Hampshire, for the purpose of amputation, but, young as I was, I utterly refused to give my assent to the operation, but I consented to their trying an experiment by removing a large portion of the bone from my left leg, which they did, and before my leg healed, fourteen additional pieces of bone were removed. During this time I was reduced so very low that my mother could carry me with ease. After I began to recover, I went about on crutches until I started for the state of New York.[8]

Lucy Smith

Joseph, our third son, having recovered from the typhus fever, after something like two weeks' sickness, one day screamed out while sitting in a chair, with a pain in his shoulder, and, in a very short time, he appeared to be in such agony, that we feared that consequence would prove to be something very serious. We immediately sent for a doctor. When he arrived, and had examined the patient, he said that it was his opinion that this pain was occasioned by a sprain. But the child declared this could not be the case, as he had received no injury in any way whatever, but that a severe pain had seized him all at once, of the cause of which he was entirely ignorant.

Nothwithstanding the child's protestations, still the physician insisted, that it must be a sprain, and consequently, he anointed his shoulder with some bone linament; but this was of no advantage to him, for the pain continued the same after the anointing as before.

When two weeks of extreme suffering has elapsed, the attendant physician concluded to make closer examination; whereupon he found that a large fever sore had gathered between his breast and shoulder. He immediately lanced it, upon which it discharged fully a quart of matter.

---

[7]The bone infection that caused Joseph Smith such pain has been identified as osteomyelitis and two of the doctors who attended to Joseph were probably doctors "Nathan Smith and Cyrus Perkins, both of Dartmouth Medical School and partners in medical practice." Dr. Nathan Smith "was the only physician in the United States at the time who had the vision, knowledge, and necessary surgical experience to deal successfully with Joseph Smith's medical problems" (Wirthlin, "Nathan Smith, Surgical Consultant to Joseph Smith," pp. 320-21).

[8]Joseph Smith, "1838 History of the Church," Note A, Church Archives.

As soon as the sore had discharged itself, the pain left it, and shot like lightning (using his own terms) down his side into the marrow of the bone of his leg, and soon became very severe. My poor boy, at this, was almost in despair, and he, cried out "Oh, father! the pain is so severe, how can I bear it!"

His leg soon began to swell, and he continued to suffer the greatest agony for the space of two weeks longer. During this period, I carried him much of the time in my arms, in order to mitigate his suffering as much as possible; in consequence of which, I was taken very ill myself. The anxiety of mind that I experienced, together with physical overexertion, was too much for my constitution, and my nature sunk under it.

Hyrum, who was rather remarkable for his tenderness and sympathy, now desired that he might take my place. As he was a good, trusty boy, we let him do so; and, in order to make the task as easy for him as possible, we laid Joseph upon a low bed, and Hyrum sat beside him, almost day and night, for some considerable length of time, holding the affected part of his leg in his hands, and pressing it between them, so that his afflicted brother might be enable to endure the pain, which was so excruciating, that he was scarcely able to bear it.

At the end of three weeks, we thought it advisable to send again for the surgeon. When he came, he made an incision of eight inches, on the front side of the leg, between the knee and the ankle. This relieved the pain in a great measure, and the patient was quite comfortable until the wound began to heal, when the pain became as violent as ever.

The surgeon was called again, and he this time enlarged the wound, cutting the leg even to the bone. It commenced healing the second time, and as soon as it began to heal, it also began to swell again, which swelling continued to rise till we deemed it wisdom to call a council of surgeons; and when they met in consultation, they decided that amputation was the only remedy.

Soon after coming to this conclusion, they rode up to the door, and were invited into a room, apart from the one in which Joseph lay. They being seated, I addressed them thus: "Gentlemen, what can you do to save my boy's leg?" They answered, "We can do nothing; we have cut it open to the bone, and find it so affected that we consider his leg incurable, and that amputation is absolutely necessary in order to save his life."

This was like a thunder bolt to me. I appealed to the principal surgeon, saying, "Dr. Stone, can you not make another trial? Can you not, but cutting around the bone, take out the diseased part, and perhaps that which is sound will heal over, and by this means you will save his leg? You will not, you must not, take off his leg, until you try once more. I will not consent to let you enter his room until you make me this promise."

After consulting a short time with each other, they agreed to do as I had requested, then went to see my suffering son. One of the doctors, on approaching his bed, said, "My poor boy, we have come again." "Yes," said Joseph, "I see you have; but you have not come to take off my leg, have you, sir?" "No," replied the surgeon, "it is your mother's request that we make one more effort, and that is what we have now come for."[9]

My husband who was constantly with the child, seemed to contemplate my countenance; then turning his eyes upon his boy [and] all his suffering together with my anxiety . . . burst into tears and sobbed like a child.[10]

The principal surgeon, after a moment's conversation, ordered cords to be brought to bind Joseph fast to the bedstead; but to this Joseph objected. The doctor, however, insisted that he must be confined, upon which Joseph said very decidedly, "No, doctor, I will not be bound, for I can bear the operation much better if I have my liberty." "Then," said Dr. Stone, "will you drink some brandy?"

"No," said Joseph, "not one drop."

"Will you take some wine?" rejoined the doctor. "You must take something, or you can never endure the severe operation to which you must be subjected."

"No," exclaimed Joseph, "I will not touch one particle of liquor, neither will I be tied down; but I will tell you what I will do—I will have my father sit on the bed and hold me in his arms, and then I will do whatever is necessary in order to have the bone taken out." Looking at me, he said, "Mother, I want you to leave the room, for I know you cannot bear to see me suffer so; father can stand it, but you have carried me so much, and watched over me so long, you are almost worn out." Then looking up into my face, his eyes swimming in tears, he continued, "Now, mother, promise me that you will not stay, will you? The Lord will help me, and I shall get through with it."

To this request I consented, and getting a number of folded sheets, and laying them under his leg, I retired, going several hundred yards from the house in order to be out of hearing.

The surgeons commenced operating by boring into the bone of his leg, first on one side of the bone where it was affected, then on the other

---

[9]Lucy Smith, *Biograpical Sketches*, pp. 62-64.

[10]Lucy Smith's manuscript history, Church Archives.

side, after which they broke it off with a pair of forceps or pincers. They thus took away large pieces of the bone. When they broke off the first piece, Joseph screamed out so loudly, that I could not forbear running to him. On my entering his room, he cried out, "Oh, mother, go back, go back; I do not want you to come in—I will try to tough it out, if you will go away."

When the third piece was taken away, I burst into the room again and oh, my God! what a spectacle for a mother's eye! The wound torn open, the blood still gushing from it, and the bed literally covered with blood. Joseph was as pale as a corpse, and large drops of sweat were rolling down his face, whilst upon every feature was depicted the utmost agony!

I was immediately forced from the room, and detained until the operation was complete; but when the act was accomplished, Joseph put upon a clean bed, the room cleared of every appearnce of blood, and the instruments which were used in the operation removed, I was permitted again to enter.

Joseph immediately commenced getting better, and from this day onward, continued to mend until he became strong and healthy.[11]

Events Following Joseph's Operation

Joseph Smith

When I was in my tenth year or thereabouts, my father left the state of Vermont [after moving from Lebanon, New Hamptshire to Norwich, Vermont] and moved to Palmyra, Ontario (now Wayne) County, New York.[12]

My father had gone to New York for the purpose of preparing a place for the removal of his family, which he effected by sending a man after us by the name of Caleb Howard. Although the snow was generally deep through the country during this journey, we performed the whole on wheels, except the first two days, when we were accompanied by my mother's mother, Grandmother Lydia Mack, who was injured by the upsetting of the sleigh and not wishing to accompany her friends west, tarried by the way with her friends in Vermont. Later we learned of her

---

[11]Lucy Smith, *Biographical Sketches*, pp. 64-65.

[12]Joseph Smith, "History of the Life of Joseph Smith," 1832, Church Archives (hereafter cited as "1832 History") and Joseph Smith, "1838 History of the Church."

death, supposing that she never recovered from the injury received by the overturn of the sleigh. After Howard had started on the journey with my mother and family, he spent the money he had received of my father in drinking, gambling, etc. Meanwhile, we fell in with a family by the name of Gates who was traveling west. Howard drove me from the waggon and made me travel in my weak state through the snow forty miles per day for several days, during which time I suffered the most excruciating weariness and pain—all this that Mr. Howard might enjoy the society of two of Mr. Gates' daughters whom he took on the waggon where I should have ridden. Thus he continued day after day through the journey. When my brothers remonstrated with Mr. Howard for his treatment to me, he knocked them down with the butt of his whip.

When we arrived at Utica, New York, Howard threw the goods out of the waggon into the street and attempted to run away with the horses and waggon, but my mother seized the horses by the reign, and, calling witnesses, forbid his taking them away, as they were her property. On our way from Utica I was left to ride on the last sleigh, belonging to the Gates family. I was knocked down by the driver, one of Gates' sons, and left to wallow in my blood until a stranger came along, picked me up, and carried me to the town of Palmyra. Since Howard had spent all our funds, my mother was compelled to pay our landlords' bills from Utica to Palmyra, in bits of cloth, clothing, etc., the last payment being made with the drops [earrings] taken from sister Sophronia's ears for that purpose. (Note A) Several years after my father's arrival at Palmyra, he moved with his family to Manchester, in the same county of Ontario. His family consisted of eleven souls: namely, my father, Joseph Smith, my mother, Lucy Smith (daughter of Solomon Mack), my brothers Alvin (who died November 18 [19], 1823, in the twenty-fifth year of his age), Hyrum, myself, Samuel Harrison, William, Don Carlos, and my sisters Sophronia, Catherine, and Lucy.[13]

Being in indigent circumstances we were obliged to labor hard for the support of a large family, having nine children. It required the exertions of all that were able to render any assistance for the support of the family. Therefore we were deprived of the benefit of an education. Suffice it to say that I was merely instructed in reading, writing and the ground rules of arithmetic; these constituted my whole literary acquirements.[14]

––––––––––––––––

[13]Joseph Smith, 1838 Manuscript History of the Church, Note A, Church Archives.

[14]"1832 History."

Lucy Smith

When health returned to us, as one would naturally suppose, it found us in quite low circumstances. We were compelled to strain every energy to provide for our present necessities, instead of making arrangements for the future, as we had previously contemplated.

Shortly after sickness left our family, we moved to Norwich, in the state of Vermont. In this place we established ourselves on a farm belonging to one Esquire Moredock. The first year our crops failed; yet, by selling fruit which grew on the place, we succeeded in obtaining bread for the family, and by making considerable exertion, we were enabled to sustain ourselves.

The crops the second year were as the year before—a perfect failure. Mr. Smith now determined to plant once more, and if he should meet with no better success than he had the two preceding years, he would then go to the state of New York, where wheat was raised in abundance.

The next year an untimely frost destroyed the crops, and being the third year in succession in which the crops had failed, it almost caused a famine. This was enough; my husband was now altogether decided upon going to New York. He came in, one day, in quite a thoughtful mood, and sat down; after meditating some time, he observed that, could he so arrange his affairs, he would be glad to start soon for New York with a Mr. [Caleb] Howard, who was going to Palmyra. He further remarked, that he could not leave consistently, as the situation of the family would not admit of his absence; besides, he was owing some money that must first be paid.

I told him it was my opinion he might get both his creditors and debtors together, and arrange matters between them in such a way as to give satisfaction to all parties concerned; and, in relation to the family, I thought I could make every necessary preparation to follow as soon as he would be ready for us. He accordingly called upon all with whom he had any dealings, and settled up his accounts with them. There were, however, some who, in the time of settlement, neglected to bring forward their books, consequently they were not balanced, or there were no entries made in them to show the settlement; but in cases of this kind, he called witnesses, that there might be evidence of the fact.

Having thus arranged his business, Mr. Smith set out for Palmyra, in company with Mr. Howard. After his departure, I and those of the family who were of much size, toiled faithfully, until we considered ourselves fully prepared to leave at a moment's warning. We shortly received a communication from Mr. Smith, requesting us to make ourselves ready to take up a journey for Palmyra. In a short time after this, a team came for us. As we were about starting on this journey, several of those gentlemen who had withheld their books in the time of settlement now brought them forth, and claimed the accounts which had been settled, and which they had, in the presence of witnesses, agreed to erase. We were all ready for the journey, and the teams were waiting on expense. Under these circumstances I concluded it would be more to our advantage to pay their unjust claims than to hazard a lawsuit. Therefore, by making considerable exertion, I raised the required sum, which was one hundred and fifty dollars, and liquidated the demand.

A gentlemen by the name of Flog, a wealthy settler, living in the town of Hanover, also a Mr. Howard, who resided in Norwich, were both acquainted with the circumstance mentioned above. They were very indignant at it, and requested me to give them a sufficient time to get the witnesses together, and they would endevour to recover that which had been taken from me by fraud. I told them I could not do so, for my husband had sent teams for me, which were on expense; moreover, there was an uncertainty in getting the money back again, and in case of failure, I should not be able to raise the means necessary to take the family where we contemplated moving.

They then proposed raising some money by subscription, saying, "We know the people feel as we do concerning this matter, and if you will receive it *we* will make you a handsome present." This I utterly refused. The idea of receiving assistance in such a way as this was indeed very repulsive to my feelings, and I rejected their offer.

My aged mother, who had lived with us some time, assisted in preparing for the journey. She came with us to Royalton, where she resided until she died, which was two years afterwards, in consequence of an injury which she received by getting upset in a waggon while travelling with us.

On arriving at Royalton I had a scene to pass through, and it was truly a severe one—one to which I shall ever look back with peculiar feelings. Here I was to take leave of my affectionate mother. The parting hour came; my mother wept over me, long and bitterly. She told me that it was not probable she should ever behold my face again; "But, my dear child," said she, "I have lived long—my days are nearly numbered—I must soon exchange the things of this world for those which pertain to another state of existence, where I hope to enjoy the society of the blessed; and now, as my last admonition, I beseech you to continue faithful in the service of God to the end of your days, that I may have the pleasure of embracing you in another and fairer world above."

This parting scene was at one Willard Pierce's, a tavern keeper. From his house my mother went to Daniel Mack's, with whom she afterwards lived until her decease.

Having travelled a short distance, I discovered that Mr. Howard, our teamster, was an unprincipled and unfeeling wretch, by the way in which he handled both our goods and money, as well as by his treatment of my children, especially Joseph. He would compel him to travel miles at a time on foot, notwithstanding he was still lame. We bore patiently with his abuse, until we got about twenty miles west of Utica, when one morning, as we were getting ready to continue our journey, my oldest son came to me and said, "Mother, Mr. Howard has thrown the goods out of the waggon, and is about starting off with the team." Upon hearing this, I told him to call the man in. I met him in the bar-room, in the presence of a large company of travellers, both male and female, and I demanded his reason for the course which he was taking. He told me the money which I had given him was all expended, and he could go no further.

I then turned to those present and said, "Gentlement and ladies, please give your attention for a moment. Now, as sure as there is a God in heaven, that team, as well as the goods, belong to my husband, and this man intends to take them from me, or at least the team, leaving me with eight children, without the means of proceeding on my journey." Then turning to Mr. Howard, I said, "Sir, I now forbid you touching the team, or driving it one step further. You can go about your own business; I have no use for you. I shall take charge of the team myself, and hereafter attend to my own affairs." I accordingly did so, and, proceeding our journey, we in a short time arrived at Palmyra, with a small portion of our effects, and barely two cents in cash.

When I again met my husband at Palmyra, we were much reduced— not from indolence, but on account of many reverses of fortune, with which our lives had been rather singularly marked. Notwithstanding our misfortunes, and the embarassments with which we were surrounded, I was quite happy in once more having the society of my husband, and in throwing myself and the children upon the care and affection of a tender companion and father.

We all now sat down, and counselled together relative to the course which was best for us to adopt in our destitute circumstances, and we came to the conclusion to unite our strength in endeavouring to obtain a piece of land. Having done considerable at painting oil-cloth coverings for tables, stands, &c., I set up the business, and did extremely well. I furnished all the provisions for the family, and, besides this, began to replenish our housbold furniture, in a very short time, by my own exertions.

My husband and his sons, Alvin and Hyrum, set themselves to work to pay for one hundred acres of land, which Mr. Smith contracted for with a land agent. In a year, we made nearly all of the first payment, erected a log house, and commenced clearing. I believe something like thirty acres of land were got ready for cultivation the first year . . . . [15]

When the time for making the second payment [of the farm] drew nigh, Alvin went from home to get work, in order to raise the money, and after much hardship and fatigue, returned with the required amount. This payment being made, we felt relieved, as this was the only thing that troubled us; for we had a snug log-house, neatly furnished, and the means of living comfortably. It was now only two years since we entered Palmyra, almost destitute of money, property, or acquaintance. The hand of friendship was extended on every side, and we blessed God, with our whole heart, for his "mercy, which endureth for ever."[16]

I now come to the history of Joseph . . . I shall say nothing respecting him until he arrived at the age of fourteen. However, in this I am aware that some of my readers will be disappointed, for I suppose, from questions which are frequently asked me, that it is thought by some that I shall be likely to tell many very remarkable incidents which attended his childhood; but, as nothing occurred during his early life, except those trivial circumstances which are common to that state of human existence, I pass them in silence.[17]

---

[15]Lucy Smith, *Biographical Sketches*, pp. 66-70.

[16]Ibid., p. 71.

[17]Ibid., p. 73.

CHAPTER TWO

The Calling of a Prophet

Surely the Lord God will do nothing, but he revealeth his secret unto his servants the prophets. (Amos 3:7.)

One of the most important events in the religious history of the world occurred in a serene grove in the spring of 1820. A young farm boy, fourteen years of age, was called by God to be a modern witness for Christ and to usher in the fulness of the everlasting gospel. In response to Joseph Smith's humble prayer, God the Eternal Father and His Son, Jesus Christ, appeared and instructed the young man. The Father introduced the Son, and the Savior unfolded a momentous message. For hundreds of years a prophet had not been available to guide God's children on earth, but now with the heavens parting, light and knowledge burst upon the inhabitants of this world. During this divine call, Joseph Smith learned more about the nature and personality of God than anyone then living. He also learned that all churches were teaching incorrect doctrines and was promised that the fulness of the gospel would be revealed to him. As he walked from the sacred grove in western New York, he was endowed with a peace and joy that he had never previously experienced and a responsibility that was distinct among men of the early nineteenth century.

On four different occasions Joseph Smith wrote or dictated a detailed account of this marvelous and sacred experience of 1820. Three of these recitals were referred to in Chapter One: the autobiography and history written in 1832 (which is the only account of the First Vision in Joseph's handwriting, the others being dictated to scribes), the history of the Church which was initiated in 1838, and the Wentworth Letter. A fourth history is the record of a conversation between Joseph Smith and a visitor to Kirtland, Ohio, a man named Matthias. This latter account was recorded in Joseph Smith's Kirtland diary by his scribe, Warren Cowdery, under the date Monday, November 9th, 1835.

As one reads the full text of the four accounts of the First vision, he should remember that the accounts are of various lengths, were prepared under different circumstances at different periods in the life of the Prophet, and were addressed to different audiences. It is not surprising, therefore, that each of them emphasize different aspects of his experience. When Latter-day Saints today explain this remarkable vision to others, their descriptions often vary according to the audience or circumstances that prompt such recitals. If one were relating the incident to a group of high priests, for example, he would undoubtedly tell it somewhat differently than he would to individuals who had never heard of Joseph Smith or the restoration of the gospel.

One can better understand and appreciate the different emphases in Joseph's four recitals of the First Vision by examining their individual historical setting, by considering Joseph's efforts to write history, and by noting his attempts to improve the form in which the basic message of the restoration was conveyed to others.[1]

For example, in the 1832 account Joseph Smith emphasized his long quest for religious truth which emerged from his desire to secure a remission of sins. A concern for the welfare of his soul led him to an investigation of religious communities, and this investigation convinced the young boy that religious leaders were teaching doctrines that did not harmonize with New Testament Christianity. In 1832 when the Prophet described what he learned during his vision, he emphasized that the Lord forgave him of his sins, instructed him concerning the atonement, and said that others had turned aside from the gospel and were not keeping his commandments.[2] Although in this account the Prophet does not refer to the appearance of the Father, the absence of this fact, along with the absence of other details, does not mean that Joseph did not behold the Father. In the two accounts addressed to non-Mormons, the Prophet said that two personages appeared to him without identifying those

---

[1]Milton V. Backman, Jr., *Joseph Smith's First Vision*, 2d ed. enlarged (Salt Lake City: Bookcraft, 1980), p. 202.

[2]Ibid.

personages. In his official history and in a number of contemporary accounts of the First Vision we read that after the two personages appeared the Father introduced the Son by saying, "This is my Beloved Son. Hear Him!" Joseph never wrote a complete description of everything he learned from the Lord in 1820, and in his official history, which is the most complete account of this experience, the Prophet concluded by declaring that "Many other things did he say unto me which I cannot write at this time."

In addition to the four accounts recorded by Joseph Smith regarding his visions, before the Prophet's death in 1844, four contemporaries wrote accounts of the First Vision based upon testimonies related to them by the Prophet. The first published account of the First Vision was written by Orson Pratt, and appeared in a work entitled *A Interesting Account of Several Remarkable Visions* (Edinburgh, 1840).

Orson Pratt was well qualified to write a history of the restoration. In addition to his capacity to write clearly and report accurately that which he observed and learned from others, following his conversion in 1830, he generally lived in the communities where Joseph Smith resided. Before and after his call in 1835 to serve as one of the members of the first quorum of the twelve apostles, he often listened as Joseph Smith in private and public gatherings unfolded the history and doctrine of the Church. He was not only a close associate of Joseph Smith but knew all of the other major participants (and members of their families) in the birth of Mormonism.

Orson Hyde, another apostle who was well acquainted with Joseph Smith, also prepared an account of the First Vision. His description of the early visions of Joseph Smith was written in German and was basically a translation of the English version prepared by Orson Pratt. This work, *A Cry from the Wilderness, A Voice From the Dust of the Earth*, was published in 1842 in Frankfurt, Germany.

A third early rendition of Joseph Smith's First Vision was written by a non-Mormon newspaper editor who visited Nauvoo and, following a conversation with the Mormon prophet, published a description of what he learned from Joseph Smith in the New York *Spectator* of September 23, 1843.

On May 24, 1844, one month prior to the death of Joseph Smith, Alexander Neibaur, another convert and friend of the Prophet, listened as Joseph Smith related to him his experience in the sacred grove. Following this conversation, Neibaur recorded in his journal his impressions of what Joseph said on that occasion.

Accounts of Josph Smith's vision of 1820 prepared by Pratt, Hyde, the non-Mormon editor, and Neibaur have been published in Backman's

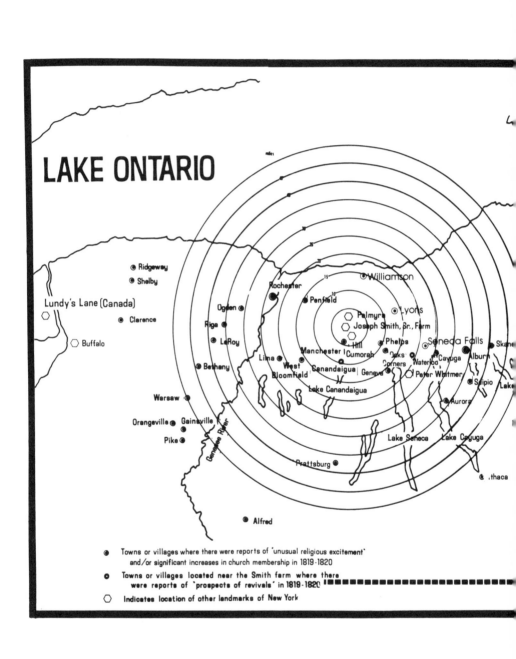

LAKE ONTARIO

miles

Ridgeway
Shelby
Lundy's Lane (Canada)
Clarence
Buffalo

Ogden
Riga
LeRoy
Bethany

Williamson
Rochester
Penfield
Palmyra
Lyons
Joseph Smith, Sr., Farm
Hill
Phelps
Seneca Falls
Skane
Manchester
Cumorah
Oaks
Cayuga
Alburn
Lima
West
Canandaigua
Corners
Waterloo
Bloomfield
Geneva
Peter Whitmer
Scipio
Lake Canandaigua
Lake

Warsaw
Aurora

Orangeville
Gainsville
Pike
Lake Seneca
Lake Cayuga

Prattsburg
,thaca

Alfred

● Towns or villages where there were reports of "unusual religious excitement"
   and/or significant increases in church membership in 1819-1820

◉ Towns or villages located near the Smith farm where there
   were reports of "prospects of revivals" in 1819-1820

○ Indicates location of other landmarks of New York

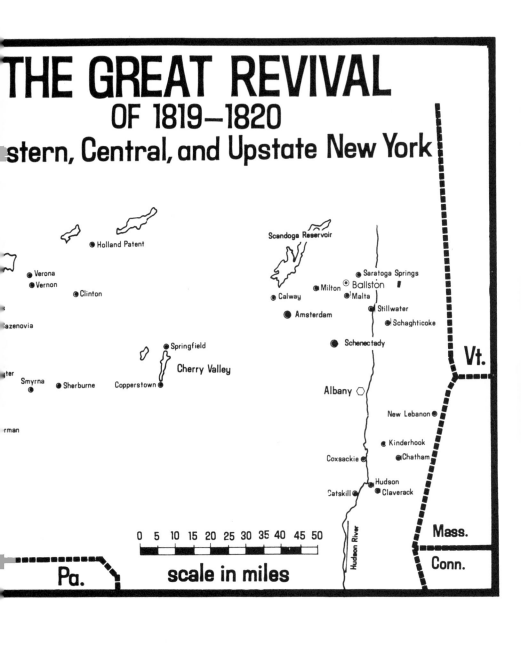

THE GREAT REVIVAL
OF 1819–1820
stern, Central, and Upstate New York

Holland Patent

Scandoga Reservoir

Verona
Vernon
Clinton

Saratoga Springs
Milton ⊙ Ballston
Calway ● Malta
Amsterdam
Stillwater
Schaghticoke

azenovia

Schenectady

Vt.

Springfield
Cherry Valley

ter
Smyrna
Sherburne
Copperstown

Albany ○

New Lebanon ●

rman

Kinderhook ●
Coxsackie ●
Chatham

Hudson
Catskill ● ● Claverack

0 5 10 15 20 25 30 35 40 45 50

Mass.

Hudson River

Pa.

scale in miles

Conn.

Joseph Smith's First Vision. Since these four accounts repeat information written by Joseph Smith, references to these contemporary versions that contain information paralleling Joseph's statements have been included in a harmony printed in Appendix A, with appropriate notations of the sources.

The contemporary accounts of the First Vision clearly substantiate Joseph Smith's narrative; nearly every concept regarding the vision related in Joseph's histories are found in accounts recorded by contemporaries before Joseph's death in 1844. Moreover, there are no major concepts regarding that vision in these secondary sources that are not found in the writings of Joseph Smith. In conclusion, the five contemporary accounts provide evidence that Joseph Smith informed others of his sacred experiences of 1820 and this testimony was the same that he recorded in his histories of the Church.

Joseph Smith also wrote an accurate account of the historical setting of the First Vision. By using the tools of secular historians, one can neither prove nor disprove a vision, but one can assess the reliability of selected statements regarding the background of events. The prophet wrote in the history which he commenced in 1838 that in the second year after his removal to Manchester there was in the place where he lived religious excitement and that in the whole region of country great multitudes united themselves to the different religious persuasions. In addition to describing the war of words and contest of opinions that occurred during this religious quickening and writing that some members of his family joined the Presbyterian church, he declared that following his First Vision he experienced intense persecution. Historical records vindicate the Prophet's writings on all of these points.[3] In conclusion, Joseph Smith not only accurately described the historical setting of his First Vision, but more importantly he accurately reported the message that God unfolded to him in 1820.

The Theophany Near Palmyra

Joseph Smith

[When I was] about...twelve years [old,] my mind became seriously impressed with regard to the all important concerns...of my immortal soul.[4] I began to reflect upon the importance of being prepared

---

[3]Ibid., pp. 92-111, 114-20, 182-83, 195-201.

[4]"1832 History."

for a future state[5] and from the age of twelve years to fifteen. . .my mind became exceedingly distressed for I became convicted [convinced] of my sins. . .I also pondered many things in my heart concerning the situation of the world of mankind, the contentions and divisions, the wickedness and abominations, and the darkness which pervaded the minds of mankind. . .Believing as I was taught that. . .the scriptures. . .contained the word of God, [I] applied myself to them. My intimate acquaintance with those of different denominations led me to marvel exceedingly.[6] I found that there was a great clash of religious sentiment concerning the plan of salvation. If I went to one society they referred me to one plan, and another to another, each one pointing to his own particular creed as the *summum bonum* of perfection.[7] I felt to mourn for my own sins and for the sins of the world.[8]

Some time in the second year after our removal to Manchester, there was in the place where we lived an unusual excitement on the subject of religion. It commenced with the Methodists, but soon became general among all the sects in that region of country. Indeed, the whole district of country seemed affected by it, and great multitudes united themselves to the different religious parties, which created no small stir and division amongst the people, some crying, "Lo, here!" and some "Lo, there!" Some were contending for the Methodist faith, some for the Presbyterian, and some for the Baptist. For, notwithstanding the great love which the converts to these different faiths expressed at the time of their conversion, and the great zeal manifested by the respective clergy, who were active in getting up and promoting this extraordinary scene of religious feelings, in order to have every body converted, as they were pleased to call it, let them join what sect they pleased; yet when the converts began to file off, some to one party, and some to another, it was seen that the seemingly good feelings of both the priests and converts were more pretended than real; for a scene of great confusion and bad feeling ensued—priest contending against priest, and convert against convert, so that all their good feelings one for another, if they every had any, were entirely lost in a

---

[5]Joseph Smith, "Church History," *T&S* 3 (March 1 1842):706-07 (hereafter cited as "1842 History").

[6]"1832 History."

[7]"1842 History."

[8]"1832 History."

strife of words, and a contest about opinions. I was at this time in my fifteenth year. My father's family was proselyted to the Presbyterian faith, and four of them joined that church, namely, my mother, Lucy, my brothers Hyrum and Samuel Harrison; and my sister Sophronia.[9]

During this time of great excitement my mind was called up to serious reflection and great uneasiness; but though my feelings were deep and often poignant, still I kept myself aloof from all these parties, though I attended their several meetings as often as occasional would permit. In process of time my mind became somewhat partial to the Methodist sect, and I felt some desire to be united with them; but so great were the confusion and strife among the different denominations, that it was impossible for a person young as I was, and so unacquainted with men and things, to come to any certain conclusion who was right and who was wrong. My mind at times was greatly excited, the cry and tumult were so great and incessant. The Presbyterians were most decided against the Baptists and Methodists, and used all the powers of either reason or sophistry to prove their errors, or, at least, to make the people think they were in error. On the other hand, the Baptists and Methodists in their turn were equally zealous in endeavoring to establish their own tenets, and disprove all others.

In the midst of this war of words and tumult of opinions, I often said to myself: What is to be done? Who of all these parties are right? Or, are they all wrong together? If any one of them be right, which is it, and how shall I know it?[10] Considering that all could not be right, and that God could not be the author of so much confusion I determined to investigate the subject more fully, believing that if God had a church it would not be split up into factions, and that if he taught one society to worship one way, and administer in one set of ordinances, he would not teach another principles which were diametrically opposed.[11]

While I was laboring under the extreme difficulties caused by the contests of these parties of religionists, I was one day reading the Epistle of James, first chapter and fifth verse, which reads: "If any of you lack wisdom, let him ask of God, that giveth to all men liberally, and

---

[9]The account of the First Vision which was initially published in the *T&S* 3 (March 15-April 1, 1842):727-28, 748-49 and later published in JS-H 1:5-26 is hereafter cited as "1838 History."

[10]"1838 History."

[11]"1842 History."

upbraideth not; and it shall be given him."[12] Never did any passage of scripture come with more power to the heart of man than this did at this time to mine. It seemed to enter with great force into every feeling of my heart. I reflected on it again and again, knowing that if any person needed wisdom from God, I did, for how to act I did not know, and unless I could get more wisdom that I then had, I would never know; for the teachers of religion of the different sects understood the same passage of scripture so differently as to destroy all confidence in settling the question by an appeal to the Bible. At length I came to the conclusion that I must either remain in darkness and confusion, or else I must do as James directs, that is, ask of God. I at length came to the determination to "ask of God," concluding that if he gave wisdom to them that lacked wisdom, and would give liberally, and not upbraid, I might venture. So, in accordance with this, my determination to ask of God, I retired to the woods to make the attempt. It was on the morning of a beautiful, clear day, early in the spring of eighteen hundred and twenty. It was the first time in my life that I had made such an attempt, for amidst all my anxieties I had never as yet made the attempt to pray vocally.[13]

After I had retired to the place where I had previously designed to go, having looked around me, and finding myself alone, I kneeled down and began to offer up the desires of my heart to God.[14] I made a fruitless attempt to pray; my tongue seemed to be swollen in my mouth, so that I could not utter. I heard a noise behind me like some person walking towards me. I sprang up on my feet and looked around, but saw no person or thing that was calculated to produce the noise of walking. I kneeled down again.[15] Immediately I was seized upon by some power which entirely overcame me, and had such astonishing influence over me as to bind my tongue so that I could not speak. Thick darkness gathered around me, and it seemed to me for a time as if I were doomed to sudden destruction. But, exerting all my powers to call upon God to deliver me out of the power of this enemy which had seized upon me, and at the very moment which I was ready to sink into despair and abandon myself to destruction—not to an imaginary ruin, but to the power of some actual

---

[12]"1838 History" and "1842 History." See also Diary of Joseph Smith, November 9, 1835, Church Archives (hereafter cited as "1835 History").

[13]"1838 History."

[14]"1832 History," "1835 History," "1838 History," and "1842 History."

[15]"1835 History."

being from the unseen world, who had such a marvelous power as I had never before felt in any being[16]—just at this moment of great alarm, I saw a pillar of light exactly over my head, above the brightness of the sun, which descended gradually until it fell upon me,[17] and I was filled with the spirit of God.[18] When the light rested upon me, I saw two Personages whose brightness and glory defy all description and who exactly resembled each other in feature and likeness.[19] One of them spake unto me, calling me by name and said pointing to the other—This is My Beloved Son. Hear Him![20] The Lord spake unto me saying, Joseph, my son thy sins are forgiven thee.[21] Go thy way, walk in my statues and keep my commandments. Behold, I am the Lord of glory. I was crucified for the world that all who believe on my name may have eternal life. Behold the world lieth in sin.[22]

My object in going to inquire of the Lord was to know which of all the sects was right, that I might know which to join. No sooner, therefore, did I get possession of myself so as to be able to speak, than I asked the personages who stood above me in the light, which of all the sects was right (for at this time it had never entered into my heart that all were wrong)—and which I should join.[23] I was answered that I must join none

---

[16]"1838 History."

[17]"1832 History," "1835 History," and "1838 History."

[18]"1832 History."

[19]"1835 History," "1838 History," and "1842 History."

[20]"1838 History."

[21]"1832 History" and "1835 History."

[22]"1832 History."

[23]"1838 History." Joseph Smith wrote in his "1832 History" that there was a time during his religious quest when he thought (or decided through an intellectual analysis) that all churches he investigated were wrong. "My mind became exceedingly distressed," he wrote, "and by searching the scriptures I found that mankind did not come unto the Lord but that they had apostatized from the true and living faith and there was no society or denomination that built upon the gospel of Jesus Christ as recorded in the New Testament." In the "1838 History" he said that it never entered his "heart" (deep down in his convictions) that all churches were wrong. At the time of the First Vision Joseph believed (in his heart) that somewhere in the world God's true church existed. Therefore, in the spring of 1820, Joseph asked the Lord, "Which church should I join?"

of them, for they were all wrong, [24] that all religious denominations were believing in incorrect doctrines. [25] The Personage who addressed me said those professors were all corrupt; that: "they draw near to me with their lips, but their hearts are far from me, they teach for doctrines the commandments of men, having a form of godliness, but they deny the power thereof." [26] After informing me that the anger of the Lord was kindled against the inhabitants of the earth because of their ungodliness, the Savior said that everything spoken of by the mouth of the prophets and apostles would be fulfilled and that he would come quickly as prophecied. [27] He again forbade me to join with any of them [28] at the same time receiving a promise that the fulness of the gospel should at some future time be made known unto me. [29] Many other things did he say unto me which I cannot write at this time. [30] I [also] saw many angels in this . . . first communication . . . [or] vision. [31] When I came to myself again, I found myself laying on my back, looking up into heaven. [32]

During this vision my soul was filled with love and for many days following this experience I rejoiced with great joy and the Lord was with me. [33] After I returned to my home, I leaned up to the fireplace. Mother enquired what was the matter. I replied, "Never mind. All is well. I am well enough off." I then told my mother that I had learned for myself that Presbyterianism is not true. [34]

Some few days after this experience, I happened to be in company with one of the Methodist preachers who was very active in the before

---

[24]"1832 History," "1835 History," "1838 History" and "1842 History."

[25]"1842 History."

[26]"1838 History."

[27]"1832 History."

[28]"1838 History," and "1842 History."

[29]"1842 History."

[30]"1838 History."

[31]"1835 History."

[32]"1838 History."

[33]"1832 History."

[34]Joseph Smith, 1838 Manuscript History of the Church, Note B, Church Archives.

mentioned religious excitement; and, conversing with him on the subject of religion, I took occasion to give him an account of the vision which I had had. I was greatly surprised at his behavior; he treated my communication not only lightly, but with great contempt, saying it was all of the devil, that there was no such thing as visions or revelations in these days; that all such things had ceased with the apostles, and that there never would be any more of them. I soon found, however, that my telling the story had excited a great deal of prejudice against me among professors of religion, and was the cause of great persecution, which continued to increase; and though I was an obscure boy, only between fourteen and fifteen years of age, and my circumstances in life such as to make a boy of no consequence in the world, yet men of high standing would take notice sufficient to excite the public mind against me and create a hot [bitter] persecution; and this was common among all the sects—all united to persecute me. It has often caused me serious reflection both then and since, how very strange it was that an obscure boy, of a little over fourteen years of age, and one, too, who was doomed to the necessity of obtaining a scanty maintenance by his daily labor, should be thought a character of sufficient importance to attract the attention of the great ones of the most popular sects of the day, so as to create in them a spirit of the most bitter persecution and reviling. But strange or not, so it was, and it was often the cause of great sorrow to myself. However, it was nevertheless a fact that I had had a vision. I have thought since that I felt much like Paul, when he made his defense before King Agrippa, and related the account of the vision he had when he saw a light, and heard a voice; but still there were but few who believed him; some said he was dishonest, others said he was mad; and he was ridiculed and reviled. But all this did not destroy the reality of his vision. He had seen a vision, he knew he had, and all the persecution under heaven could not make it otherwise; and though they should persecute him unto death, yet he knew and would know to his latest breath, that he had both seen a light and heard a voice speaking unto him, and all the world could not make him think or believe otherwise. So it was with me. I had actually seen a light, and in the midst of that light I saw two Personages, and they did in reality speak to me, or one of them did; and though I was hated and persecuted for saying that I had seen a vision, yet it was true; and while they were persecuting me, reviling me, and speaking all manner of evil against me falsely for so saying, I was led to say in my heart: Why persecute me for telling the truth? I have actually seen a vision; and who am I that I can withstand God, or why does the world think to make me deny what I have actually seen? For I had seen a vision; I knew it, and I knew that God knew it, and I could not deny it, neither dare I do it; at least I knew that by so doing I would offend God, and come under condemnation. I had now got my mind satisfied so far as the sectarian world was concerned, that it was not my duty to join with any of them, but to continue as I was until further directed. I had found the testimony of James to be true, that a man who lacked wisdom might ask of God, and obtain and not be upbraided. I continued to pursue my common vocations in life until the twenty-first of September, one thousand eight hundred and twenty-three, all the time suffering severe persecution at the hands of all classes of men, both religious and irreligious, because I continued to affirm that I had seen a vision.[35]

During the space of time which intervened between the time I had the vision and the year eighteen hundred and twenty-three—having been forbidden to join any of the religious sects of the day, and being of very tender years, and persecuted by those who ought to have been my friends and to have treated me kindly, and if they supposed me to be deluded to have endeavored in a proper and affectionate manner to have reclaimed me—I was left to all kinds of temptations; and, mingling with all kinds of society, I frequently fell into many foolish errors, and displayed the weakness of youth, and the foibles of human nature; which, I am sorry to say led me into divers temptations, to the gratification of many appetites, offensive in the sight of God.[36]

In making this confession, no one need suppose me guilty of any great or malignant sins. A disposition to commit such was never in my nature. But I was guilty of levity, and sometimes associated with jovial company, etc., not consistent with that character which ought to be maintained by one who was called of God as I had been. But this will not seem very strange to any one who recollects my youth, and is acquainted with my native cherry temperment.[37]

Lucy Mack Smith's Confirmation of Joseph's Writings and Her
Descriptions of Selected Events that Transpired About 1819 and 1820

Lucy Smith

Shortly after my husband received the foregoing vision, [a vision which Lucy reported he had received in 1819] there was a great revival in

---

[35]"1832 History" and "1838 History."

[36]"1838 History."

[37]Joseph Smith, "1838 History of the Church," Note C.

religion, which extended to all the denominations of Christians in the surrounding country in which we resided. Many of the world's people, becoming concerned about the salvation of their souls, came forward and presented themselves as seekers after religion. Most of them were desirous of uniting with some church, but were not decided as to the particular faith which they would adopt. When the numerous meetings were about breaking up, and the candidates and the various leading church members began to consult upon the subject of adopting the candidates into some church or churches, as the case might be, a dispute arose, and there was a great contention among them. . . .[38]

At the age of fourteen, an incident occurred which alarmed us much, as we knew not the cause of it. Joseph being a remarkably quiet, well disposed child, we did not suspect that any one had aught against him. He was out one evening on an errand, and, on returning home, as he was passing through the door yard, a gun was fired across his pathway, with the evident intention of shooting him. He sprang to the door much frightened. We immediately went in search of the assassin, but could find no trace of him that evening. The next morning we found his tracks under a waggon, where he lay when he fired; and the following day we found the balls, which were discharged from the gun, lodged in the head and neck of a cow that was standing opposite the waggon, in a dark corner. We have not as yet discovered the man who made this attempt at murder, neither can we discover the cause thereof.[39]

Conclusion

Orson Pratt

What are the circumstances that enabled him [Joseph Smith] to have manifestations from heaven at that early period of his life? He was very anxious, as most of mankind are, to be saved; and he was also very anxious to understand how to be saved . . .He was a farmer's boy; he was not brought up and educated in high schools, academies or colleges . . .First one and then another of the different persuasions would come and converse with him and try to influence him to join his lot with them; and seeing so much confusion, each sect claiming that they were the true people of God, he became at a loss what to do. He occasionally

---

[38]Lucy Smith, *Biographical Sketches*, p. 74.

[39]Ibid., p. 73.

devoted an hour, when his labors on the farm would permit, to reading the Bible, and while doing so his eyes happened to fall on a certain passage of scripture, recorded in the epistle of James, which says that if any man lack wisdom let him ask of God who giveth liberally to all men and upbraideth not. Now this youth . . . believe[d] that that passage really meant what it said. He went out into a little grove near his father's house, . . . and there he knelt down in all the simplicity of a child and prayed to the Father in the name of Jesus that He would show him which, among all the churches, was the true one. . . .

He had now come to a Person who was able to teach him. All his inquiries previously had been futile and vain, but he now applied to the right source. Did the Lord hear him? Yes. But he had to exercise faith. . . . The Lord hearkened. Being the same God who lived in ancient times, He was able to hear and answer prayers that were offered up in this sincere manner, and He answered the prayers of this youth. The heavens, as it were, were opened to him . . . and he was filled with the visions of the Almighty, and he saw, in the midst of this glorious pillar of fire, two glorious personages, whose countenances shone with an exceeding great lustre. One of them spoke to him, saying, while pointing to the other, "This is my beloved Son in whom I am well pleased, hear ye him."

Now here was a certainty; here was something that he saw and heard; here were personages capable of instructing him, and of telling him which was the true religion. How different this from going to an uninspired man! . . . One minute's instruction from personages clothed with the glory of God coming down from the eternal worlds is worth more than all the volumes that ever were written by uninspired men. . . .

He was told there was no Christian church on the face of the earth according to the ancient pattern, as recorded in the New Testament; but they had all strayed from the ancient faith and had lost the gifts and power of the Holy Ghost; they had lost the spirit of revelation and prophecy, [and] the power to heal the sick. . . . "Go not after them," was the command given to this young man, and he was told that if he would be faithful in serving the true and living God, it should be made manifest to him, in a time to come, the true church that God intended to establish.

Now we can see the wisdom of God in not revealing everything to him on that occasion. He revealed as much as Joseph was capacitated to receive. . . .[40]

---

[40]Orson Pratt in *Journal of Discourses*, 26 vols. (London: Latter-day Saints' Book Depot, 1855-1886), 12:353-55 (hereafter cited as *JD*).

When he related [to others] that which he had received in this vision, the ministers immediately made light of it, and said to him, "God does not reveal anything in our days; he revealed all that was necessary in ancient times; he has not spoken for 1800 years to anyone." From that time forth he was persecuted. . . . This seemed to be the feeling manifested, not only by professors, but by all; but yet he knew that God had manifested himself to him; he could not be persuaded to the contrary, any more than Paul could when he heard Jesus in his first vision.[41]

---

[41]Ibid., 14:141. For additional descriptions (by contemporaries) of what Joseph Smith saw and learned during his First Vision see JD 2:170-71; 2:196-97; 7:220-21; 8:354; 11:1-2; 12:67; 12:302; 12:352-54; 13:65-67; 13:77-78; 14:140-41; 14:261-62; 15:180-82; 18:239; 20:167; 21:161-65; 22:29; 24:371-73; and 25:155-57. In the early history of the Church, some leaders referred to Jesus as an angel (a messenger from the Father).

CHAPTER THREE

Unfolding Cumorah's Hidden Treasure

1823-1827

And I saw another angel fly in the midst of heaven, having the
everlasting gospel to preach unto them that dwell on the earth, and to every
nation, kindred, and tongue, and people. (Rev. 14:6.)

Following the First Vision, three years passed before Joseph Smith received additional instructions from a heavenly being. In the spring of 1820 Joseph learned that the fulness of the gospel would be revealed to him, and after waiting three years he thought his transgressions might have prevented the fulfillment of that promise. On the night of September 21-22, 1823, while the seventeen-year-old boy was seeking forgiveness and petitioning the Lord, the heavens were again opened; and Joseph Smith beheld a series of visions. Moroni, a prophet who had lived on the American continent, appeared to him and told Joseph that an ancient record was deposited in a hill near his home. This religious history, he said, contained the fulness of the everlasting gospel as taught by the Savior and his prophets to the early inhabitants of America. Joseph Smith learned that following Christ's resurrection, the Savior appeared as he predicted to his other sheep living on the American continent, and they heard his voice (John 10:16, 3 Nephi 15:21). This record which had been compiled by Mormon, the father of Moroni, is a new witness for Christ, a fifth gospel, and is a work which unfolds the teachings of Christ with clarity and purity.

The coming forth of the Book of Mormon is in harmony with a divine law of witnesses. Joseph Smith does not stand alone in bearing witness to the restoration of Christ's gospel. In other dispensations, prophets were supported by witnesses. Methuselah proclaimed the same warning message as Noah. Aaron served as a spokesman for Moses. Many witnesses testified of events in the life of the Savior, including his resurrection. The Book of Mormon is a modern witness for Christ, but it is also a witness of the divine calling of Joseph Smith. This work contains predictions of a gospel restoration following the American Revolution by a person named Joseph who was the son of a Joseph. (2 Nephi 3:11-15 and 1 Nephi 13:18-23.) The book itself also serves as a powerful, tangible evidence of the authenticity of this latter-day prophet. Moreoever, the Book of Mormon is a witness of the validity of the basic message of the Bible.

> Know ye not that there are more nations than one? Know ye not that I, the Lord your God, have created all men, and that I remember those who are upon the isles of the sea; and that I rule in the heavens above and in the earth beneath; and I bring forth my word unto the children of men, yea, even upon all the nations of the earth?
>
> Wherefore murmur ye, because ye shall receive more of my word? Know ye not that the testimony of two nations is a witness unto you that I am God, that I remember one nation like unto another? Wherefore, I speak the same words unto one nation like unto another. And when the two nations shall run together the testimony of the two nations shall run together also. (2 Nephi 29:7-8.)

While the Book of Mormon is a witness to the authenticity of the Bible and the divine calling of Joseph Smith, the Bible is a witness to the restoration. The Bible predicted the scattering of Israel, declaring that the descendents of Joseph would run over the wall (ocean) (Genesis 11:9 and 49:22-26.) Ancient prophets also predicted that the writings of Judah (the Bible) and the writings of Joseph (the Book of Mormon) would be one in the hands of others (Ezekiel 37:15-20 and 2 Nephi 3:12), that a book would be delivered to one who was unlearned, and that the unlearned would bring forth a marvelous work and a wonder (Isaiah 29:11-14, 18, 24). The

Bible further predicted that Elijah would come before the great and dreadful day of the Lord (Malachi 4:5-6), that Elias would come and restore all things (Matthew 17:11 and Mark 9:12), and that another angel would come, bringing to the earth the everlasting gospel (Revelation 14:6).

Before obtaining the record which was a modern witness for Christ, Joseph Smith was visited by many heavenly beings who had lived anciently on this continent. These angelic messengers instructed him concerning life in ancient America, so that between 1823 and 1827, through visions and revelations, Joseph Smith became an authority on the religious, social, and political history of several American civilizations that were disrupted through multiple internal and external forces.[1]

In addition to the four histories written by the Prophet other contemporary accounts are included in this chapter which confirm Joseph Smith's writings and amplify our understanding of his religious experiences during this 1823-1827 period.

Included among these other accounts are the writings of Lucy Smith and other members of the Smith family, Orson Pratt, Joseph Knight (an employer and friend of the Prophet), and Oliver Cowdery. The Oliver Cowdery history cited in this chapter was initially printed in the *Latter Day Saints' Messenger and Advocate* in Kirtland, Ohio, in 1834-1835 and subsequently reprinted in the *Times and Seasons* in Nauvoo, Illinois, in 1840-1841. Oliver Cowdery was a school teacher who met Joseph Smith in April 1829. After becoming one of the major witnesses to the restoration movement, he wrote the first major history describing Joseph Smith's religious experiences of 1823. Although Oliver Cowdery testified that his writings were based upon what he learned from Joseph Smith, there is no evidence that the Prophet carefully read this manuscript before its publication in order to correct possible mistakes. Nevertheless, the general accuracy of this history is attested to by its harmony with the writings of Joseph Smith, the similarity in this history to the one prepared by Orson Pratt, and its republication in the official Latter-day Saints' newspaper, the *Times and Seasons*, while Joseph was living in Nauvoo. The harmony which exists in the writings of Joseph Smith (describing his religious experiences between 1823 and 1827) and the histories written by Lucy Smith, Orson Pratt, and Oliver Cowdery provide confirming evidence of Moroni's appearances to the young prophet. (See Appendix B)

---

[1]*HC*, 4:537; John Taylor, *JD*, 17:374; 21:94, 161 and George Q. Cannon, *JD*, 13:47.

Emma Hale Smith (*Courtesy RLDS Church*)

Joseph Smith (*Courtesy RLDS Church*)

THE HILL CUMORAH

The earliest known artist's sketch of the hill Cumorah, published in J. W. Barber and Henry Howe's *Historical Collections of the State of New York* (1841)

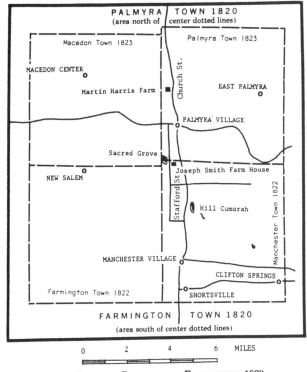

PALMYRA TOWN 1820
(area north of center dotted lines)

Macedon Town 1823

Palmyra Town 1823

MACEDON CENTER

Martin Harris Farm

Church St.

EAST PALMYRA

PALMYRA VILLAGE

Sacred Grove

NEW SALEM

Joseph Smith Farm House

Stafford St.

Hill Cumorah

Manchester Town 1822

MANCHESTER VILLAGE

CLIFTON SPRINGS

Farmington Town 1822

SHORTSVILLE

FARMINGTON TOWN 1820
(area south of center dotted lines)

0   2   4   6   MILES

TOWNS OF PALMYRA AND FARMINGTON, 1820

★★★

The Message of Moroni

Joseph Smith

On the evening of September 21, 1823,[2] when I was seventeen years of age, I retired to my bed for the night and while praying unto God asked for forgiveness of all my sins and follies and for a manifestation to me, that I might know of my state and standing before him.[3] I had not been asleep, but was meditating upon my past life and experience. I was very conscious that I had not kept the commandments and I repented heartily of all my sins and transgressions and humbled myself before Him whose eyes are in all things.[4] I had full confidence in obtaining a divine manifestation, as I had previously had one.[5]

While I was thus in the act of calling upon God,[6] I discovered a light appearing in my room which continued to increase until the room was

---

[2]Since Lucy included in her history of Joseph the account of the visions of September 21-22, 1823, which the Prophet in 1838 and published in the *Times and Seasons*, the quotes in her writings from that recital have not been cited in this harmony. Nevertheless, Lucy confirms Joseph's testimony of these visions by including this information in her history. Various comments by Lucy that are not direct quotes from Joseph's history are included in this chapter. The description of the Moroni visitation recorded in the "1842 History" was initially published in *T&S* 3 (March, 1842):707, and the same vision as reported in Joseph Smith's "1838 History" was printed in *T&S* 3 (April 1-May 2, 1842):749, 753-54, 771 and JS-H 1:27-54.

[3]"1832 History," "1835 History," "1838 History," and "1842 History."

[4]"1835 History."

[5]"1838 History."

[6]While describing the time when the vision commenced, Oliver wrote: "In this situation hours passed unnumbered—how many or how few I know not, neither is he [Joseph Smith] able to inform me; but supposes it must have been eleven or twelve, and, perhaps later, as the noise and bustle of the family, in retiring, had long since ceased." (*The Latter-day Saints' Messenger and Advocate* 1 [February 1835]:79, hereafter cited as *M&A*.)

lighter than at noonday. Indeed the first sight was as though the house was filled with consuming fire; the appearance produced a shock that affected my whole body. In a moment a personage stood before me, surrounded with a glory yet greater than that with which I was already surrounded.[7] An angel appeared[8] at my bedside and stood in the air, for his feet did not touch the floor.[9]

He had on a loose robe of most exquisite whiteness. It was a whiteness beyond anything earthly I had ever seen, nor do I believe that any earthly thing could be made to appear so exceedingly white and brilliant. His hands were naked, pure and white, and his arms also, a little above the wrists; so, also were his feet naked, as were his legs, a little above the ankles. His head and neck were also bare. I could discover that he had no other clothing on but this robe, as it was open so that I could see into his bosom.[10]

Not only was his robe exceedingly white, but his whole person was glorious beyond description and his countenance truly like lightning.[11] When I first looked upon him, I was afraid; but the fear soon left me.[12] He called me by name and said unto me that he was a messenger sent from the presence of God to me to bring joyful tidings[13] and that his name was

---

[7]"1835 History," "1838 History," and "1842 History."

[8]"1832 History," "1835 History," "1838 History," and "1842 History."

[9]"1838 History."

[10]"1835 History," and "1838 History."

[11]"1838 History." While describing this angel and his dress, Oliver wrote: "The stature of this personage was a little above the common size of men in this age; his garment was perfectly white, and has the appearance of being without seam" (*M&A* 1 [February 1835]:79). Oliver also described this angel by writing: "Though his countenance was as lightning, yet it was of a pleasing, innocent and glorious appearance, so much so, that every fear was banished from the heart, and nothing but calmness pervaded the soul" (*Ibid*).

[12]"1838 History."

[13]"1832 History," "1835 History," "1838 History," and "1842 History."

Moroni.[14] He told me that the Lord had forgiven me of my sins[15] and said, "Be faithful and keep His commandments in all things."[16] I was informed that I was a chosen instrument in the hands of God to bring about some of his purposes in this glorious dispensation.[17]

Oliver Cowdery

The messenger also informed Joseph Smith that the Lord had chosen him to be an instrument in His hand to bring to light that which shall perform his act, His strange act, and bring to pass a marvelous work and a wonder. He further said that Joseph Smith's prayers were heard that the scriptures might be fulfilled, which say—"God has chosen the foolish things of the world to confound the things which are mighty; and base things of the world, and things which are despised, has God chosen; yea, and things which are not, to bring to nought things which are, that no flesh should glory in his presence. Therefore, says the Lord, I will proceed to do a marvelous work among this people, even a marvelous work and a wonder; the wisdom of their wise shall perish, and the understanding of their prudent shall be hid;" [Isa. 29:14] for according to this covenant which he made with his ancient saints, his people, the house of Israel,

---

[14]In the manuscript history of the Church (which Joseph Smith began writing in 1838) the heavenly messenger who appeared to Joseph on September 21-22, 1823, was called "Nephi" (in one instance) and this name was printed in the *Times and Seasons* when the history was initially published. In other writings, Joseph Smith identified the angel who appeared to him on that occasion as "Moroni." (See D&C 27:5; 128:20; and *Elder's Journal* 1 [July 1838]:42-43.) Early leaders of the Church recognized that the reference to Nephi in the *Times and Seasons* was an error. In a letter discussing this problem, Orson Pratt wrote that he believed that the angel who appeared to Joseph Smith in 1823 was "Moroni." The discrepancy in the history, he suggested, was due to the "ignorance or carelessness of the historian or transcriber" and Joseph Smith's probable failure to proofread carefully that text before it was printed. When other church leaders (who were close associates of the Prophet) identified the angel who appeared in 1823 and held the keys of the unfolding of the Book of Mormon they consistently called this messenger "Moroni," (See *T&S* 3 [April 15, 1842]:753 and Orson Pratt to John Christensen, March 11, 1876, Orson Pratt Papers, Church Archives. See also *M&A* 1 [April 1835]:112; *T&S* 2 [April 1, 1841]:363; and *JD*, 6:29; 17:281; 18:326; 26:106.)

[15]"1832 History."

[16]"1835 History."

[17]"1838 History" and "1842 History."

must come to a knowledge of the gospel, and own that Messiah whom their fathers rejected, and with them the fulness of the Gentiles be gathered in, to rejoice in one fold under one Shepherd.[18]

Joseph Smith

He further told me that my name should be had for good and evil among all nations, kindreds and tongues, or that it should be both good and evil spoken of among all people.[19]

He said there was a book deposited, written upon gold plates by Moroni and his father, containing an abridgment of the records of the ancient prophets who had lived on this continent, giving an account of these people; and I was shown who they were and from whence they came, learning that the Indians were literal descendants of Abraham. He also said that the fulness of the everlasting gospel was contained in it, as delivered by the Savior to the ancient inhabitants. A brief sketch of their origin, progress, civilization, laws, governments, of their righteousness and iniquity, and the blessings of God being finally withdrawn from them as a people was make known unto me.[20]

Orson Pratt

It was also made manifest to him that the "American Indians" were a remnant of Israel; that when they first emigrated to America, they were an enlightened people, possessing a knowledge of the true God, enjoying his favor and peculiar blessings from his hand; that the prophets and inspired writers among them were required to keep a sacred history of the most important events transpiring among them: which history was handed down for many generations, till at length they fell into great

---

[18]*M&A* 1 (February 1835):79. In the discussion of what Joseph Smith learned from the angel Moroni when "he was directed to go and obtain the record of the Nephites," Oliver explained that although he was not able to record the order in which the information was unfolded to Joseph Smith nor "the precise words" spoken by Moroni he believed that he accurately recorded the general principles (or "the facts in substance") related to the Prophet on that occasion. "You are aware", he added, "that to give a minute rehearsal of a lengthy interview with a heavenly messenger, is very difficult, unless one is assisted immediately with the gift of inspiration" (*M&A* 1 [April 1835]:109, 112).

[19]"1838 History."

[20]"1832 History," "1835 History," "1838 History," and "1842 History."

wickedness: the most part of them were destroyed, and the records, (by commandment of God, to one of the last prophets among them) were safely deposited, to preserve them from the hands of the wicked, who sought to destroy them. He was informed that these records contained many sacred revelations pertaining to the gospel of the kingdom, as well as prophecies relating to the great events of the last days; and that to fulfill his [God's] promises to the ancients, who wrote the records, and to accomplish his purposes, in the restitution of their children, etc., they were to come forth to the knowledge of the people. If faithful, he [Joseph] was to be the instrument, who should be thus highly favoured in bringing these sacred things to light.[21]

Joseph Smith

The messenger further told me that two transparent stones in silver bows were deposited with the plates; and these stones, which were fastened to a breastplate, constitued what is called the Urim and Thummim.[22] The angel said that possession and use of these stones was what constituted seers in ancient or former times and that God had prepared them for the purpose of translating the book.[23]

After telling me these things, he commenced quoting the prophecies of the Old Testament. He first quoted part of the third chapter of Malachi; and he quoted also the fourth or last chapter of the same prophecy, though with a little variation from the way it reads in our Bibles.[24] Instead of quoting the first verse of chapter four as it reads in our books, he quoted it thus: "For behold, the day cometh that shall burn as an oven, and all the proud, yea, and all that do wickedly shall burn as stubble; for the day that cometh shall burn them, saith the Lord of Hosts, that it shall leave them neither root nor branch.

---

[21]Orson Pratt, *An Interesting Account of Several Remarkable Visions* (Edinburg, 1840), p. 7 (hereafter cited as Orson Pratt, *Account of Several Remarkable Visions*).

[22]"1838 History" and "1842 History." When describing the breastplate, Oliver Cowdery wrote: "This box (in which the Book of Mormon plates had been placed) was sufficiently large to admit a breast-plate, such as was used by the ancients to defend the chest, & the arrows and weapons of their enemy" (*M&A* 2 [October 1835]:196).

[23]"1835 History" and "1838 History."

[24]"1835 History" and "1838 History."

And again, he quoted the fifth verse thus: "Behold, I will reveal unto you the Priesthood, by the hand of Elijah the prophet, before the coming of the great and dreadful day of the Lord."

He also quoted the next verse differently: "And he shall plant in the hearts of the children the promises made to the fathers, and the hearts of the children shall turn to their fathers. If it were not so, the whole earth would be utterly wasted at his coming."[25]

In addition to these, he quoted the eleventh chapter of Isaiah, saying that it was about to be fulfilled. He quoted also the third chaper of Acts, twenty-second and twenty-third verses, precisely as they stand in our New Testament. He said that that prophet was Christ; but the day had not yet come when "they who would not hear His voice should be cut off from among the people," but soon would come.

He also quoted the second chapter of Joel, from the twenty-eighth verse to the last. He also said that this was not yet fulfilled, but was soon to be. And he further stated that the fulness of the Gentiles was soon to come in. He quoted many other passages of scripture, and offered many explanations which cannot be mentioned here.[26]

The messenger, therefore, told me that the covenant which God made with ancient Israel was at hand to be fulfilled; that the preparatory work for the second coming of the Messiah was speedily to commence; that the time was at hand for the gospel, in all its fulness to be preached in power, unto all nations that a people might be prepared for the millennial reign.[27]

Oliver Cowdery

Moreover, the messenger declared that before the history of the aborigines of this country is translated, the scripture must be fulfilled

---

[25]"1838 History." See also the Doctrine and Covenants of The Church of Jesus Christ of Latter-day Saints (Salt Lake City: The Church of Jesus Christ of Latter-day Saints, 1981), 2:2-3 (hereafter cited as D&C).

[26]"1838 History." In the most lengthy description of Moroni's first visitation to Josph Smith, Oliver Cowdery identified many scriptures that Moroni possibly quoted that are not mentioned in Joseph Smith's accounts. Upon reading Oliver's history, however, it is not clear whether Oliver is quoting Moroni or merely explaining, with scriptural references, themes emphasized by Moroni. Included among the scriptures quoted by Oliver, not mentiond by Joseph, are the following: Isaiah 2:2-3; 4:5-6; 29:11, 14; Jeremiah 16:16; 30:18-21; 31:27-28; 31:33; and John 10:16. I have included in the text of this work the references that seem to have been quoted by Moroni.

[27]"1842 History."

which says that the words of a book which were sealed were presented to the learned; [Isa. 29:11] for thus has God determined to leave men without excuse, and show to the meek that his arm is not shortened that it cannot save.[28]

The angel instructed Joseph concerning the blessings, promises and covenants to Israel, and the great manifestations of favor to the world in the ushering in of the fulness of the gospel to prepare the way for the second advent of the Messiah.[29] Most clearly was it shown to the prophet that the righteous should be gathered from all the earth before the great and dreadful day of the Lord and be taught the fulness of the gospel.[30]

Joseph Smith

Again, he told me that when I got those plates of which he had spoken [for the time that they should be obtained was not yet fulfilled] I should not show them to any person, neither the breastplate wit the Urim and Thummim, only to those to whom I should be commanded to show them; if I did, I should be destroyed. While he was conversing with me about the plates, the vision was opened to my mind that I could see the place where the plates were deposited, and that so clearly and distinctly that I knew the place again when I visited it.

After this communication, I saw the light in the room begin to gather immediately around the person of him who had been speaking to me, and it continued to do so until the room was again left dark, except just around him; when, instantly I saw, as it were, a conduit open right up into heaven, and he ascended up till he entirely disappeared. After the messenger gradually vanished out of my sight or the vision closed, the room was left as it had been before this heavenly light had made its appearance.[31]

I lay musing on the singularity of the scene, and marveling greatly at what had been told me by this extraordinary messenger; when, in the midst of my meditation, I suddenly discovered that my room was again beginning to get lighted, and in an instant, as it were, the same heavenly messenger was again by my bedside.

He commenced, and again stated the very same things which he had done at his first visit, without the least variation, and much more; which

---

[28]*M&A* 1 (February 1835):79.

[29]*M&A* 1 (July 1835):155.

[30]*M&A* 1 (April 1835):109.

[31]"1835 History" and "1838 History."

having done, he informed me of great judgments which were coming upon the earth, with great desolations by famine, sword, and pestilence; and that these grievous judgments would come on the earth in this generation. Having related these things he again ascended as he had done before.[32]

By this time, so deep were the impressions made on my mind, that sleep had fled from my eyes, and I lay overwhelmed in astonishment at what I had both seen and heard. But what was my surprise when again I beheld the same messenger at my bedside, and heard him rehearse or repeat over again to me the same things as before;[33] and added a caution to me, telling me that Satan would try to tempt me (in consequence of the indigent circumstances of my father's family), to get the plates for the purpose of getting rich. This he forbid me, saying that I must have no other object in view in getting the plates but to glorify God, and must not be influenced by any other motive but that of building his Kingdom; otherwise I could not get them.[34]

After this third visit[35] he again ascended into heaven as before, and I was again left to ponder on the strangeness of what I had just experienced; when almost immediately after the heavenly messenger had ascended from me for the third time, the cock crowed, and I found that day was approaching, so that our interviews must have occupied the whole of the night.[36]

The Vision in the Field

Joseph Smith

I shortly after arose from my bed, and, as usual, went to the necessary labors of the day; but, in attempting to labor as at other times, I found my strength so exhausted as rendered me entirely unable. My father, who was laboring along with me, discovered something to be wrong with me, and told me to go home. I started with the intention of going to the house; but, in attempting to cross the fence out of the field

---

[32]"1835 History" and "1838 History."

[33]"1832 History," "1835 History," "1838 History," and "1842 History."

[34]"1838 History."

[35]"1832 History," "1835 History," "1838 History," and "1842 History."

[36]"1838 History."

where we were, my strength entirely failed me, and I fell helpless on the ground, and for a time was quite unconscious of anything.[37]

The first thing that I can recollect was a voice speaking unto me, calling me by name. I looked up, and beheld the same messenger standing over my head, surrounded by light as before. He then again related unto me all that he had related to me the previous night, and commanded me to go to my father and tell him of the vision and commandments which I had received.[38]

I obeyed; I returned to my father in the field, and rehearsed the whole matter to him. He replied to me that it was of God, and [told me] to go and do as commanded by the messenger.[39] I left the field, and went to the

---

[37]"1838 History." While describing this same incident, Lucy wrote: "The next day, my husband, Alvin, and Joseph, were reaping together in the field, and as they were reaping Joseph stopped quite suddenly, and seemed to be in a very deep study. Alvin, obsrving it, hurried him, saying, 'We must not slacken our hands or we will not be able to complete our task.' Upon this Joseph went to work again, and after labouring a short time, he stopped just as he had done before. This being quite unusual and strange, it attracted the attention of his father, upon which he discovered that Joseph was very pale. My husband, supposing that he was sick, told him to go to the house and have his mother doctor him. He accordingly ceased his work, and started, but on coming to a beautiful green, under an apple-tree, he stopped and lay down, for he was so weak he could proceed no further" (Lucy Smith, *Biographical Sketches*, p. 81-82).

[38]"1832 History," "1835 History," and "1838 History." Describing this vision, Lucy Smith wrote: "He was here but a short time [lying near the fence], when the messenger whom he saw the previous night, visited him again, and the first thing he said was,—'Why did you not tell your father that which I commanded you to tell him?'—Joseph replied, "I was afraid my father would not believe me." The angel rejoined, 'He will believe every word you say to him.' Joseph then promised the angel that he would do as he had been commanded. Upon this, the messenger departed" (Lucy Smith, *Biographical Sketches*, p. 82).

[39]"1835 History" and "1838 History." Lucy included in her history the positive response of Joseph Smith's father to his son's report of having received a message from a heavenly being. Describing her husband's reaction, Lucy wrote that following the vision under an apple tree, "Joseph returned to the field, where he had left my husband and Alvin; but when he got there, his father had just gone to the house, as he was somewhat unwell. Joseph then desired Alvin to go sraightaway and see his father, and inform him that he had something of great importance to communicate to him, and that he wanted him to come out into the field where they were at work. Alvin did as he was requested, and when my husband got there, Joseph related to him all that had passed between him

place where the messenger had told me that the plates were deposited; and owing to the distinctness of the vision which I had had concerning it, I knew the place the instant that I arrived there.[40]

Oliver Cowdery

As you pass on the mail-road, from Palmyra, Wayne County, to Canadaigua, Ontario County, New York, before arriving at the little village of Manchester, say from three to four, or about four miles from Palmyra, you pass a large hill on the east side of the road. Why I say large, is because it is as large, perhaps, as any in that country.

The north end rises quite suddenly until it assumes a level with the more southernly extremity; and I think I may say, an elevation higher than at the south, a short distance, say half or three-fourths of a mile. As you pass towards Canadaigua, it lessens gradually, until the surface assumes its common level, or is broken by other smaller hills or ridges, water-courses and ravines. I think I am justified in saying that this is the highest hill for some distance round, and I am certain that its appearance, as it rises so suddenly from a plain on the north end, which has been described as rising suddenly from the plain, forms a promontory without timber, but covered with grass. As you pass to the south, you soon come to scattering timber, the surface having been cleared by art or wind; and short distance further left, you are surrounded with the common forest of the country. It is necessary to observe that even the part cleared was only occupied for pasturage; its steep ascent and narrow summit not admitting the plough of the husbandman with any degree of ease or profit.[41]

Joseph Rebuked

Joseph Smith

On the west side of this hill, not far from the top, under a stone of considerable size, lay the plates, deposited in a stone box. This stone was

---

and the angel the previous night and that morning. Having heard this account, his father charged him not to fail in attending strictly to the instruction which he had received from this heavenly messenger" (Lucy Smith, *Biographical Sketches*, p. 82).

[40]"1832 History" and "1838 History."

[41]*M&A* 1 (July 1835):158.

thick and rounding in the middle on the upper side, and thinner toward the edges, so that the middle part of it was visible above the ground, but the edge all around was covered with earth.

Having removed the earth, I obtained a lever, which I got fixed under the edge of the stone, and with a little exertion raised it up. I looked in, and there indeed did I behold the plates, the Urim and Thummim, and the breastplate, as stated by the messenger. The box in which they lay was formed by laying stones together in some kind of cement. In the bottom of the box were laid two stones crossways of the box, and on these stones lay the plates and the other things with them.[42]

Oliver Cowdery

At each edge [of the smooth stone cover] was placed a large quantity of cement, and into this cement, at the four edges of this stone, were placed erect, four other; their bottom edges resting in the cement, at the outer edges of the first stone. The four last names, when placed erect, formed a box: the corners, or where the edges of the four came in contact, were also cemented so firmly that the moisture from without was prevented from entering. It is to be observed, also, that the inner surfaces of the four erect or side stones were smooth . . .From the bottom of the box, or from the breastplate, arose three small pillars, composed of the same description of cement used on the edges, and upon these three pillars were placed the record of the children of Joseph.[43]

Joseph Smith

[I] made three attempts to get [take] them but was forbidden by the messenger. I cried unto the Lord in the agony of my soul, [asking] why I could not obtain them, and the angel said unto me that I had not kept the commandments of the Lord . . .for . . .I had been tempted . . .[by] the adversary and sought the plates to obtain riches and kept not the commandment that I should have an eye single to the glory of God. Therefore, I was chastened.[44]

---

[42]"1838 History." See also *M&A* 2 (October 1835):196. Orson Pratt included in his history Oliver Cowdery's description of the angel's visitation to Joseph Smith on the Hill Cumorah on September 22, 1823. (See Orson Pratt, *Account of Several Remarkable Visions*, pp. 8-11.)

[43]*M&A* 2 (October 1835):196.

[44]"1832 History," "1835 History," and "1838 History."

Lucy Smith

While Joseph...[was] at the place where the plates were deposited...the angel showed him, by contrast, the difference between good and evil, and likewise the consequences of both obedience and disobedience to the commandments of God, in such a striking manner that the impression was always vivid in his memory until the very end of his days; and in giving a relation of this circumstance, not long prior to his death, he remarked, that "ever afterwards he was willing to keep the commandments of God."[45]

Oliver Cowdery

[After making three attempts to secure the plates, Joseph Smith saw] the angel who had previously given him the directions concerning this matter. In an instant, all the former instructions, the great intelligence concerning Israel and the last days, were brought to his mind. He had come, to be sure, and found the word of angel fulfilled concerning the reality of the record, but he had failed to remember the great end for which they had been kept, and in consequence could not have power to take them into his possession and bear them away.

At that instant he looked to the Lord in prayer, and as he prayed darkness began to disperse from his mind and his soul was lit up as it was the evening before, and he was filled with the Spirit; and again did the Lord manifest his condescension and mercy: the heavens were opened and the glory of the Lord shone round about and rested upon him. While he thus stood gazing and admiring, the angel said, "Look!" and as he thus spake he beheld the prince of darkness, surrounded by his innumerable train of associates. All this passed before him, and the heavenly messenger said, "All this is shown, the good and the evil, the Holy and impure, the glory of God and the power of darkness, that you may know hereafter the two powers and never be influenced or overcome by that wicked one. You now see why you could not obtain this record. The plates are not deposited here for the sake of accumulating gain and wealth for the glory of the world.[46]

---

[45]Lucy Smith, *Biographical Sketches*, p. 82-83.

[46]*M&A* 2 (October 1835):198.

Aftermath of Five Visions

Joseph Smith

The angel also informed me that the time for bringing forth the record had not yet arrived, neither would until four years from that time, but he told me that I should come to that place precisely in one year from that time, and that he would there meet with me, and that I should continue to do so until the time should come for obtaining the plates.[47]

Lucy Smith

The ensuing evening, [September 22, 1823] when the family were all together, Joseph made known to them all that he had communicated to his father in the field, and also of his finding the Record, as well as what passed between him and the angel while he was at the place where the plates were deposited.

Sitting up late that evening, in order to converse upon these things, together with over-exertion of mind, had much fatigued Joseph; and when Alvin observed it, he said, "Now, brother, let us go to bed, and rise early in the morning, in order to finish our day's work at an hour before sunset, then, if mother will get our suppers early, we will have a fine long evening, and we will all sit down for the purpose of listening to you while you tell us the great things which God has revealed to you."

Accordingly, by sunset the next day we were all seated, and Joseph commenced telling us the great and glorious things which God had manifested to him; but, before proceeding, he charged us not to mention

---

[47]"1835 History" and "1838 History." One of the friends of Joseph Smith, Joseph Knight, wrote that after the young prophet had removed a book from a box (buried in a hill), he placed the record by his side. He was then told to take the book, but after he had covered the box from which the work had been taken, he was astonished because it had disappeared. Joseph decided to open the box a second time and to his amazement he relocated the record. When Joseph attempted to lift the book a second time, he was unable to move it. A messenger then told him, "You can't have it now." When Joseph inquired when he could secure the record, the messenger said to return on the 22nd of September, 1824. According to Joseph Knight, each year for several years Joseph Smith returned to the hill anticipating on each occasion that he would be given the sacred record. ("Reminiscences of Joseph Knight," Church Archives. This manuscript written between 1833 and 1847 has been published in Dean C. Jessee, "Joseph Knight's Recollections of Early Mormon History," *BYU Studies* 17 [Autumn 1976]:30-39.)

out of the family that which he was about to say to us, as the world was so wicked that when they came to a knowledge of these things they would try to take our lives; and that when we should obtain the plates, our names would be cast out as evil by all people. Hence the necessity of suppressing these things as much as possible, until the time should come for them to go forth to the world.

After giving us this charge, he proceeded to relate further particulars concerning the work which he was appointed to do, and we received them joyfully, never mentioning them except among ourselves, agreeable to the instructions which we had received from him.

From this time forth, Joseph continued to receive instructions from the Lord, and we continued to get the children together every evening for the purpose of listening while he gave us a relation of the same. I presume our family presented an aspect as singular as any that ever lived upon the face of the earth—all seated in a circle, father, mother, sons, and daughters, and giving the most profound attention to a boy, eighteen years of age, who had never read the Bible through in his life: he seemed much less inclined to the perusal of books than any of the rest of our children, but far more given to meditation and deep study.

We were now confirmed in the opinion that God was about to bring to light something upon which we could stay our minds, or that would give us a more perfect knowledge of the plan of salvation and the redemption of the human family. This caused us greatly to rejoice, the sweetest union and happiness pervaded our house, and tranquility reigned in our midst.

During our evening conversations, Joseph would occasionally give us some of the most amusing recitals that could be imagined. He would describe the ancient inhabitants of this continent, their dress, mode of travelling, and the animals upon which they rode; their cities, their buildings, with every particular; their mode of warfare; and also their religious worship. This he would do with as much ease, seemingly, as if he had spent his whole life with them. [48]

Joseph Smith

Accordingly, as I had been commanded, I went at the end of each year, and at each time I found the same messenger there, and received instruction and intelligence from him at each of our interviews,

---

[48]Lucy Smith, *Biographical Sketches*, pp. 83-87.

respecting what the Lord was going to do, and how and in what manner His Kingdom was to be conducted in the last days.[49]

Lucy Smith

On the twenty-second of September, 1824, Joseph again visited the place where he found the plates the year previous; and supposing at this time that the only thing required, in order to possess until the time for their translation, was to be able to keep the commandments of God—and he firmly believed he could keep every commandment which had been given him—he fully expected to carry them home with him. Therefore, having arrived at the place, and uncovering the plates, he put forth his hand and took them up, but, as he was taking them hence, the unhappy thought darted through his mind that probably there was something else in the box besides the plates, which would be of some pecuniary advantage to him. So, in the moment of excitement, he laid them down very carefully, for the purpose of covering the box, lest some one might happen to pass that way and get whatever there might be remaining in it. After covering it, he turned round to take the Record again, but behold it was gone, and where he knew not, neither did he know the means by which it had been taken from him.

At this, as a natural consequence, he was much alarmed. He kneeled down and asked the Lord why the Record had been taken from him; upon which the angel of the Lord appeared to him, and told him that he had not done as he had been commanded, for in a former revelation he had been commanded not to lay the plates down, or put them for a moment out of his hands, until he got into the house and deposited them in a chest or trunk, having a good lock and key, and, contrary to this, he had laid them down with the view of securing some fancied or imaginary treasure that remained.

In the moment of excitement, Joseph was overcome by the powers of darkness, and forgot the injuction that was laid upon him.

Having some further conversation with the angel on this occasion, Joseph was permitted to raise the stone again, when he beheld the plates as he had done before. He immediately reached forth his hand to take them, but instead of getting them, as he anticipated, he was hurled back upon the ground with great violence. When he recovered, the angel was gone, and he arose and returned to the house, weeping for grief and disappointment.

---

[49]"1838 History."

As he was aware that we would expect him to bring the plates home with him, he was greatly troubled, fearing that we might doubt his having seen them . . . .

Joseph then related the circumstance in full, which gave us much uneasiness, as we were afraid that he might utterly fail of obtaining the Record through some neglect on his part. We, therefore, doubled our diligence in prayer and supplication to God, in order that he might be more fully instructed in his duty, and be preserved from all the wiles and machinations of him "who lieth in wait to deceive."[50]

Katharine Salisbury (Joseph Smith's sister)

I well remember the trials my brother had, before he obtained the records. After he had the vision, he went frequently to the hill, and upon returning would tell us, "I have seen the records, also the brass plates and the sword of Laban with the breast plate and interpreters." He would ask father why he could not get them. The time had not yet come.[51]

Joseph Smith

As my father's worldly circumstances were very limited, we were under the necessity of laboring with our hands, hiring out by day's work and otherwise, as we could get opportunity. Sometimes we were at home, and sometimes abroad, and by continuous labor were enabled to get a comfortable maintenance. In the year 1823 my father's family met with a great affliction by the death of my eldest brother, Alvin. In the month of October, 1825, I hired with an old gentleman by the name of Josiah Stoal, [Stowell], who lived in Chenango County, state of New York. He had heard something of a silver mine having been opened by the Spaniards in Harmony, Susquehanna County, state of Pennsylvania; and had, previous to my hiring to him, been digging in order, if possible, to discover the mine. After I went to live with him, he took me, with the rest of his hands, to dig for the silver mine, at which I continued to work for nearly a month, without success in our

---

[50]Lucy Smith, *Biographical Sketches*, pp. 85-86.

[51]Katharine Salisbury to "Dear Sisters," cited in *The Saints' Herald* 33 (May 1, 1886):260. I have used the spelling of "Katharine" as she wrote her name during the latter part of her life.

undertaking, and finally I prevailed with the old gentleman to cease digging after it. Hence arose the very prevalent story of my having been a money-digger.[52]

During the time that I was thus employed, I was put to board with a Mr. Isaac Hale, of that place; it was there I first saw my wife (his daughter) Emma Hale. On the 18th of January, 1827, we were married, while I was yet employed in the service of Mr. Stoal [Stowell]. Owing to my continuing to assert that I had seen a vision, persecution still followed me, and my wife's father's family were very much opposed to our being married at the house of Squire Tarbill [Tarbell], in South Bainbridge, Chenango County, New York. Immediately after my marriage, I left Mr. Stoal's [Stowell's] and went to my father's, and farmed with that season.[53]

Emma Smith

I was married at South Bainbridge, New York; at the house of Squire Tarbell...when I was in my 22nd or 23rd year...I was visiting at Mr. Stowell's, who lived in Bainbridge, and saw your father there. I had no intention of marrying when I left home; but, during my visit at Mr. Stowell's [Joseph]...urged me to marry him, and preferring to marry him to any other man I knew, I consented. We went to Squire Tarbell's and were married...The account in Mother Smith's History is substantially correct as to date and place.[54]

Joseph Knight

Joseph then went to Mr. Stowel's [Stowell] where he had lived sometime before. But Mr. Stowel could not pay him money for his work very well and he came to me perhaps in November [1826] and worked for me until about the time that he was married, which I think was in

---

[52]"1838 History."

[53]"1838 History." See also "1832 History."

[54]"Last Testimony of Sister Emma," *The Saints' Herald* 26 (October 1, 1879):289-90. See also Joseph Smith III to James T. Cobb, February 14, 1879, Church Archives, Reorganized Church of Jesus Christ of Latter Day Saints, Letterbook 2:85-88 (hereafter cited as RLDS Library-Archives). This and other accounts which are based on interviews with witnesses of the restoration are identified with the word "Interview."

February [January]. And I paid him the money and I furnished him with a horse and cutter [sleigh] to go and see his girl down to Mr. Hail's [Hale's]. And soon after this he was married and Mr. Stowel moved him and his wife to his father's in Palmyra, Ontario County.[55]

Conclusion

Lucy Smith

Perhaps you [Solomon Mack, brother of Lucy Smith] will inquire how this revelation [the Book of Mormon] came forth. It has been hid...in the earth fourteen hundred years, and was placed there by Moroni one of the Nephites, [and] it was engraven upon plates which have the appearance of gold. He being a prophet of the Lord, and seeing the wickedness of the people and knowing that they must be destroyed, and also knowing that if the plates fell into the hands of the Lamanites that they would destroy them, for they sought to destroy all sacred writings, therefore he hid them...in the earth having obtained a promise of the Lord that they should come forth in his own due time unto the world, and I feel to thank my God that he hath spared my life to see this day.[56]

Orson Pratt

In what manner did Joseph Smith declare that a dispensation of the gospel was committed to him? He testified that an angel of God, whose name was Moroni, appeared unto him. It was not merely something speaking in the dark; it was not something wrapped up in mystery, with no glory attending it; but a glorious angel whose countenance shone like a vivid flash of lightning and who was arrayed in a white robe stood before him. He [also] testified that Moroni revealed unto him where he deposited the sacred records of his nation some fourteen hundred years ago; that these records contained the "everlasting gospel" as...anciently taught and recorded by this branch of Israel; and that the

---

[55]Reminiscences of Joseph Knight, published in Dean C. Jessee, "Joseph Knight's Recollection of Early Mormon History," *BYU STudies* 17 (Autumn 1876):30-39. In Jessee's publication and in this work minimal punctuation has been added to facilitate reading.

[56]Lucy Smith to Solomon Mack, January 6, 1831, Church Archives.

time was at hand for the record to be brought forth by the gift and power of God.

Here, then, was a reality—something great and glorious, and after having received from time to time, visits from . . .glorious personages, and talking with them, as one man would talk with another, face to face, beholding their glory, he was permittd to go and take these plates from the place of their deposit—plates of gold—records, some of which were made nearly six hundred years before Christ. And then, to show still further a reality . . .[he] obtained with the record . . .something tangible, the Urim and Thummim, a glorious instrument, used by ancient seers, through which, by the gift and power of the Holy Ghost and by the commandment of Almight God, he translated that record into our language, and the book was published in the fore part of the year 1830 . . .

How does this testimony of Joseph Smith agree with the book of John's prophecy given on the Isle of Patmos? John testifies that when the dispensation of the gospel is again committed to the nations, it shall be through the medium of an angel from heaven. J[oseph] Smith testifies that a dispensation of the gospel for all nations has been committed to him by an angel. The one uttered the prediction; the other testified its fulfillment.[57]

---

[57]Orson Pratt, *Divine Authority, or the Question, Was Joseph Smith Sent of God?* No. 1 (Liverpool: R. James, 1848), p. 4; Orson Pratt in JD, 13:66. In this harmony of the writings and discourses of Orson Pratt, I have changed a few verb tenses for sake of clarity.

CHAPTER FOUR

A Sealed Book and a Lost Manuscript
September 1827 to April 1829

And thou shalt be brought down . . .and thy speech shall whisper out of the dust . . . .And the vision of all is become unto you as the words of a book that is sealed, which men deliver to one that is learned, saying, Read this, I pray thee: and he saith, I cannot; for it is sealed: And the book is delivered to him that is not learned, saying, Read this, I pray thee: and he saith, I am not learned . . . .Behold, I will proceed to do a marvellous work among this people, even a marvellous work and a wonder: for the wisdom of their wise men shall perish, and the understanding of their prudent men shall be hid. (Isaiah 29:4, 11-12, 14 and 2 Nephi 27:6-10.)

After waiting four years, Joseph Smith rode to the Hill Cumorah, and on September 22, 1827, the twenty-one-year-old prophet obtained the Urim and Thummim and a set of plates containing a religious history of ancient America. Upon securing this record, persecution intensified, and in December of that year Joseph and his wife, Emma, decided to move to Harmony, Pennsylvania. There he began a serious translation of a new witness for Christ.

During the eighteen month period that commenced with Joseph Smith's securing the plates, two major developments occured which centered around the activities of Martin Harris. The first of these was Martin Harris' journey to New York City where he met scholars who were unable to translate characters which Joseph had copied from the plates. The other major development was the loss of 116 pages of the Book of Mormon manuscript and the subsequent loss of the power to translate. Even though an unlearned young man was beginning to accomplish a marvelous work, this work proceeded slowly, so that in April 1829, the translation was still in a preliminary stage.

Many contemporary accounts which describe this eighteen month period were written by members of Joseph Smith's family and other close associates. All of them substantiate the Prophet's history. Joseph's contemporaries have stated that persecution intensified in the fall of 1827, and that after Joseph had secured the record on September 22, 1827, some of them assisted him in hiding the plates. Contemporaries also believed Martin Harris when he told them about his journey to New York City, and they accepted his account of losing 116 pages of the manuscript. Although no one except Joseph Smith claimed to have seen the plates during these months, others said they felt the plates (which were wrapped in cloth) and examined the Urim and Thummim. There are no primary sources which suggest that prior to the fall of 1827 Joseph Smith possessed metal plates, a Urim and Thummim, a script containing characters that appeared like ancient writing, nor a manuscript containing a religious history of ancient America. Nor are there any primary sources which indicate that before or during these eighteen months Joseph Smith was composing (by writing and rewriting) a history or studying scholarly publications that might have aided him in writing about the past.

The earliest reports of Joseph Smith's visions by non-Mormons also date to the autumn of 1827. Shortly after Joseph Smith obtained the metal plates, Martin Harris informed others of this event and of the remarkable visions that preceded the coming forth of the Book of Mormon. One writer who described this narrative, as it was related to him by Harris in 1827 and 1828, was the Episcopal minister of Palmyra, Rev. John A. Clark. Rev. Clark's account was written in 1840 after he had moved to Philadelphia. At that time he was serving as rector of St. Andrews Church and as one of the editors and proprietors of the *Episcopal Recorder*, a religious periodical published in Philadelphia. His account was also included in a book which he wrote, entitled *Gleanings by the Way* (1842). Although this report was based on Clark's memory and was written thirteen years after the incident had occurred, Clark did state that his memory of some of the details concerning the rise of Mormonism was refreshed during a visit to Palmyra in the late 1830s.[1]

Rev. Clark's recollection of his conversation with Martin Harris, early one morning in the autumn of 1827, includes many details that harmonize with Joseph Smith's testimony of the coming forth of the Book of Mormon. For example, the Episcopal clergyman wrote that Harris told him of Joseph Smith's nocturnal vision in which he was "assured" by an angel that he was chosen of the Lord to be a prophet of the Most High God. He (Joseph) was further told that he would "bring to light hidden things that would prove of unspeakable benefit to the world." During this vision, Clark continued, Joseph learned about the "golden Bible" that had been kept on "metallic plates covered with characters embossed in gold." This book had been deposited in a chest, ark, or box.[2] According to Clark, Martin Harris also said that during this vision Joseph saw the place where the book was deposited and was instructed to "follow implicitly the divine direction or he would draw down upon him the wrath of heaven." While explaining the process of translation, Clark said that he learned that Joseph Smith would translate the record with the aid of "two transparent stones that had been laid with the golden Bible." Clark reported Harris' sincere interest and belief in this "divine manifestation" and his declaration that Joseph Smith had recently obtained the record and that a "great flood of light was about to burst upon the world."[3] (See Appendix C.)

Joseph Smith and some of his contemporaries wrote accounts of the coming forth of the Book of Mormon and described Harris' experience in New York in February 1828. Before journeying to New York City, Martin Harris secured from the Prophet a page of characters that Joseph had transcribed from the Book of Mormon plates and Joseph's translation of these characters. Harris was interested in securing professional opinions of these documents from America's leading scholars of classical languages. Among the scholars visited by Harris during this trip to New

---

[1]John A. Clark *Gleanings By the Way* (Philadelphia: W. J. & J. K. Simon, 1842), pp. 216, 222, 225, 229, 230-231.

[2]Ibid., pp. 223, 225-26.

[3]Ibid., pp. 223, 225-26, 228.

York City were Professor Charles Anthon and Dr. Mitchell (probably Samuel Lathan Mitchill).[4]

Charles Anthon (1797-1867) and Samuel L. Mitchill (1764-1831) were well known for their knowledge of ancient languages. Anthon knew Latin, Greek, French, and German, and Mitchill could translate German and Latin and had a keen interest in many ancient languages. Both of these men were born, reared, and educated in or near New York City. Dr. Samuel Mitchill's early studies were in the classics, and, after studying science and medicine in New York and Edinburgh, he became a celebrated physician and scientist and wrote scholarly books, articles, and pamphlets on a variety of subjects. Because of his extensive knowledge in so many different areas, Dr. Mitchill was known as a "living encyclopedia."[5]

Charles Anthon was also well known by 1828 for his many accomplishments. After graduating from Columbia College with highest honors, he was admitted to the practice of law in 1819. Shortly after entering this practice and serving as a judge, he accepted a teaching position at Columbia. During the 1820s, Professor Anthon gained distinction for his knowledge of Greek and Roman languages and culture and for his interest in Egyptology and other specialized studies of the ancient world. The work that established Anthon as the foremost classicist in early nineteenth-century America was his edition of J. Lempriere's *Classical Dictionary*. This popular work, translated and enlarged by Anthon, was published in 1825 and went through six or more editions by 1828.[6]

Since Martin Harris was a western New York farmer without any special training in ancient languages, he did know the extent nor the limitations of contemporary scholars' knowledge in this area. Harris could not read the characters which he was carrying to New York City,

---

[4]Stanley H. B. Kimball, "Charles Anthon and the Egyptian Language," *The Improvement Era* 63 (October 1960): 708 and Stanley H. B. Kimball, "I Cannot Read a Sealed Book," *The Improvement Era* 60 (January 1957): 80-82.

[5]Kimball, "Charles Anthon and the Egyptian Language," p. 709-710; Kimball, "I Cannot Read a Sealed Book," pp. 81-82, 106; Allen Johnson and Dumas Malone, eds., *Dictionary of American Biography*, 20 vols. (New York: Charles Scribner's Sons, 1957), 1:313-14 and 7:69-71; and *The National Encyclopedia of American Biography*, 57 vols. (New York and Clifton, N.J.: James T. White, 1882-1977), 4:409 and 6:345-7.

[6]Kimball, "Charles Anthon and the Egyptian Language," p. 709.

and when he started on this journey he probably did not know that scholars in America could not read them either. Many of the Book of Mormon characters were in a "reformed" (possibly meaning modified) Egyptian script. Mormon, one of the last prophets to write on the plates, stated that he wrote in a language that was not understood by other people (Mormon 9:34). Moreover, scholars in America and other parts of the world could not read ancient Egyptian writings in 1828, so that even if the characters which Martin Harris took to New York were Egyptian script, no one in this country could have translated them.

Although Charles Anthon and Samuel Mitchill could not read ancient Egyptian in 1828, they were acquainted with this "mysterious" language. They owned books that contained many examples of Egyptian characters and they knew that scholars in Europe, aided by the Rosetta stone, were beginning to translate Egyptian.[7]

The Rosetta stone had enabled scholars to resolve many of the mysteries of Egyptian script. This monumental stone was discovered in the Nile Valley in 1799 near the town of Rosetta. It measured about 3.75 inches long, 2.5 feet wide and 11 inches thick and contained an inscription written in 196 B.C. by a group of priests praising King Ptolemy V. The decree was written in three different kinds of writing. On the top panel was the hieroglyphic or pictographic script (sacred picture writing) used by the priests. The middle panel repeated the account in the demotic script of spoken Egyptian. The bottom panel contained the same decree in a Greek script that could be easily translated by scholars. After others had unsuccessfully tried to solve the riddle of the Rosetta stone, Jean-Francois Champollion, in 1808, began to study the stone. Eventually, he was able to translate many of the Egyptian characters by comparing the Greek writing with the two Egyptian scripts.[8]

Before meeting Martin Harris, Charles Anthon had studied one book which Champollion had published—*Precis du Systems Hieroglyphique des Anciens Egyptiens* (Paris, 1824). Although in the early 1820s Champollion was beginning to translate some of the characters, such as royal titles, there was little actual translation in the *Precis*. This work, however, informed Anthon and other readers that Champollion was beginning to break a formidable language barrier.[9]

---

[7]Ibid., p. 710.

[8]Fred Gladstone Bratton, *A History of Egyptian Archaeology* (New York: Thomas Y. Crowell Co., 1972), pp. 37-41.

[9]Kimball, "Charles Anthon and the Egyptian Language," p. 710.

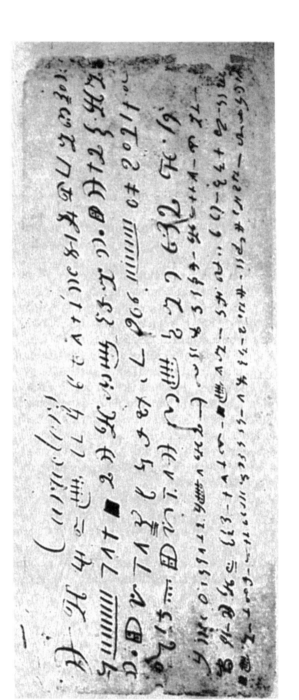

BOOK OF MORMON CHARACTERS

A copy of the characters on the plates from which the Book of Mormon was translated. Following the death of David Whitmer, this transcript passed to members of the Whitmer family. Eventually, it was given to the Reorganized Church of Jesus Christ of Latter Day Saints.

Martin Harris

Charles Anthon

Samuel L. Mitchill

Rosetta Stone

Martin Harris testified that after examining the characters and reading the accompanying translation, Professor Anthon "stated that the translation was correct, more so than any he had before seen translated from the Egyptian." Harris further stated that Charles Anthon gave him a "certificate certifying to the people of Palmyra that they were true characters, and that the translation of such of them as had been translated was also correct." Before leaving, Harris added, Professor Anthon asked him to explain the origin of the manuscripts. After Martin Harris told Anthon about the coming forth of the Book of Mormon through an angelic visitation and that a portion of the plates were sealed and were not to be translated at that time, Harris said that Anthon took the certificate, tore it to pieces, and said, "I cannot read a sealed book."

Harris also said that he showed the characters and the translation to a "Dr. Mitchell" who verified the opinion of Anthon regarding both the characters and the translation.[10] It is possible that Martin Harris visited Dr. Mitchill before conversing with Professor Anthon. Perhaps Harris took to Anthon a letter of introduction from Mitchill, and then returned to Mitchill's home or office after meeting with Anthon. At any rate, Martin Harris returned from this trip to New York City convinced that Joseph Smith was a prophet of God, that he possessed a set of golden plates, and that by the power of God he was able to translate the sacred record. Fortified by this conviction, and learning from Joseph that his journey fulfilled a prophecy that had been recorded by Isaiah centuries before the birth of Christ, Martin Harris was prepared to give his time, his energy, and his material wealth to help Joseph Smith bring forth "a marvelous work and a wonder."

A question that has often been asked is "Why did Anthon inform Harris that the translation of the characters was correct if he could not have read the ancient American script?" Perhaps, when Charles Anthon compared the characters on the manuscript with other ancient scripts, he recognized that many of the characters appeared genuine and that when he saw the Prophet's translation he did not want to admit that he could not decipher the characters.[11] In light of the discovery of the Rosetta stone, perhaps he thought there was already someone who could

---

[10]*T&S* 3 (May 2, 1842):773. In Joseph Smith's manuscript history and in the initial publication of this history in the *Times and Seasons* Anthon was spelled "Anthony" and Mitchill, "Mitchel."

[11]Ariel L. Crowley, "The Anthon Transcript: An Evidence of the Truth of the Prophet's Account of the Origin of the Book of Mormon," *The Improvement Era* 45 (January-March 1942): 14-15, 58-60, 76-79, 124-25, 150-51, and 182-83.

translate Egyptian. He must have been puzzled as he read the manuscript but, as Martin Harris declared, Anthon did indicate to him that the translation appeared correct. Perhaps Anthon was interested in securing an ancient document, thereby enhancing his reputation by being personally involved in an important discovery.[12] After learning about the unusual circumstances surrounding the Book of Mormon and that a portion of the plates was sealed and not to be translated, Anthon undoubtedly recognized his mistake, destroyed the certificate that he had prepared, and said that he could not read a sealed book.

At the request of others, Charles Anthon wrote two known letters describing Martin Harris' visit with him in which he was shown a transcript from the Book of Mormon plates. The first of these letters was published by its recipient, E. D. Howe of Painesville, Ohio, in *Mormonism Unvailed* (1834), and the second was sent to Rev. Dr. Thomas Winthrop Coit, Rector of Trinity Church, Rochelle, Westchester County, New York, and later published in Rev. John A. Clark's *Gleanings by the Way* (1842).[13]

There are several obvious contradictions in Anthon's letters. In the second letter (1841), Anthon wrote that "until the present time" no one had ever requested from him a "statement in writing" about his encounter with Martin Harris, as if to say that he had never written the 1834 Howe letter. This seems even more puzzling when one compares the two letters which contain similar words and phrases. There are so many similarities that it appears as though Anthon might have used the first letter as basis for the second, even copying portions of the first letter. In Anthon's 1834 letter, he reported that he had declined to give Harris ("the stranger") any opinion regarding the ancient characters, yet, in the 1842 letter he wrote that at the request of the "plain looking countryman," he had given his "opinion in writing about the paper which he had shown" him without hesitation.

There are also conflicts in the writings of Anthon and statements of Harris. Anthon denied saying that the characters were authentic and did not refer in his letters to examining a translation. A basic theme of the Anthon letters is that this professor convinced the stranger that the manuscript was a hoax while statements of Harris reveal that, at least during part of the visit, Anthon indicated to him that the characters appeared genuine and the translation seemed to be correct. Since both

---

[12]Orson Pratt, *Account of Several Remarkable Visions*, p. 14.

[13]E. D. Howe, *Mormonism Unvailed* (Painesville: E. D. Howe, 1834), pp. 270-72 and Clark, *Gleanings By the Way*, pp. 233, 237-38.

accounts cannot be entirely correct, why should one believe Harris rather than Anthon? Copies of the characters taken to New York City which have been preserved provide evidence that these inscriptions appear like ancient Egyptian script. Moreover, if Anthon would have convinced Harris that the manuscript was a hoax, then why would Harris have immediately returned to Pennsylvania to assist Joseph Smith with the translations, and why would Harris have sacrificed financially to pay for the publication of the Book of Mormon and contributed much of his material wealth to the advancement of the restored gospel? Undoubtedly, Charles Anthon was embarrassed by some of the things which he had said to Harris, especially for that which he had written on a certificate, and therefore, he wrote some inaccurate statements. Despite his original interest (according to Harris) and his later vehement denial of the characters' authenticity, Anthon never pursued the matter any further. He refused to investigate the history and doctrines of the restored church. He refused to attend any meeting conducted by a Mormon preacher, even after he learned that his name was being mentioned in the sermons delivered by missionaries of the church.[14]

Although there are contradictions in the two letters written by Anthon and conflicts between the statements of Anthon and Harris, these letters substantiate some aspects of Martin Harris' testimony. They clearly prove that Harris did take characters which had been copied from the Book of Mormon plates to New York City and that he showed them to Professor Anthon and Dr. Samuel Mitchell, and that these scholars were unable to translate the characters. (See Appendix D.)

Many contemporary records, some written by critics of the Church, identify Martin Harris as the individual who showed Charles Anthon the characters which Joseph Smith copied from the golden plates as well as a translation of this script. One non-Mormon contemporary who verified many aspects of the visit of Martin Harris to New York was Pomeroy Tucker. Tucker was a resident of Palmyra who became acquainted with the Smith family shortly after they arrived in Palmyra from Vermont in 1816. His acquaintance with the Smiths continued after they moved to Manchester township in 1818. He was editor and proprietor of the *Wayne Sentinel* when the Book of Mormon was being printed on the press which produced his paper. He assisted in the printing of the Book of Mormon and claimed that he had frequent interviews with Martin Harris, Oliver Cowdery, and members of the Smith family.[15] According to Tucker,

---

[14]Clark, *Gleanings By the Way*, pp. 233, 237-38.

[15]Pomeroy Tucker, *Origin, Rise, and Progress of Mormonism* (New York: D. Appleton and Co., 1867), p. 4.

Martin Harris desired to secure the opinion of scholars regarding the ancient characters before he invested his money in the Book of Mormon project. Therefore, he procured from Joseph Smith *"some resemblances of antique characters of hieroglyphics* purporting to be exact copies from the plates; which, *together with the translations* . . .he carried to New York City, where he sought for them the interpretation and bibliogical scrutiny of such scholars as Hon. Luther Bradish, Dr. Mitchell, Professor Anthon, and others."[16] Tucker quoted Anthon's 1834 letter in a critical work which he published in 1867 (*Origin, Rise, and Progress of Mormonism*), and he concluded that the scholars of New York had pronounced Joseph Smith's claims as fraudulent. Yet he also wrote that Harris had always been known for his "honesty" and stated that, following the trip to New York, Harris was willing to make substantial financial sacrifices to bring forth the "golden Bible." In Tucker's opinion, the Book of Mormon would not have been published without Harris' financial aid.[17]

Rev. John Clark another critic, also stated that Martin Harris had shown Book of Mormon characters to Professor Anthon and returned from this experience with a determination to help Joseph Smith publish the Book of Mormon. Clark identified the approximate date of the New York trip by writing that Harris had visited him soon after his interview with Anthon and had discussed the Anthon conversation with him (Clark). According to Rev. Clark, Martin Harris had not doubts regarding Joseph Smith's commission and was willing "to sustain Smith in carrying on this work of the lord; and that he was determined that the book should be published, though it consumed all his worldly substance."[18]

Another non-Mormon who identified Martin Harris as the individual who showed characters that appeared like ancient writings to scholars in New York City was James Gordon Bennett. He was a writer for the *New York Courier and Enquirer* and became one of America's most renowned early journalists. While traveling in western New York in August 1831, Bennett interviewed Charles Butler, a lawyer and philanthropist of Geneva, New York; Egbert B. Grandin, publisher of the

---

[16]Ibid., pp. 41-42 (italics added). Luther Bradish (1783-1863) was a diplomat and statesman who had traveled extensively in Europe and Asia (including Egypt) before 1826 and then settled in Franklin County, New York, where he owned extensive properties. From 1827 to 1830 he served in the state legislature. (*Dictionary of American Biography* 1:567-68.)

[17]Tucker, *Origin, Rise, and Progress of Mormonism*, pp. 42, 45, 54-55, 71.

[18]Clark, *Gleanings By the Way*, pp. 228-31.

Book of Mormon; and others living in the Finger Lake Country. Employing notes taken during his interviews, Bennett wrote a feature story on August 15, 1831, that appeared in two issues of the *Morning Courier and Enquirer*. According to this account, Harris showed "several manuscripts" to one of the professors of Columbia who "thought them very curious . . .[but] admitted that he could not decypher them," and counseled Harris to take the manuscripts to Dr. Mitchell. Complying with this suggestion, Harris visited Dr. Mitchell who examined the characters and "compared them with the hieroglyphics discovered by Champollion in Egypt—and set them down as the language of a people formerly in existence in the East, but now no more."[19]

In addition to the writings of Joseph Smith, Lucy Smith, and Orson Pratt, this chapter contains other contemporary accounts which substantiate Joseph Smith's statements regarding events that transpired in 1827 and 1828. Martin Haris did not keep a diary during this period (nor did he write an autobiography describing events in which he was involved during the 1820s. Therefore, his experiences are based on a few of his letters and on various reports of interviews with him.

Joseph Obtains the Plates

Joseph Smith

After I had received many visits from the angels of God unfolding the majesty and glory of the events that should transpire in the last days, on the morning of September 22, 1827, the angel of the Lord delivered the records, the Urim and Thummim, and breastplate into my hands. [I had] gone as usual at the end of another year to the place where they [the plates] were deposited, and the same heavenly messenger delivered them up to me with this charge: that I should be responsible for them; that if I should let them go carelessly, or through any neglect of mine, I should

---

[19]Leonard J. Arrington, "James Gordon Bennett's 1831 Report on 'The Mormonites,'" *BYU Studies* 10 (Spring 1970): 353-56, 362. A portion of this article was reprinted in the *Hillsborough Gazette* (Ohio), October 29, 1831, and is on file at Oberlin College. See also Milton V. Backman, Jr., "Contemporary Accounts of the Latter-day Saints and Their Leaders Appearing in Early Ohio Newspapers, 1830-1838," Vol. II, Task Paper, Church Archives and Brigham Young University Library.

be cut off; but that if I would use all my endeavors to preserve them, until he, the messenger, should call for them, they should be protected.[20]

William Smith

After my father's family moved to New York State, in about five years they cleared sixty acres of land, and fenced it. The timber on this land was very heavy. Some of the elms were so large that we had to nigger them off. They were too large to be cut with a cross-cut saw. We built a frame dwelling house and out buildings. My brothers Joseph and Hyrum had to work. Joseph did not have time to make gold plates.

The time to receive the plates came at last. When Joseph received them, he came in and said: "Father, I have got the plates." All believed it was true, father, mother, brothers and sisters. You can tell what a child is.

---

[20]JS-H 1:59 and *T&S* 3 (May 2, 1842):772. See also "1832 History" and "1842 History." According to Lucy, when Joseph first obtained the plates, the angel of the Lord instructed him, saying:

> Now you have got the Record into your own hands, and you are but a man, therefore you will have to be watchful and faithful to your trust, or you will be overpowered by wicked men, for they will lay every plan and scheme that is possible to get it away from you, and if you do not take heed continually, they will succeed. While it was in my hands, I could keep it, and no man had power to take it away; but now I give it up to you. Beware, and look well to your ways, and you shall have power to retain it, until the time for it to be translated. (Lucy Smith, *Biographical Sketches*, p. 106.)

Orson Pratt described attempts by others to secure the plates as follows:

> After having obtained those sacred things, while proceeding home through the wilderness and fields, he [Joseph Smith] was waylaid by two ruffians, who had secreted themselves for the purpose of robbing him of the records. One of them struck him with a club before he perceived them; but being a strong man, and a large in stature, with great exertion he cleared himself from them, and ran towards home, being closely pursued until he came near his father's house, when his pursuers, for fear of being detected, turned and fled the other way. (Orson Pratt, *Account of Several Remarkable Visions*, p. 13.)

Parents know whether their children are truthful or not. . . .Father knew his child was telling the truth. When the plates were brought in they were wrapped up in a tow frock. My father then put them into a pillow case. Father said, "What, Joseph, can we not see them?"

"No, I was disobedient the first time, but I intend to be faithful this time; for I was forbidden to show them until they are translated, but you can feel them. . . ."[21]

I was permitted to lift them as they laid in a pillow case; but not to see them, as it was contrary to the commands he had received. They weighed about sixty pounds according to the best of my judgment. . . .[22] They were not quite as large as this Bible. . . .One could easily tell that they were not stone, hewn out to deceive, or even a block of wood. Being a mixture of gold and copper, they were much heavier than stone, and very much heavier than wood.[23]

Katharine Salisbury, Sister of the Prophet

When [the time to secure the plates had] arrived, he [Joseph Smith] was commanded to go on the 22nd day of September 1827 at 2'clock. We had supposed that when he should bring them home, the whole family would be allowed to see them, but he said it was forbidden of the Lord. They could be seen only by those who were chosen to bear their testimony to the world. We had therefore to be content until they were translated and we could have the book to read.[24]

Lucy Smith

On the twentieth of September, Mr. [Joseph] Knight and his friend Stoal [Josiah Stowell], came to see how we were managing matters with

---

[21]"The Old Soldier's Testimony," sermon preached by Bro. William B. Smith, in the Saints' Chapel, Deloit, Iowa, June 8, 1884, and reported by C. E. Butterworth. *The Saint's Herald* 31 (1884):643-44. See also William Smith, *William Smith On Mormonism: A True Account of the Origin of the Book of Mormon* (Lamoni, Iowa: Herald, 1883), pp. 10-11.

[22]William Smith, *On Mormonism*, p. 12.

[23]"The Old Soldier's Testimony," p. 644.

[24]Letter of Katharine Salisbury, March 10, 1886 cited in *Saints' Herald* 33 (1886):260.

Stoddard and Co.; and they tarried with us until the twenty-second. On the night of the twenty-first, I sat up very late, as my work rather pressed upon my hands. I did not retire until after twelve o'clock at night. About twelve o'clock, Joseph came to me and asked me if I had a chest with a lock and key. I knew in an instant what he wanted it for, and not having one, I was greatly alarmed, as I thought it might be a matter of considerable moment. But Joseph, discovering my anxiety, said, "Never mind, I can do very well for the present without it—be calm—all is right."

Shortly after this, Joseph's wife passed through the room with her bonnet and riding dress; and in a few minutes they left together, taking Mr. Knight's horse and waggon. I spent the night in prayer and supplication to God, for the anxiety of my mind would not permit me to sleep. At the usual hour, I commenced preparing breakfast. My heart fluttered at every footstep, as I now expected Joseph and Emma momentarily, and feared lest Joseph might meet with a second disappointment.

When the male portion of the family were seated at the breakfast table, Mr. Smith enquired for Joseph, for he was not aware that he had left home. I requested my husband not to call him, for I would like to have him take breakfast with his wife that morning.

"No, no;" said my husband, "I must have Joseph sit down here and eat with me."

"Well, now, Mr. Smith," continued I, "*do* let him eat with his wife *this* morning; he almost always takes breakfast with you."

His father finally consented, and eat without him, and no further inquiries were made concerning his absence, but in a few minutes Mr. Knight came in quite disturbed.

"Why, Mr. Smith," exclaimed he, "my horse is gone, and I can't find him on the premises, and I wish to start for home in a half an hour."

"Never mind the horse," said I. "Mr. Knight does not know all the nooks and corners in the pastures; I will call William, he will bring the horse immediately."

This satisfied him for the time being; but he soon made another discovery. His waggon also was gone. He then concluded, that a rogue had stolen them both.

"Mr. Knight said I, do be quiet; I would be ashamed to have you go about, waiting upon yourself—just go out and talk with Mr. Smith until William comes, and if you really must go home, your horse shall be brought, and you shall be waited upon like a gentleman. He accordingly went out, and while he was absent Joseph returned.

I trembled so with fear, lest all might be lost in consequence of some failure in keeping the commandments of God, that I was under the necessity of leaving the room in order to conceal my feelings. Joseph saw this, and said, "Do not be uneasy mother, all is right."[25]

Joseph Knight

[In] the forepart of September [1827], I went to Rochester on business and returned by Palmyra to be there by the 22nd of September. I was there several days.... That night we went to bed and in the morning I got up and my horse and carriage were gone....After a while he [Joseph Smith] came home [with] the horse. All came into the house to breakfast but nothing [was] said about where they had been. After breakfast Joseph called me into the other room....He set his foot on the bed, leaned his head on his hand and said, ..."It is ten times better than I expected." Then he went on to tell length and width and thickness of the plates; and said he, "They appear to be gold." But he seemed to think more of the glasses or the Urim and Thummim than he did of the plates, for, said he, "I can see anything; they are marvellous. Now they are written in characters and I want them translated."[26]

Joseph Knight, Jr.

In 1827 [the winter of 1826-1827] he [my father] hired Joseph Smith. Joseph and I worked and slept together. My father said Joseph was the best hand he ever hired. We found him a boy of truth. He was about 21 years of age. I think it was in November [1826] he made known to my father and I that he had seen a vision, that a personage had appeared to him and told him where there was a gold book of ancient date buried, and if he would follow the directions of the angel he could get it. We were told it in secret; I being the youngest son, my two older brothers did not believe in such things. My father and I believed what he told us. I think we were the first [to believe] after his father's family [and probably Martin Harris]....At last he got the plates, and rode in my father's wagon and carried them home.[27]

---

[25]Lucy Smith, *Biographical Sketches*, pp. 99-101.

[26]Reminiscenses of Joseph Knight, Church Archives. This manuscript written between 1833 and 1847 has been published in Dean Jessee, "Joseph Knight's Recollection of Early Mormon History," *BYU Studies* 17 (Autumn 1976):30-39. In this and other quotations from this manuscript, spelling, verb tenses, and punctuation changes have been made to harmonize with current English usage.

[27]Autobiography of Joseph Knight, Jr., p. 1, Church Archives.

A Description of the Plates, Urim and Thummim, and Breastplate

Joseph Smith

These records were engraven on plates which had the appearance of gold; each plate was six inches wide and eight inches long and not quite so thick as common tin. They were filled with engravings in Egyptian characters and bound together in a volume, as the leaves of a book, with three rings running through the whole. The volume was something near six inches in thickness, a part of which was sealed. The characters on the unsealed part were small and beautifully engraved. The whole book exhibited many marks of antiquity in its construction and much skill in the art of engraving. With the records was found a curious instrument which the ancients called "Urim and Thummim," which consisted of two transparent stones set in the rim of a bow fastened to a breastplate.[28]

Lucy Smith

[On the morning of September 22, after Joseph had returned from the hill, he placed] the article [the Urim and Thummim] of which he spoke into my hands, and, upon examination, [I] found that it consisted of two smooth three-cornered diamonds set in glass, and the glasses were set in silver bows, which were connected with each other in much the same way as old fashioned spectacles.

That of which I spoke, which Joseph termed a key, was indeed, nothing more nor less than the Urim and Thummim, and it was by this that the angel showed him many things which he saw in vision; by which he could also ascertain, at any time, the approach of danger, either to himself or the Record, and on account of which he always kept the Urim and Thummim about his person.

After bringing home the plates, Joseph commenced working with his father and brothers on the farm, in order to be as near as possible to the treasure which was confided to his care.

Soon after this, he came in from work, one afternoon, and . . .handed me the breastplate spoken of in his history.

It was wrapped in a thin muslin handkerchief, so thin that I could see the glistening metal, and ascertain its proportions without any difficulty.

It was concave on one side, and convex on the other, and extended from the neck downwards, as far as the centre of the stomach of a man of

---

[28]*T&S* 3 (March 1 1842):707 and Orson Pratt, *Account of Several Remarkable Visions*, pp. 12-13.

extraordinary size. It had four straps of the same material, for the purpose of fastening it to the breast, two of which ran back to go over the shoulders, and the other two were designed to fasten to the hips. They were just the width of two of my fingers, (for I measured them,) and they had holes in the end of them, to be convenient for fastening.

The whole plate was worth at least five hundred dollars: after I had examined it, Joseph placed it in the chest with the Urim and Thummim.[29]

Persecution Intensifies

Joseph Smith

I soon found out the reason why I received such strict charges to keep them safe, and why it was that the messenger had said that when I had done what was required at my hand, he would call for them. For no sooner was it known that I had them, than the most strenuous exertions were used to get them from me, and false reports, misrepresentations and slander flew as on the wings of the wind in every direction. Rumor with her thousand tongues was all the time employed in circulating tales about my father's family, and about myself. If I were to relate a thousandth part of them, it would fill up volumes. The house was frequently beset by mobs and evil designing persons. Several times I was shot at and very narrowly escaped. The persecution became more bitter and severe than before, and multitudes were on the alert continually to get them [the plates] from me if possible. But by the wisdom of God, they remained safe in my hands until I had accomplished by them what was required.[30]

Joseph Knight

Now he [Joseph Smith] was commanded not to let [anybody] see those things [plates and the Urim and Thummim] except for a few witnesses at a given time. Now it soon got about that Joseph had found the plates and people came to see them, but he told them they could not, for he must not show them. But many insisted and offered money and property to see them. [And] for keeping them from the people, they [others] persecuted and abused him. The Smiths were obliged to hide

---

[29]Lucy Smith, *Biographical Sketches*, pp. 101, 106, 107.

[30]JS-H 1:60-61 and *T&S* 3 (May 2, 1842):772. See also "1842 History."

them [the plates], and they hid them under a brick hearth in the west room.[31]

Lucy Smith

[A few days after Joseph obtained the Record], one of the neighbours asked Mr. Smith many questions concerning the plates. I will here observe, that no one ever heard anything from us respecting them, except a confidential friend, whom my husband had spoken to about them some two or three years previous. It appeared that Satan had now stirred up the hearts of those who had gotten a hint of the matter from our friend, to search into it, and make every possible move towards thwarting the purposes of the Almighty . . . .

[One day Joseph] sent Carlos, my youngest son, to his brother Hyrum's, to have him come up immediately, as he desired to see him. When he came, Joseph requested him to get a chest, having a good lock and key, and to have it there by the time he (Joseph) should return. And, after giving these instructions, Joseph started for the plates.

The plates were secreted about three miles from home, in the following manner. Finding an old birch log much decayed, excepting the bark, which was in a measure sound, he took his pocket knife and cut the bark with some care, then turned it back, and made a hole of sufficient size to receive the plates, and laying them in the cavity thus formed, he replaced the bark; after which he laid across the log, in several places, some old stuff that happened to lay near, in order to conceal, as much as possible, the place in which they were deposited.

Joseph, on coming to them, took them from their secret place, and, wrapping them in his linen frock, placed them under his arm and started for home.

After proceeding a short distance, he thought it would be more safe to leave the road and go through the woods. Travelling some distance after he left the road, he came to a large windfall, and as he was jumping over a log, a man sprang up from behind it, and gave him a heavy blow with a gun. Joseph turned around and knocked him down, then ran at the top of his speed. About half a mile further he was attacked again in the same manner as before; he knocked this man down in like manner as the former, and ran on again; and before he reached home he was assaulted the third time. In striking the last one he dislocated his thumb, which,

---

[31]Reminiscences of Joseph Knight, Church Archives.

however, he did not notice until he came within sight of the house, when he threw himself down in the corner of the fence in order to recover his breath. As soon as he was able, he arose and came to the house. He was still altogether speechless from fright and the fatigue of running.

After resting a few moments, he desired me to send Carlos . . .to Hyrum's, to tell him to bring the chest.

I did as I was requested, and when Carlos arrived at Hyrum's, he found him at tea, with two of his wife's sisters. Just as Hyrum was raising a cup to his mouth, Carlos touched his shoulder. Without waiting to hear one word from the child, he dropped the cup, sprang from the table, caught the chest, turned it upside down, and emptying its contents on the floor, left the house instantly with the chest on his shoulder.

The young ladies were greatly astonished at his singular behaviour, and declared his wife—who was then confined to her bed, her oldest daughter, Lovina, being but four days old—that he was certainly crazy.

His wife laughed heartily, and replied, "Oh, not in the least, he has just thought of something which he has neglected, and it is just like him to fly off in a tangent when he thinks of anything in that way."

When the chest came, Joseph locked up the Record, then threw himself upon the bed, and after resting a little, so that he could converse freely, he arose and went into the kitchen, where he related his recent adventure to his father, Mr. Knight, and Mr. Stoal [Stowell], besides many others, who had by this time collected, with the view of hearing something in regard to the strange circumstance which had taken place. He showed them his thumb, saying, "I must stop talking, father, and get you to put my thumb in place, for it is very painful . . . ."

Shortly after this circumstance, Joseph . . .determined that a portion of the hearth should be taken up, and the Record and breast-plate should be buried under the same, and then the hearth be relaid, to prevent suspicion.

This was done as speedily as possible, but the hearth was scarcely relaid when a large company of men well armed came rushing up to the house. Joseph threw open the doors, and taking a hint from the stratagem of his grandfather Mack, halloowed as if had a legion at hand, in the meanwhile, giving the word of command with great emphasis; while all the male portion of the family, from the father down to little Carlos, ran out of the house with such fury upon the mob, that it struck them with terror and dismay, and they fled before the little Spartan band into the woods, where they dispersed themselves to their several homes.

In a short time Joseph received another intimation of the approach of a mob, also of the necessity of removing the Record and breast-plate from the place wherein they were secreted, consequently he took them out of the box in which they were placed, and wrapping them in clothes, carried them across the road to a cooper's shop, and laid them in a quantity of flax which was stowed in the shop loft. After which he nailed up the box again, then tore up the floor of the shop, and put it under the same.

As soon as night came, the mob came also, and commenced ransacking the place. They rummaged round the house, and all over the premises, but did not come into the house. After making satisfactory search they went away.

The next morning we found the floor of the cooper's shop torn up, and the box which was laid under it shivered in pieces.[32]

The Move to Pennsylvania

Joseph Smith

Persecution became so intolerable that I was under the necessity of leaving Manchester, and going with my wife to Susquehanna County, in the state of Pennsylvania. While preparing to start—being very poor, and the persecution so heavy upon us that there was no probability that we would ever be otherwise—in the midst of our afflictions we found a friend in a gentleman by the name of Martin Harris, who came to us and gave me fifty dollars [to bear my expenses]. Mr. Harris was a resident of Palmyra Township, Wayne County, in the state of New York, and a farmer of respectability. By this timely aid, I was enabled to reach the place of my destination in Pennsylvania.[33]

Lucy Smith

Soon afterwards, Alva Hale, Joseph's brother-in-law, came to our house, from Pennsylvania, for the purpose of moving Joseph to his father-in-law's, as word had been sent to them, that Joseph desired to move there as soon as he could settle up his business. During the short interval of Alva's stay with us, he and Joseph were one day in Palmyra, at a public-house, transacting some business. As they were thus engaged, Mr. Harris came in: he stepped immediately up to my son, and taking him by the hand, said, "How do you do, Mr. Smith." After which, he took a bag of silver from his pocket, and said again, "Here, Mr. Smith, is fifty

---

[32]Lucy Smith, *Biographical Sketches*, pp. 102, 104-09.

[33]JS-H 1:61-62 and *T&S* 3 (May 2, 1842):772.

dollars; I give this to you to do the Lord's work with; no, I give it to the Lord for his own work."

"No," said Joseph, "We will give you a note, Mr. Hale, I presume, will sign it with me."

"Yes," said Alva, "I will sign it."

Mr. Harris, however, insisted that he would give the money to the Lord, and called those present to witness the fact that he gave it freely, and did not demand any compensation, that it was for the purpose of helping Mr. Smith to do the Lord's work. And as I have been informed, many were present on that occasion, who witnessed the same circumstance.

Joseph, in a short time, arranged his affairs, and was ready for the journey. [He placed] the Record and breast-plate . . .[in a box and] nailed up . . .(the) box and then put . . .[the box] into a strong cask; and filling the cask with beans, headed it up again

When it became generally known that Joseph was about moving to Pennsylvania, a mob of fifty men collected themselves together, and they went to one Dr. McIntyre, and requested him to take the command of the company, stating, that they were resolved on following "Joe Smith," and taking his "gold bible" from him. The doctor's ideas and feelings did not altogether harmonize with theirs, and he told them they were a pack of devilish fools, and to go home and mind their own business; that, if Joseph Smith had any busines of that sort to attend to, he was capable of doing it, and that it would be better for them to busy themselves about that which more concerned them.

After this, a quarrel arose among them respecting who should be captain, and it ran so high that it broke up the expedition.[34]

Orson Pratt

[After packing] his goods [and] putting the plates into a barrel of beans [Joseph] proceeded upon his journey. He had not gone far before he was overtaken by an officer with a search-warrant, who flattered himself with the idea that he should surely obtain the plates; after searching very diligently, he was sadly disappointed at not finding them. Mr. Smith then drove on, but before he got to his journey's end, he was again overtaken by an officer on the same business, and after ransacking

---

[33]JS-H 1:61-62 and *T&S* 3 (May 2 1842): 772.

[34]Lucy Smith, *Biographical Sketches*, pp. 112-13.

the wagon very carefully, he went his way, as muchg chagrined as the first at not being able to discover the object of his research. Without any further molestation, [Joseph] pursued his journey until he came into the northern part of Pennsylvania, near the Susquehannah River, in which part his father-in-law resided.[35]

William Smith

We were all very much scoffed at and persecuted during all this time, while Joseph was receiving his visions and translating the plates . . . .In consequence of his vision and his having the golden plates and refusing to show them [to others], a great persecution arose against the whole family, and he [Joseph] was compelled to remove to Pennsylvania with the plates, where he translated them by means of the Urim and Thummim, which he obtained with the plates.[36]

Martin Harris' Experience in New York City

Joseph Smith

Immediately after my arrival there [Harmony, Pennsylvania], I commenced copying the characters off the plates. I copied a considerable number of them, and by means of the Urim and Thummim, I translated some of them, [which I did] between the time I arrived at the house of my wife's father, in the month of December, and the following February. [Meanwhile,] because of [the] faith and righteous deed of Martin Harris [in giving financial assistance for the move to Pennsylvania], the Lord appeared to him in a vision and showed him the marvelous work which he [the Lord] was about to do. He [Martin Harris] immediately came to Susquehannah sometime in the month of February, and said that the Lord had shown him that he must go to New York City with some of the characters. [After I had given him] the characters which I had drawn off the plates, he started with them to the city of New York.

While in New York City, Martin Harris showed the manuscript to the learned, saying, "Read this, I pray thee." The learned replied, "I cannot," but said that if Martin Harris would bring the plates to him, he would read it. But the Lord forbade it. After Martin Harris' return to Pennsylvania, I

---

[35]Orson Pratt, *Account of Several Remarkable Visions*, pp. 13-14.

[36]William Smith, *On Mormonism*, pp. 11-12.

told the Lord that I was not learned and could not translate the record, but the Lord [had] prepared spectacles (the Urim and Thummim) for me to read the book by, therefore I commenced translating the characters. Thus, the prophecy of Isaiah which is written in the 29th chapter of that book was fulfilled.

For [a descrition of] what took place [in New York City,] I refer to his [Martin Harris'] own account of the circumstances, as he related them to me after his return:

> I went to the city of New York, and presented the characters which had been translated, with the translation thereof, to Professor Anthon, a gentleman celebrated for his literary attainments. Professor Anthon stated that the translation was correct, more so than any he had before seen translated from the Egyptian. I then showed him those which were not yet translated, and he said that they were Egyptian, Chaldaic, Assyriac, and Arabic; and he said that they were true characters. He gave me a certificate, certifying to the people of Palmyra that they were true characters, and that the translation of such of them as had been translated was also correct. I took the certificate and put it into my pocket, and was just leaving the house when Mr. Anthon called me back and asked me how the young man found that there were gold plates in the place where he found them. I answered that an angel of God had revealed it unto him. He then said to me, "Let me see the certificate." I accordingly took it out of my pocket and gave it to him, when he took it and tore it to pieces, saying that there was no such thing now as ministering of angels, and that if I would bring the plates to him he would translate them. I informed him that part of the plates were sealed, and that I was forbidden to bring them. He replied, "I cannot read a sealed book." I left him and went to Dr. Mitchel [probably Mitchill], who sanctioned what Professor Anthon had said respecting both the characters and translation.[37]

---

[37]JS-H 1;64-65; *T&S* 3 (May 2, 1842):772-73; "1832 History," and Hofmann Manuscript, Church Archives. For changes in the text (spelling of Anthon), see footnote 10.

Additional Contemporary Accounts of Martin Harris' Trip to New York

Lucy Smith

Not long after the circumstance of the mob's going into the cooper's shop, and splitting in pieces the box, Joseph began to make arrangements to accomplish the translation of the Record. The first step that he was instructed to take in regard to this work, was to make a *fac-simile* of some of the characters, which were called reformed Egyptian, and to send them to some of the most learned men of this generation, and ask them for the translation thereof.

The reader will here observe, that on a preceding page of this volume, I spoke of a confidential friend to whom my husband merely mentioned the existence of the plates, some two or three years prior to their coming forth. This was no other than Martin Harris, one of the witnesses to the book subsequent to its being translated . . . .

When Joseph had had a sufficient time to accomplish the journey, and transcribe some of the Egyptian characters, it was agreed that Martin Harris should follow him—and that he (Martin) should take the characters to the East, and, on his way, he was to call on all the professed linguists, in order to give them an opportunity to display their talents in giving a translation of the characters.[38]

Martin Harris - Interviews

I took a transcript of the characters of the plates to Dr. Anthon of New York. When I arrived at the house of Professor Anthon, I found him in his office and alone, and [I] presented the transcript to him and asked him to read it . . . .Professor Anthon . . .pronounced them [the characters copied from the golden plates] correct Egyptian characters, but somewhat changed and gave me a certificate, . . .certifying that the characters were Arabic, Chaldaic, and Egyptian . . . .he said if I would bring [him] the plates, he would assist in the translation. I told him I could not, for they were sealed . . . .I then [was preparing to leave] . . .and was near the door, when he said, "How did the young man know the plates were there?" I said an angel had shown them to him. Professor Anthon then said, "Let me see the certificate:"—upon which I took it from my waistcoat pocket and unsuspectingly gave it to him. He then tore it up in anger, saying there was no such thing as angels now—it was all a hoax. I then went to

---

[38]Lucy Smith, *Biographical Sketches*, pp. 109, 113-14.

Dr. Mitchell with the transcript, and he confirmed what Professor Anthon had said . . . .

[David Whitmer has] a transcript of a portion of the characters as found on the golden plates taken or copied on a small piece of paper, perhaps about six or seven inches by four or five. Seven or eight lines of them were very carefully transmitted to this paper as the words of this book which were taken [by me] to Professor Charles Anthon of New York . . . . Oliver Cowdery . . . left this relic with David Whitmer . . . shortly before his demise [death].[39]

Orson Pratt

The perfect agreement between the prediction of Isaiah (chap. xxix) and Mr. Smith's account of the finding and translation of the Book of Mormon is another collateral proof that he was divinely commissioned. Mr. Smith testifies that the plates from which that book was translated were *taken out of the ground*, from where they were originally deposited by the prophet Moroni; that the box containing them was composed of stone, so constructed as to exclude, in a great degree, the moisture of the soil; that with the plates he discovered a Urim and Thummim, through the aid of which he afterward was enabled to translate the book into the English language. Soon after obtaining the plates, a few of the original characters were accurately transcribed and translated by Mr. Smith, which, with the translation, were taken by a gentleman by the name of Martin Harris to the city of New York, where they were presented to some of the most learned individuals in the United States to see if they could translate them. Among the rest, they were presented to Professor Anthon of New York City, who professed to be extensively acquainted with many languages, both ancient and modern. He examined them but was unable

---

[39]This testimony is a harmony of two reports based upon interviews with Martin Harris. While traveling on a mission to the British Isles in 1853, Elder David B. Dille interviewed Martin Harris in Kirtland, Ohio, and published what he learned in the *Millennial Star*. The second interview was also conducted and reported by a missionary, Elder Edward Stevenson. (See *Latter-day Saints Millennial Star* 21 [August 20, 1859]: 545 [hereafter cited as *MS*] and *MS* 48 [July 5 1886]: 421-22.) In a letter written by Martin Harris in 1870, Harris mentioned his journey to New York in 1828 by writing: "I do say that . . . the translation that I carried to Prof. Anthon was copied from these same [Book of Mormon] plates; also, that the Professor did testify to it being a correct translation" (Martin Harris to H. B. Emerson, Nov. 23, 1870, cited in *The Latter Day Saints' Herald* 22 [1875]:630).

to decipher them correctly, but he presumed that if the original records could be brought, he could assist in translating them. No man was found able to read them by his own learning or wisdom. Mr. Smith, though an unlearned man, testifies that he was commanded to translate them, through the inspiration of the Holy Ghost, by the aid of the Urim and Thummim and that the Book of Mormon is that translation. Now, Isaiah says to Israel, "Thou shalt be brought down, and shalt speak out of the ground, and thy speech shall be low out of the dust, and thy voice shall be as of one that hath a familiar spirit, out of the ground, and they speech shall whisper out of the dust." (Isaiah 29:4.)[40]

The Translation Resumes

Joseph Smith

Having returned from this tour, he [Martin Harris] left me and went home to Palmyra, arranged his affairs and returned again to my house about the twelfth of April, eighteen hundred and twenty eight.[41]

Lucy Smith

[After Martin Harris returned from his journey to New York City, Mrs. Harris] endeavoured to dissuade her husband from taking any further part in the publication of the Record; however, Mr. Harris paid no attention to her, but returned [to Harmony] and continued writing

Immediately after Martin Harris left home for Pennsylvania, his wife went from place to place, and from house to house, telling her grievances,

---

[40]Orson Pratt, *Divine Authority, or the Question, was Joseph Smith Sent of God?* (Liverpool, England: R. James, 1848), p. 8 and Orson Pratt, *Account of Several Remarkable Visions*, p. 14. This account combines the writings of Orson Pratt as published in two different pamphlets. For additional accounts of the Martin Harris visit to New York based on interviews with Martin Harris see Reminiscences of Joseph Knight, Church Archives; William Pilkington, "They Dying Testimony of Martin Harris," p. 2, photocopy included in Wayne Cutler Gunnell, "Martin Harris: Witness and Benefactor to the Book of Mormon" Master's thesis, Brigham Young University, 1955, pp. 104-11; Simon Smith to President Joseph Smith, December 29, 1880, cited in *The Saints' Herald* 28 (1881):43; and Affidavit of John E. Godfrey, photocopy, Special Collections Library, Brigham Young University (hereafter cited as BYU).

[41]*T&S* 3 (May 16, 1842): 785.

and declaring that Joseph Smith was practising a deception upon the people, which was about to strip her of all that she possessed, and that she was compelled to deposit a few things away from home in order to secure them. So she carried away her furniture, linen, and bedding; also other moveable articles, until she nearly stripped the premises of every thing that could conduce either to comfort or convenience, depositing them with those of her friends and acquaintances, in whom she reposed sufficient confidence to assure her of their future safety.[42]

Success and Failure

Joseph Smith

[After returning to Harmony in April 1828, Martin Harris] commenced writing for me, while I translated the plates. We continued until the fourteenth of June following, by which time he had written one hundred and sixteen pages of manuscript on foolscap paper [typically 13 × 17 inches].[43]

Martin Harris - Interview

The Prophet Joseph Smith . . . possessed a seer stone by which he was enabled to translate, as well as from the Urim and Thummim, and for convenience he then used the seer stone . . . . The seer stone differed in appearance entirely from the Urim and Thummim that was obtained with the plates (which was two clear stones set in two rims, very much resembling spectacles) . . . . After continued translation, we would become weary, and would go down to the river and exercise by throwing stones out on the river, etc. While so doing on one occasion, I found a stone very much resembling the one used for translating, and on resuming our labor of translation, I put in place the stone that I had found . . . . The Prophet remained silent, unusually and intently gazing in darkness . . . . Much surprised, Joseph exclaimed, "Martin! What is the matter? All is as dark as Egypt!" My countenance betrayed me, and the Prophet asked me why I had done so. I said, to stop the mouths of fools, who had told me that the Prophet had learned those sentences and was

---

[42]Lucy Smith, *Biographical Sketches*, pp. 116-17.

[43]*T&S* 3 (May 16 1842): 785 and "1835 History."

merely repeating them...Not many pages [were] translated while I wrote.[44]

Joseph Smith

Some time after Mr. Harris had begun to write for me, he began to tease me to give him liberty to carry the writings home and show them, and he desired of me that I would enquire of the Lord through the Urim and Thummim if he might not do so. I did enquire, and the answer was that he must not. However, he was not satisfied with this answer and desired that I should enquire again. I did so, and the answer was as before. Still he could not be contented but insisted that I should enquire once more. After much solicitation, I again enquired of the Lord and permission was granted him to have the writings on certain conditions, which were that he show them only to his brother, Preserved Harris, his own wife, his father, and his mother, and a Mrs. Cobb, a sister to his wife. In accordance with this last answer, I required of him that he should bind himself in a covenant to me in the most solemn manner that he would not do otherwise than had been directed. He did so. He bound himself as I required of him, took the writings and went on his way.[45]

Lucy Smith

After leaving Joseph he [Martin Harris] arrived at home with the manuscript in safety. Soon after he exhibited the manuscript to his wife and family. His wife was so pleased with it, that she gave him the privilege of locking it up in her own set of drawers, which was a special favour, for she had never before this allowed him even the privilege of looking into them . . .

Shortly after Mr. Harris left [Harmony], Joseph's wife became the mother of a son, which, however, remained with her but a short time before it was snatched from her arms by the hand of death. And the mother seemed, for some time, more like sinking with her infant into the mansion of the dead, than remaining with her husband among the living.

---

[44]Edward Stevenson, "Incidents in the Life of Martin Harris," *MS* 44 (February 6, 1882): 86-87. This statement has been placed in the first person instead of the third person as originally published, and the tense of one verb was changed to harmonize with correct English usage.

[45]*T&S* 3 (May 16, 1842): 785.

Her situation was such for two weeks, that Joseph slept not an hour in undisturbed quiet. At the expiration of this time she began to recover, but as Joseph's anxiety about her began to subside, another cause of trouble forced itself upon his mind. Mr. Harris had been absent nearly three weeks, and Joseph had received no intelligence whatever from him, which was altogether aside of the arrangement when they separated. But Joseph kept his feelings from his wife, fearing that if she became acquainted with them it might agitate her too much.

In a few days, however, she mentioned the subject herself, and desired her husband to go and get her mother to stay with her, while he should repair to Palmyra, for the purpose of learning the cause of Mr. Harris's absence as well as silence. At first Joseph objected, but seeing her so cheerful, and so willing to have him leave home, he finally consented.[46]

Joseph Smith

In the mean time while Martin Harris was gone with the writings, I went to visit my father's family at Manchester.[47]

Lucy Smith

He [Joseph Smith] set out in the first stage that passed for Palmyra, and, when he was left to himself, he began to contemplate the course which Martin had taken, and the risk which he (Joseph) had run in letting the manuscript go out of his own hand—for it could not be obtained again, in case Martin had lost it through transgression, except by the power of God, which was something Joseph could hardly hope for—and that, by persisting in his entreaties to the Lord, he had perhaps fallen into transgression, and thereby lost the manuscript. When, I say, he began to contemplate these things, they troubled his spirit, and his soul was moved with fearful apprehensions. And, although he was now nearly worn out, sleep fled from his eyes, neither had he any desire for food, for he felt that he had done wrong, and how great his condemnation was he did not know.[48]

---

[46]Lucy Smith, *Biographical Sketches*, pp. 118, 122.

[47]*T&S* 3 (May 16, 1842): 786.

[48]Lucy Smith, *Biographical Sketches*, pp. 118-119.

The Loss of 116 Pages

Joseph Smith

Notwithstanding the great restrictions which he [Martin Harris] had been laid under and the solemnity of the covenant which he had made with me, he did show them[116 pages of the manuscript] to others, and by stratagem they got them away from him, and they never have been recovered nor obtained back again unto this day.[49]

Lucy Smith

When Joseph had taken a little nourishment [after his arrival from Harmony]...he requested us to send immediately for Mr. Harris. This we did without delay...

For a short time previous to Joseph's arrival, Mr. Harris had been otherwise engaged, and thought but little about the manuscript. When Joseph sent for him, he went immediately to the drawer where he had left it, but, behold it was gone! He asked his wife where it was. She solemnly averred that she did not know anything respecting it. He then made a faithful search throughout the house...

[After we had sent for Martin Harris], we commenced preparing breakfast for the family; and we supposed that Mr. Harris would be there, as soon as it was ready, to eat with us, for he generally came in such haste when he was sent for. At eight o'clock we set the victuals on the table, as we were expecting him every moment. We waited till nine, and he came not—till ten, and he was not there—till eleven, still he did not make his appearance. But at half-past twleve we saw him walking with a slow and measured tread towards the house, his eyes fixed thoughtfully upon the ground. On coming to the gate, he stopped, instead of passing through, and got upon the fence, and sat there some time with his hat drawn over his eyes. At length he entered the house. Soon after which we sat down to the table, Mr. Harris with the rest. He took up his knife and fork as if he were going to use them, but immediately dropped them. Hyrum, observing this, said "Martin, why do you not eat; are you sick? Upon which, Mr. Harris pressed his hands upon his temples, and cried out, in a tone of deep anguish, "Oh, I have lost my soul! I have lost my soul!"

Joseph, who had not expressed his fears till now, sprang from the table, exclaiming, "Martin, have you lost that manuscript? have you

---

[49]*T&S* 3 (May 16, 1842): 786 and "1832 History."

broken your oath, and brought down condemnation upon my head, as well as your own?"

"Yes, it is gone," replied Martin, "and I know not where."

"Oh, my God!" said Joseph, clinching his hands. "All is lost! all is lost! What shall I do? I have sinned—it is I who tempted the wrath of God. I should have been satisfied with the first answer which I received from the Lord; for he told me that it was not safe to let the writing go out of my possession." He wept and groaned, and walked the floor continually.

At length he told Martin to go back and search again.

"No," said Martin, "it is all in vain; for I have ripped open beds and pillows; and I know it is not there."

"Then must I," said Joseph, "return to my wife with such a tale as this? I dare not do it, lest I should kill her at once. And how shall I appear before the Lord? Of what rebuke am I not worthy from the angel of the Most High?"

I besought him not to mourn so, for perhaps the Lord would forgive him, after a short season of humiliation and repentance. But what could I say to comfort him, when he saw all the family in the same situation of mind as himself; for sobs and groans, and the most bitter lamentation filled the house. However, Joseph was more distressed than the rest, as he better understood the consequences of disobedience. And he continued, pacing back and forth, meantime weeping and grieving, until about sunset, when, by persuasion, he took a little nourishment . . .

The manuscript [Martin Harris lost] has never been found; and there is no doubt but Mrs. Harris took it from the drawer, with the view of retaining it, until another translation should be given, then, to alter the original translation, for the purpose of showing a discrepancy between them, and thus make the whole appear to be a deception.[50]

Lucy Smith's Description of the Contents of the 116 Pages of the Early Translation of the Book of Mormon

Lucy Smith

I now come to say something of the record it was placed in the earth many hundred years ago by the forefathers of our Indians, they

---

[50]Lucy Smith, *Biographical Sketches*, pp. 120-21, 123. Additional accounts of the loss of 116 pages of the manuscript based on conversations with those involved in this incident are found in the following works: Reminiscences of Joseph Knight, Church Archives and William Pilkington, "The Dying Testimony of Martin Harris," p. 3.

descended from a prophet of the Lord whose name was Lehi he fled from Jerusalem with his family and also his wife's brother's family a few days before Nebuchadnezzar besieged the city and layed it in ashes, for although Lehi prophesied unto the Jews in the name of the Lord that they must repent of their sins yet they would not, neither would they believe the wonders which were shown to him in dreams concerning Christ that he should be Crucified, therefore God commanded the people of Lehi to get out of Jerusalem and flee into the wilderness and at length they were directed to enter upon the Land of America: now a part of the people of Lehi whose head was named Laman (a son of Lehi) became savage and they sought to exterminate their more virtuous brethren who were called the people of Nephi therefore God cast off the people of Laman and he cursed them with a dark skin but the people of Nephi he preserved and prospered so long as they obeyed his commandments, and they were not unskilled workmen having a knowledge of the arts together with the sciences. But they had among them that same secret society which had brought Jerusalem and the whole nation of the Jews to destruction; and after many years they became the more wicked than their accursed brethren, and God seeing that they would not repent of the evil he visited them with extinction.[51]

Joseph Returns to Pennsylvania

Joseph Smith

I continued there [Joseph's parents' home in Manchester] for a short season and then returned to my place in Pennsylvania.[52]

Lucy Smith

We parted with heavy hearts, for it now appeared that all which we had so fondly anticipated, and which had been the source of so much secret gratification, had in a moment fled, and fled for ever . . . .

It seemed as though Martin Harris, for his transgression, suffered temporally as well as spiritually. The same day on which the foregoing

---

[51]Lucy Smith to Mary Pierce, January 23 1829, in possession of Brent F. Ashworth, Provo, Utah. In this quote I have placed the the word "City" in lower case and corrected the spelling of "brethren."

[52]*T&S* 3 (May 16, 1842): 786.

circumstance took place, a dense fog spread itself over his fields, and blighted his wheat while in the blow, so that he lost about two-thirds of his crop, whilst those fields which lay only on the opposite side of the road, received no injury whatever.

I well remember that day of darkness, both within and without. To us, at least, the heavens seemed clothed with blackness, and the earth shrouded with gloom. I have often said within myself, that if a continual punishment, as severe as that which we experienced on that occasion, were to be inflicted upon the most wicked characters who ever stood upon the footstool of the Almighty—if even their punishment were no greater than that, I should feel to pity their condition.[53]

An Interruption in the Translation

Joseph Smith

Since the Lord suffered the writings to fall into the hands of wicked men, Martin was chastened for his transgression and I also was chastened for my transgression for asking the Lord a third time. Therefore, the plates and the Urim and Thummim were taken from me by the power of God and I was not able to obtain them for a season. [A short time later,] I was walking a little distance when the former heavenly messenger appeared and handed to me the Urim and Thummim again. I enquired of the Lord through them and obtained the following revelation.[54]

Revelation to Joseph Smith, Jr. given July 1828 concerning certain manuscripts on the first part of the Book of Mormon, which had been taken from the possession of Martin Harris. [See D&C Section 3:9-15]

---

[53]Lucy Smith, *Biographical Sketches*, pp. 122-24.

[54]*T&S* 3 (May 16, 1842): 786 and "1832 History." Although quotations of the revlations, headings, and paragraph divisions appearing in this work are from the '1838 History" as printed in the *Times and Seasons*, for sake of clarity, spelling, punctuation, and word usage (such as pronoun usage and verb tenses) have been changed to harmonize with current English usage as generally printed in the 1981 edition of The Doctrine and Covenants. When the first word of a verse begins in upper case in the D&C which would in a paragraph be written in lower case, the lower has been used. And for consistency, throughout this work, "Jr." has been used as an abbreviation for "Junior" and "Sr." for "Senior."

Behold, thou art Joseph, and thou wast chosen to do the work of the Lord, but because of transgression, if thou art not aware thou wilt fall. But remember, God is merciful; therefore, repent of that which thou hast done which is contrary to the commandment which I gave you and thou art chosen, and art again called to the work; except thou do this, thou shalt be delivered up and become as other men, and have no more gift.

And when thou deliveredst up that which God had given thee sight and power to translate, thou deliveredst up that which was sacred into the hands of a wicked man, who has set at nought the counsels of God, and has broken the most sacred promises which were made before God, and has depended upon his own judgment and boasted in his own wisdom. And this is the reason that thou has lost thy privileges for a season—for thou hast suffered the counsel of thy director to be trampled upon from the beginning.

After I had obtained the above revelation [D&C Section 3], both the plates and the Urim and Thummim were taken from me again: but in a few days they were returned to me, when I enquired of the Lord, and the Lord said unto me.[55]

Revelation given to Joseph Smith, Jr., informing him of the alteration of the manuscript of the forepart of the Book of Mormon. [See D&C Section 10:1-3, 7-11, 30][56]

Now, behold, I say unto you, that because you delivered up those writings which you had power given unto you to translate by the means of the Urim and Thummim, into the hands of a wicked man, you have lost them. And you also lost your gift at the same time, and your mind became darkened. Nevertheless, it is now restored unto you again; therefore see that you are faithful and continue on unto the finishing of the

---

[55]*T&S* 3 (June 1, 1842): 801.

[56]It is possible that Section 10 of the D&C was recorded in May 1829 and contains several revelations. An earlier revelation relating to the alteration of the manuscript of the Book of Mormon may have been received by the Prophet in the fall of 1828 and then included in a later revelation that was possibly received a few months after the Book of Mormon manuscript had been lost. (See Max H. Parkin, "A Preliminary Analysis of the Dating of Section 10," *Sidney B. Sperry Symposium*, January 27, 1979 [Provo: Brigham Young University, 1979].)

remainder of the work of translation as you have begun. . . . And for this cause I said that he is a wicked man, for he has sought to take away the things wherewith you have been entrusted; and he has also sought to destroy your gift. And because you have delivered the writings into his hands, behold, wicked men have taken them from you. Therefore, you have delivered them up, yea, that which was sacred, unto wickedness. And, behold, Satan has put it into their hearts to alter the words which you have caused to be written, or which you have translated, which have gone out of your hands. And behold, I say unto you, that because they have altered the words, they read contrary from that which you translated and caused to be written . . . .

Behold, I say unto you that you shall not translate again those words which have gone forth out of your hands; for, behold, they shall not accomplish their evil deisgns in lying against those words. For, behold, if you should bring forth the same words they will say that you have lied [and] that you have pretended to translate, but that you have contradicted yourself. And, behold, they will publish this, and Satan will harden the hearts of the people to stir them up to anger against you, that they will not believe my words. Thus Satan thinketh to overpower your testimony in this generation.[57]

Lucy Smith

For nearly two months after Joseph returned to his family, in Pennsylvania, we heard nothing from him, and become anxious about him, Mr. Smith and myself set off to make him a visit. When we came within three-quarters of a mile of the house, Joseph started to meet us, telling his wife, as he left, that father and mother were coming. When he met us, his countenance wore so pleasant an aspect, that I was convinced he had something agreeable to communicate with regard to the work in which he was engaged. When I entered, the first thing which attracted my attention was a red morocco trunk, lying on Emma's bureau, which

---

[57]*T&S* 3 (June 1, 1842): 801-804.

Joseph shortly informed me contained the Urim and Thummim, and the plates. And, in the evening, he gave us the following relation of what had transpired since our separation:—

"On leaving you," said Joseph, "I returned immediately home. Soon after my arrival, I commenced humbling myself in mighty prayer before the Lord, and, as I was pouring out my soul in supplication to God, that if possible, I might obtain mercy at his hands, and be forgiven of all that I had done contrary to his will, an angel stood before me, and answered me, saying, that I had sinned in delivering the manuscript into the hands of a wicked man, and, as I had ventured to become responsible for his faithfulness, I would of necessity have to suffer the consequences of his indiscretion, and I must now give up the Urim and Thummim into his (the angel's) hands."

"This I did as I was directed, and as I handed them to him, he remarked, 'If you are very humble and penitent, it may be you will receive them again; if so it will be on the twenty-second of next September.'"

Joseph then related a revelation which he received soon after the angel visited him. [See D&C Section 3] . . .

While on this visit we became acquainted with Emma's father, whose name was Isaac Hale; also his family, which consisted of his wife, Elizabeth, his sons, Jesse, David, Alva, Isaac Ward, and Reuben; and his daughters, Phebe, Elizabeth, and A----[Tryal and Emma].

They were an intelligent and highly respectable family. They were pleasantly situated, and lived in good style, in the town of Harmony, on the Susquehannah river, within a short distance of the place where Joseph resided.

The time of our visit with them, we passed very agreeably, and returned home relieved of a burden which was almost insupportable, and our present joy far overbalanced all our former grief.[58]

Return of the Plates

Joseph Smith

[After the angel returned the plates and Urim and Thummim to me] I did not go immediately to translating, but went to laboring with my

---

[58]Lucy Smith, *Biographical Sketches*, pp. 124-25, 127.

hands upon a small farm which I had purchased of my wife's father, in order to provide for my family.[59]

Lucy Smith

"After the angel left me," said he [Joseph], "I continued my supplications to God, without cessation, and on the twenty-second of September, I had the joy and satisfaction of again receiving the Urim and Thummim, with which I have again commenced translating, and Emma writes for me, but the angel said that the Lord would send me a scribe, and I trust his promise will be verified. The angel seemed pleased with me when he gave me back the Urim and Thummim, and he told me that the Lord loved me, for my faithfulness and humility."[60]

Joseph Smith

In March 1829 I obtained the following revelation: [see D&C Section 5:4.][61]

---

[59]*T&S* 3 (June 15, 1842): 817. Shortly after arriving in Harmony, Pennsylvania, Joseph and Emma moved from Emma's parents' home to a home of their own. This house (which was located near the residence of Isaac Hale belonged to Jesse Hale (Emma'a brother) and had been built on property owned by Isaac Hale. "Your father bought your uncle Jesse's place, off father's farm," Emma told her son, Joseph Smith III, "and we lived there till the Book of Mormon was translated; and I think published." Although Joseph settled on this farm during the winter of 1827-1828, he did not secure title to the property until August 25, 1830, paying $200 for approximately thirteen acres. After moving to Kirtland, Ohio, Joseph sold this land (on June 8, 1833) for $300. (See "Last Testimony of Sister Emma," *The Saint's Herald* 26 [October 1, 1879]:289 and Larry C. Porter, "A Study of the Origins of The Church of Jesus Christ of Latter-day Saints in the States of New York and Pennsylvania, 1816-1831" [Ph.D. diss., Brigham Young University, 1971], pp. 132-134.)

[60]Lucy Smith, *Biographical Sketches*, p. 126.

[61]Although this revelation was received following a request by Martin Harris and most of the information in the revelation is directed to him, only portions relating to Joseph Smith are cited in this chapter. In Chapter 6, references in the revelations to Martin Harris and other witnesses to the Book of Mormon will be cited.

And you [Joseph Smith] have a gift to translate the plates; and this is the first gift that I bestowed upon you; and I have commanded that you should pretend to no other gift until my purpose is fulfilled in this; for I will grant unto you no other gift until it is finished.

Conclusion

Orson Pratt

Joseph Smith...was a farmer by occupation. His advantages for acquiring scientific knowledge were exceedingly small, being limited to a slight acquaintance with two or three of the common branches of learning. He could read without much difficulty, and write a very imperfect hand; and had a very limited understanding of the elementary rules of arithmetic. These were his highest and only attainments; while the rest of those branches, so universally taught in the common schools throughout the United States, were entirely unknown to him ....

[After] he frequently received instructions from the mouth of the heavenly messenger,...on the morning of the 22d of September, A.D. 1827, the angel of the Lord delivered the records into his hands ....Having provided himself with a home, he commenced translating the record, by the gift and power of God, through the means of the Urim and Thummim; and being a poor writer, he was under the necessity of employing a scribe, to write a translation as it came from his mouth.[62]

Joseph Smith's accounts of the restoration of the gospel by an angel, of his taking out of the ground the sacred records of the tribe of Joseph, [and] of their subsequent translation by the gift of God...are all events clearly predicted by the ancient Jewish apostles and prophets ....If Joseph Smith [, for example,] was an imposter and wished to palm himself off upon the world as the great prophet who was to usher in the preparatory dispensation for the coming of the Lord, how came he to discover all the...minute particulars contained in Isaiah's prophecy [29th chapter]....He sent the "words of a book" which he found, as before stated, to Professor Anthon. But it was a sealed writing to the learned professor—the aboriginal language of ancient America could not be deciphered by him. He [Charles Anthon] was as much puzzled as the wise men of Babylon were to interpret the unknown writing upon the wall. Human wisdom and learning, in this case, were altogethr insufficient. It required another Daniel, who was found in the person of

---

[62]Orson Pratt, *Remarkable Visions*, (Liverpool, 1848), pp. 1, 6.

Mr. Smith. What a marvellous work! What a wonder! How the wisdom of the wise and learned was made to perish by the gift of interpretation given to the unlearned! . . . .[In conclusion,] Joseph Smith presents the world with the fulfillment [of Biblical prophecies] at the predicted time, in the predicted manner, and for the predicted purpose as anciently specified.[63]

---

[63]Orson Pratt, *Divine Authority*, No. 1, pp. 9, 11, 16.

CHAPTER FIVE

Three Remarkable Months

April 7 - Early July 1829

Moreover, thou son of man, take thee one stick, and write upon it, for Judah, and for the children of Israel his companions: then take another stick, and write upon it, for Joseph, the stick of Ephraim, and for all the house of Israel his companions:
And join them one to another into one stick; and they shall become one in thine hand . . . .
And the sticks whereon thou writest shall be in thine hands before their eyes. (Ezekiel 37:16-17, 20.)
No man taketh this honour unto himself, but he that is called of God, as was Aaron. (Hebrews 5:4.)

One of the most remarkable periods in the history of Christianity began on April 7, 1829. Between April and early July of that year, five of the most significant events in the history of the restoration movement occurred. The writings of Joseph Smith, Oliver Cowdery, Lucy Smith, and David Whitmer and reported interviews with individuals who were closely associated with the Prophet in 1829 affirm that nearly all of the Book of Mormon (excluding the 116 pages of the Book of Lehi) was translated during these three months. Moreover, these writings inform us that, with the possible exception of Oliver Cowdery's translation of a few words, Joseph Smith was the sole translator of that record.[1] While various individuals served as scribes to the Prophet, there are no primary historical sources which indicate that any person assisted Joseph Smith in the composition of the Book of Mormon. The young man had received only a meager formal education, and he did not have access to any major library. In 1829 he could not dictate a coherent letter nor write a series of well-structured English sentences. Yet day after day, for approximately three months, he dictated a manuscript (containing more than five hundred pages) describing the religious history of a people spanning more than two thousand years.[2]

Some critics have suggested that Sidney Rigdon was a principle author of the Book of Mormon. They have argued that he used as a guide, for the historical portions of this work, a romance written by Solomon Spaulding. However, no records have been located which indicate that Sidney Rigdon knew Joseph Smith before 1830. A preponderance of evidence shows that Sidney Rigdon himself certified that he first learned the Book of Mormon. While testifying of the divine authenticity of the Book of Mormon, Sidney Rigdon himself asserted that he first learned about that sacred record when it was presented to him by Parley P. Pratt in the fall of 1830.[3] Others have declared that when Rigdon was initially

---

[1] D&C 9:5.

[2] A description of the libraries and the educational opportunities available to Joseph Smith while he was living in Manchester is found in Milton V. Backman, Jr., *Joseph Smith's First Vision*, 2nd ed. enlarged (Salt Lake City: Bookcraft, 1980), pp. 48-51 and in Robert Paul, "Joseph Smith and the Manchester (New York) Library," *BYU Studies* 22 (Summer 1982):333-56. The "1832 History" of Joseph Smith provides a sample of Joseph Smith's literary abilities at a time when he was not aided by the Lord and before he had seriously studied English grammar. His capacity to express himself in writing improved during the late 1830s and early 1840s as is evident from his various writings. Nevertheless, Joseph Smith did not have the knowledge nor the literary skill to have produced the Book of Mormon at any time in his life without divine assistance.

[3] *Painesville Telegraph* (Ohio), February 15, 1831; Letter of Sidney Rigdon, July 1868, Stephen Post Collection, microfilm copy, Church Archives; Josiah Jones, "History of the Mormonites," *The Evangelist* 9 (June 1, 1844):132-34; Parley P. Pratt, *Mormonism Unveiled* (New York: O. Pratt and E. Fordham, 1838), pp. 40-41; Sidney Rigdon to editors of the *Boston Journal*, May 27, 1839, cited in Samuel M. Smucker, ed., *The Religious, Social, and Political History of the Mormons, or Latter-day Saints* (New York: Miller, Orton and Co., 1857), pp. 45-47; and Sidney Rigdon to Joseph H. Newton, July 1, 1868, Stephen Post Collection, Church Archives. See also the account of Sidney Rigdon's conversion published in Nauvoo when he had an opportunity to review this history. (*T&S* 4 [August 15 and September 1, 1843]:289-90, 305.)

given a copy of that book his response was negative. Like many other restorationist preachers of the 1820s, Rigdon taught that the Bible was the sole standard of faith. For this reason he "partly condemned it,"[4] and, as Parley P. Pratt recalled, Rigdon questioned the proclamation of a new book containing the teachings of Christ. "He was much surprised," Parley added, "and it was with much persuasion and argument that he was prevailed on to read it."[5] Nevertheless, as many contemporaries have noted, following his careful examination of that book, Rigdon publicly announced his conversion to Mormonism.[6]

Shortly after he joined the restored Church and traveled to western New York to meet the Prophet Joseph Smith, critics accused Rigdon of being the author of the Book of Mormon. Many of Joseph Smith's non-Mormon contemporaries refused to believe that the young prophet or his known associates of the 1820s, could have written that work. Therefore, critics in 1831 selected Sidney Rigdon as the author.[7] However, individuals who were closely associated with Joseph Smith before 1831 deny this theory. For example, Rigdon's son, John Wickliffe Rigdon, reported that his father repeatedly told friend and foe alike that he did not write the Book of Mormon. Rigdon insisted that he "never saw the Book of Mormon until Parley Pratt presented it to him," and that he met Joseph Smith for the first time *after* his baptism. When others suggested that Rigdon had used Solomon Spaulding's manuscript as a basis for writing the historical portions of the Book of Mormon, he urged that never in his life had he seen the Spaulding manuscript.[8]

---

[4]*Painesville Telegraph* (Ohio), February 15, 1831, p. 1.

[5]Parley P. Pratt, *Mormonism Unveiled Zion's Watchman Unmasked* (New York, 1838), pp. 41-42.

[6]Ibid.; *Painesville Telegraph* (Ohio), February 15, 1831, pp. 1-2; and Josiah Jones, "History of the Mormonites," *The Evangelist* 9 (1844):132-34. See also Milton V. Backman, Jr., "The Quest for a Restoration: The Birth of Mormonism in Ohio," *BYU Studies* 12 (Summer 1972):356-64 and Richard L. Anderson, "The Impact of the First Preaching in Ohio," *BYU Studies* 11 (Summer 1971):474-96.

[7]Diary of James Gordon Bennett, August 7, 1831, cited in Leonard J. Arrington, "James Gordon Bennett's 1831 Report on 'The Mormonites,'" *BYU Studies* 10 (Spring 1870):355; *Morning Courier and Enquirer* (New York), August 31, 1831; and *Hillsborough Gazette* (Ohio), October 29, 1831.

[8]Karl Keller, ed. "The Life and Testimony of Sidney Rigdon," *Dialogue* 1 (Winter 1966):19, 25. See also Parley P. Pratt, *Mormonism Unveiled*, pp. 40-42 and Sidney Rigdon to editors of the *Boston Journal*, May 27, 1839, cited in Smucker, ed., *History of the Mormons*, pp. 45-47.

There are no significant parallels in the known writings of Solomon Spaulding and the Book of Mormon.[9] In fact, except for the King James Version of the Bible, there are no quotations in the Book of Mormon from any book available in any library or any published manuscript written before 1830. Portions of the Old Testament and the writings of Isaiah and other prophets were recorded on the Book of Mormon plates as well as some of the same sermons which Christ had unfolded to audiences in the land of Palestine. Because of this and the fact that the Book of Mormon contains these messages in the Biblical language popular during the early nineteenth century,[10] its credibility has been challenged. It was also during the same months that most of the Book of Mormon was translated that the Aaronic and Melchizedek priesthoods were restored. These two events are without a parallel in the annals of modern religious history. In these visions the power and authority to act in the name of God were restored to man on earth. Joseph Smith and Oliver Cowdery testified that they beheld angelic messengers who gave them verbal instructions and that they felt the hands of the heavenly beings upon their heads as they received the holy priesthood. No other individuals in the modern history of Christianity have made such claims. Whenever, as far as we know, Joseph Smith received priesthood keys, another witness was present to

---

[9]Solomon Spaulding, Manuscript, Oberlin College Archives, Oberlin, Ohio; Lester E. Bush, Jr., "The Spalding Theory: Then and Now," *Dialogue* 10 (Autumn 1977):41-63; and James H. Fairchild, *Manuscript of Solomon Spaulding and the Book of Mormon* (Cleveland: Western Reserve Historical Society, 1886).

[10]"Approximately one-third of the biblical writings of Isaiah are quoted in the Book of Mormon," but of these, half (or 229 verses) are quoted differently from those in the King James Version while 196 are identical. There are also quotations in the Book of Mormon which are similar to verses in Matthew (the Sermon on the Mount) and from the letters of Paul, but again the quotations are not identical. Possibly Paul quoted from the teachings of the Savior on love and gifts of the spirit or received information on these subjects from revelations and Moroni quoted from the same sources, either from the teachings of the Savior or possibly from revelations which he received which were similar to those unfolded to Paul. Possibly when Joseph Smith was translating the Book of Mormon he learned concepts that were similar to those recorded in the Bible and was influenced by the wording of the Bible, thereby using the language found in the King James Version, the version most popular in the United States during the early nineteenth century. (Monte S. Nyman, *Great are the Words of Isaiah* [Bookcraft: Salt Lake City, 1980], pp. 2, 7, 282 and Sidney B. Sperry, *The Problems of the Book of Mormon* [Bookcraft: Salt Lake City, 1964], pp. 99-106, 112-21.)

verify the reality of the experience and to receive the same power and authority.

Several other important events that took place during the months of April-July 1829, related to the Book of Mormon. For example, eleven men testified that in the presence of Joseph Smith they saw the plates from which the Book of Mormon had been translated. An account of their experiences and a harmony of their testimonies has been included in Chapter Seven.

Translation of a Sacred Record

Joseph Smith

The Lord appeared to a young man by the name of Oliver Cowdery and showed [the plates] to him in a vision and also the truth of the work and what the Lord was about to do through me, his unworthy servant. Therefore, he was desirous to come and write for me [as I translated.] Now, my wife had written some for me and also my brother, Samuel H. Smith, but we had become reduced in property and my wife's father was about to turn me out of doors. . . .I had nowhere to go. . . .I cried unto the Lord that he would provide for me to accomplish the work whereunto he had commanded me.[11]

On the fifteenth [5th] day of April, 1829, Oliver Cowdery [whom I had never previously seen] came to my house [Harmony], Pennsylvania]. . . .He stated to me that having been teaching school in the neighborhood where my father resided, and my father being one of those who sent to the school, he went to board for a season at his [my father's] house, and while there the family related to him the circumstance of my having received the plates . . . .Accordingly he had come to make enquiries of me.[12]

Lucy Smith

Soon after we returned from [visiting Joseph in] Harmony, a man by the name of Lyman Cowdery, came into the neighborhood, and applied

---

[11]"1832 History." Although a few words have been changed in this quotation, so that the sentences flow according to proper modern English usage, the basic ideas written by the Prophet have not been changed. Words which have been added have been placed in brackets as in other parts of this work.

[12]JS-H 1:66 and *T&S* 3 (July 1, 1842):832.

to Hyrum, (as he was one of the trustees,) for the district school. A meeting of the trustees was called, and Mr. Cowdery was employed. But the following day, this Mr. Cowdery brought his brother Oliver to the trustees, and requested them to receive him instead of himself, as circumstances had transpired which rendered it necessary for him to disappoint them, or which would not allow of his attending to the school himself; and he would warrant the good conduct of the school under his brother's supervision. All parties being satisifed, Oliver commenced his school, boarding for the time being at our house. He had been in the school but a short time, when he began to hear from all quarters concerning the plates, and as soon began to importune Mr. Smith upon the subject, but for a considerable length of time did not succeed in eliciting any information. At last, however, he gained my husband's confidence, so far as to obtain a sketch of the facts relative to the plates.

Shortly after receiving this information, he told Mr. Smith that he was highly delighted with what he had heard, that he had been in a deep study upon the subject all day, and that it was impressed upon his mind, that he should yet have the privilege of writing for Joseph. Furthermore, that he had determined to pay him a visit at the close of the school, which he was then teaching.

On coming in on the following day, he said, "The subject upon which we were yesterday conversing seems working in my very bones, and I cannot, for a moment, get it out of my mind, finally, I have resolved on what I will do. Samuel, I understand, is going down to Pennsylvania to spend the spring with Joseph; I shall make my arrangements to be ready to accompany him thither, by the time he recovers his health; for I have made it a subject of prayer, and I firmly believe that it is the will of the Lord that I should go. If there is a work for me to do in this thing, I am determined to attend to it." . . . . In April, Samuel, and Mr. Cowdery set out for Pennsylvania. The weather, for some time previous, had been very wet and disagreeable—raining, freezing, and thawing alternately, which had rendered the roads almost impassable, particularly in the middle of the day. Notwithstanding, Mr. Cowdery was not to be detained, either by wind or weather, and they persevered until they arrived at Joseph's.

Joseph had been so hurried with his secular affairs, that he could not proceed with his spiritual concerns so fast as was necessary for the speedy completion of the work; there was also another disadvantage under which he laboured, his wife had so much of her time taken up with the care of her house, that she could write for him but a small portion of the time. On account of these embarrassments, Joseph called upon the Lord, three days prior to the arrival of Samuel and Oliver, to send him a scribe, according to the promise of the angel; and he was informed that the same should be forth coming in a few days. Accordingly, when Mr. Cowdery told him the business that he had come upon, Joseph was not at all surprised.[13]

Joseph Smith

Two days after the arrival of Mr. Cowdery (being the 17th of April), [7th], I commenced to translate the Book of Mormon, and he commenced to write for me. [This] having continued for some time, I enquired of the Lord, through the Urim and Thummim, and obtained the following revelation.[14]

Revelation given April 1829 to Oliver Cowdery and Joseph Smith, Jr. [see D&C Section 6:10-13, 18-19, 22-25].

Behold thou [Oliver Cowdery] has a gift [the spirit of revelation], and blessed art thou because of thy gift. Remember it is sacred and cometh from above—And if thou wilt inquire, thou shalt know mysteries which are great and marvelous; therefore thou shalt exercise thy gift, that thou mayest find out mysteries, that thou mayest bring many to the knowledge of the truth, yea, convince them of the error of their ways. Make not thy gift known unto any save it be those who are of thy faith. Trifle not with sacred things. If thou wilt do good, yea, and hold out faithful to the end, thou shalt be saved in the kingdom of God, which is the greatest of all the gifts of God; for there is no gift greater than the gift of salvation . . . .

Therefore be diligent; stand by my servant Joseph, faithfully, in whatsoever difficult circumstances he may be for the word's sake. Admonish him in his faults, and also receive admonition of him . . . .

Verily, verily, I say unto you, if you desire a further witness, cast your mind upon the night that you cried unto me in your heart, that you might know concerning the truth of these things. Did I not speak peace to your mind concerning the matter? What greater witness can you have than from God? And now, behold, you have received a witness; for if I

---

[13]Lucy Smith, *Biographical Sketches*, pp. 128-31.

[14]*T&S* 3 (July 1, 1842):832.

have told you things which no man knoweth have you not received a witness? And, behold, I grant unto you a gift [to translate the record], if you desire of me, to translate, even as my servant Joseph.

After we had received this revelation, he [Oliver Cowdery], stated to me that after he had gone to my father's to board, and after the family communicated to him concerning my having got the plates, that one night, after he had retired to bed, he called upon the Lord to know if these things were so and that the Lord manifested to him that they were true, but that he had kept the circumstance entirely secret and had mentioned it to no being, so that after this revelation having been given, he knew that the work was true, because no being living knew of the thing alluded to in the revelation but God and himself.[15]

During the month of April, I continued to translate and he to write with little cessation. . . .While continuing the work of translation . . .Oliver Cowdery became exceedingly anxious to have the power to translate bestowed upon him, and in relation to this desire, the following revelations were obtained.[16]

Revelation given April 1829
[See D&C Section 8:1-2, 5-8, 11]

Oliver Cowdery, verily, verily, I say unto you, that assuredly as the Lord liveth, who is your God and your Redeemer, even so surely shall you receive a knowledge of whatsoever things you shall ask in faith, with an honest heart, believing that you shall receive a knowledge concerning the engraving of old records, which are ancient, which contain those parts of my scripture of which has been spoken by the manifestation of my Spirit. Yea, behold, I will tell you in your

---

[15]*T&S* 3 (July 15, 1842):853.

[16]Ibid. In April 1829 Joseph Smith received the revelation that is now section 7 of the D&C. The following introduction to this revelation was included in Joseph Smith's history: "A difference of opinion arising between us [Joseph and Oliver] about the account of John the Apostle, mentioned in the New Testament (John 21:22) whether he [John] died or continued to live, we mutually agreed to settle it by the Urim and Thummim, and the following is the word which we received" (*HC* 1:35-36).

mind and in your heart, by the Holy Ghost, which shall come upon you and which shall dwell in your heart . . . .

Oh, remember these words, and keep my commandments. Remember, this is your gift. Now this is not all thy gift; for you have another gift, which is the gift of Aaron;[17] behold, it has told you many things; behold, there is no other power, save the power of God, that can cause this gift of Aaron to be with you. Therefore, doubt not, for it is the gift of God; and you shall hold it in your hands, and do marvelous works; and no power shall be able to take it away out of your hands, for it is the work of God.

. . .Ask that you may know the mysteries of God, and that you may translate and receive knowledge from all those ancient records which have been hid up, that are sacred; and according to your faith shall it be done unto you.

Revelation given to Oliver Cowdery, April 1829[18]
[See D&C Section 9:1-2, 4-5, 7-11]

Behold, I say unto you, my son, that because you did not translate according to that which you desired of me, and did commence again to write for my servant, Joseph Smith, Jun., even so I would that ye should continue until you have finished this record, which I have entrusted unto him. And then, behold, other records have I, that I will give unto you power that you may assist to translate . . . .

Behold, the work which you are called to do is to write for my servant Joseph. And, behold, it is because that you did not

---

[17]Oliver Cowdery received two gifts: one was the gift of revelation and the other was the gift of Aaron. Possibly this gift of Aaron was a power to be a mouthpiece for Joseph Smith, even as Aaron had been for Moses, or this gift might have been "the rod of Aaron"—a tangible, sacred instrument that one could hold in his hand. This rod could assist the holder to receive revelations from the Lord. (Richard O. Cowan, *Doctrine and Covenants: Our Modern Scripture* [Provo: Brigham Young University Press, 1978], pp. 28-29 and Sidney B. Sperry, *Doctrine and Covenants Compendium* [Salt Lake City: Bookcraft, 1960], p. 71.

[18]*T&S* 3 (July 15, 1842):854.

continue as you commenced, when you began to translate, that I have taken away this privilege from you . . . .[19]

Behold, you have not understood; you have supposed that I would give it unto you, when you took no thought save it was to ask me. But, behold, I say unto you, that you must study it out in your mind; then you must ask me if it be right, and if it is right I will cause that your bosom shall burn within you; therefore, you shall feel it is right. But if it be not right you shall have no such feelings, but you shall have a stupor of thought that shall cause you to forget the thing which is wrong; therefore, you cannot write that which is sacred save it be given you from me.

Now, if you had known this you could have translated; nevertheless, it is not expedient that you should translate now. Behold, it was expedient when you commenced; but you feared, and the time is past, and it is not expedient now . . . .

Oliver Cowdery

Near the time of the setting of the sun, Sabbath evening, April 5th, 1829, my natural eyes, for the first time beheld this brother [Joseph Smith]. On Monday the 6th, I assisted him in arranging some business of a temporal nature, and on Tuesday the 7th, commenced to write the Book of Mormon. These were days never to be forgotten—to sit under the sound of a voice dictated by the inspiration of heaven, awakened the utmost gratitude of this bosom! Day after day I continued, uninterrupted, to write from his mouth, as he translated, with the Urim and Thummim, or, as the Nephites would have said, "Interpreters," the history, or record, called the Book of Mormon.[20]

---

[19]This revelation reveals that Oliver Cowdery translated a few words, and therefore, prior to his viewing the plates as one of the three special witnesses, he undoubtedly saw and handled the plates. In a discourse quoted at the end of this chapter, Oliver Cowdery testified (as reported by Reuben Miller) that he handled with his hands the golden plates. (Journal of Reuben Miller, 1848, Church Archives and *MS* 21 [August 20, 1859]:544.)

[20]*M&A* 1 (October 1834):14.

Emma Smith - Interview

[During the translation] the plates often lay on the [table in our home], without any attempt at concealment, wrapped in a small linen tablecoth, which I had given him [Joseph Smith] to fold them in. I once felt . . .the plates, as they thus lay on the table, tracing their outline and shape. They seemed to be pliable like thick paper, and would rustle with a metalic sound when the edges were moved by the thumb, as one does sometimes thumb the edges of the book . . . .I did not attempt to handle the plates, other than [through the linen cloth] . . .I was satisfied that it was the work of God, and therefore did not feel it to be necessary to do so. I knew that he [Joseph Smith] had them, and was not specially curious about them. I moved them from place to place on the table, as it was necessary in doing my work . . . .Oliver Cowdery and . . .[Joseph Smith] wrote in the room where I was at work . . . .[21]

Restoration of the Aaronic Priesthood

Joseph Smith

We still continued the work of translation, when, in the ensuing month, (May, 1829), we on a certain day went into the woods to pray and inquire of the Lord respecting baptism for the remission of sins, that we found mentioned in the translation of the plates. While we thus employed, praying and calling upon the Lord, a messenger from heaven descended in a cloud of light, and having laid his hands upon us, he ordained us, saying: "Upon you my fellow servants, in the name of Messiah, I confer the Priesthood of Aaron, which holds the keys of the ministering of angels, and of the gospel of repentance, and of baptism by immersion for the remission of sins; and this shall never be taken again from the earth, until the sons of Levi do offer again an offering unto the Lord in righteousness" [see D&C Section 13]. He said this Aaronic priesthood had not the power of laying on of hands for the gift of the Holy Ghost, but that this should be conferred on us hereafter; and he commanded us to go and be baptized and gave us directions that I should baptize Oliver Cowdery, and that afterwards he should baptize me.[22]

---

[21]Statement of Emma Smith to her son, Joseph Smith III, February 4-10, 1879, cited in *The Saints' Herald* 26 (October 1, 1879):289-90.

[22]JS-H 1:68-69 and *T&S* 3 (August 1, 1842):865-66.

Oliver Cowdery

Restoration of the Melchizedek Priesthood

Accordingly we went and were baptized. I baptized him first, and afterwards he baptized me—after which I laid my hands upon his head and ordained him to the Aaronic Priesthood, and afterwards he laid his hands on me and ordained me to the same priesthood—for so we were commanded.

The messenger who visited us on this occasion and conferred this Priesthood upon us, said that his name was John, the same that is called John the Baptist in the New Testament, and that he acted under the direction of Peter, James and John, who held the keys of the Priesthood of Melchizedek, which Priesthood, he said, would in due time be conferred on us. [At that time] I should be called the first Elder of the Church and he (Oliver Cowdery) the second. It was on the fifteenth day of May, 1829, that we were ordained under the hand of this messenger and baptized. Immediately upon our coming up out of the water after we had been baptized, we experienced great and glorious blessings from our Heavenly Father. No sooner had I baptized Oliver Cowdery, than the Holy Ghost fell upon him, and he stood up and prophesied many things which should shortly come to pass. And again, so soon as I had been baptized by him, I also had the spirit of prophecy . . .[and], standing up, I prophesied concerning the rise of this Church and many other things connected with the Church, and this generation of the children of men. We were filled with the Holy Ghost, and rejoiced in the God of our salvation.[23]

Oliver Cowdery

After writing the account given of the Savior's ministry to the remnant of the seed of Jacob, upon this continent, it was easily to be seen. . .that amid the great strife and noise *concerning* religion, none had authority from God to administer the ordinances of the gospel. For, the question might be asked, have men authority to administer in the name of Christ, who deny revelations? when his testimony is no less than the spirit of prophecy? and his religion based, built, and sustained by immediate revelations in all ages of the world, when he has had a people on earth? . . .Our souls were driven out in mighty prayer to know how we might obtain the blessings of baptism and of the Holy Spirit, according to the order of God, and we diligently sought for the right of the fathers, and

---

[23]JS-H 1:71-73 and *T&S* 3 (August 1, 1842):866.

the authority of the holy priesthood...We...waited for the commandment to be given, "Arise and be baptized."[24]

This was not long desired before it was realized. He [Joseph Smith]...in company with myself, in the town of Harmony, Susquehanna County, Pennsylvania, on Friday, the 15th of May 1829...called upon him [God] in a fervent manner, aside from the abodes of men, [and the Lord] condescended to manifest to us his will. On a sudden, as from the midst of eternity, the voice of the Redeemer spake peace to us, while the veil was parted and the angel of God came down clothed in glory, and delivered the anxiously looked for message, and the keys of the gospel of repentance! What joy! what wonder! what amazement! While the world were [was] racked and distracted—while millions were grouping [groping] as the blind for the wall, and while all men were resting upon uncertainty, as a general mass, our eyes beheld—our ears heard. As in the "blaze of day"; yes, more—above the glitter of the May sun beam, which then shed its brilliancy over the face of nature! Then his voice, though mild, pierced to the center, and his words, "I am thy fellow servant," dispeled every fear. We listened—we gazed—we admired! 'Twas the voice of the angel of glory—'twas a message from the Most High! and as we heard we rejoiced, while his love enkindled upon our souls, and we were rapt in the vision of the Almighty! Where was room for doubt? No where: uncertainty had fled, doubt had sunk, no more to rise, while faction and deception had fled forever!...What joy filled our hearts and with what surprise we must have bowed...when we received under his hand the holy priesthood, ...[or were] ordained by the angel John unto the lesser or Aaronic priesthood...as he said, "upon you my fellow servants, in the name of Messiah I confer this priesthood and this authority, which shall remain upon earth, that the sons of Levi may yet offer an offering unto the Lord in righteousness!"...[25]

Earth, nor men, with the eloquence of time, cannot begin to cloth language in as interesting and sublime a manner as this holy personage. No; nor has this earth power to give the joy, to bestow the peace, or

---

[24]*M&A* 1 (Oct. 1834):15 and Book of Patriarchal Blessings, September 1835, Church Archives. The quotations from this manuscript have not been taken from a patriarchal blessing but from a testimony written in that record by Oliver Cowdery following one of the blessings.

[25]*M&A* 1 (1834):15 and Book of Patriarchal Blessings, September 1835.

comprehend the wisdom which was contained in each sentence as they were delivered by the power of the Holy Spirit! . . .The assurance that we were in the presence of an angel; the certainty that we heard the voice of Jesus, and the truth unsullied as it flowed from a pure personage, dictated by the will of God, is to me, past description . . . .

After . . .[we were ordained] we repaired to the water, even to the Susquehannah River, and were baptized, he first ministering unto me and after I to him.[26]

Orson Pratt

In the year 1829, Mr. Smith and Mr. Cowdery, having learned the correct mode of baptism, from the teachings of the Saviour to the ancient Nephites, as recorded in the "Book of Mormon," had a desire to be baptized, but knowing that no one had authority to administer that sacred ordinance in any denomination, they were at a loss to know how the authority was to be restored, and while calling upon the Lord with a desire to be informed on the subject, a holy angel appeared and stood before them, and laid his hands upon their heads, and ordained them, and commanded them to baptize each other, which they accordingly did.[27]

Restoration of the Melchizedek Priesthoood

Joseph Smith

I received the holy priesthood by the ministering of angels to administer the letter of the gospel. I received the high priesthood after the holy order of the son of the living God. I received the power [and the authority] to preach the gospel and administer in the ordinances [thereof]. The keys of the kingdom [were also] conferred upon me.[28]

---

[26]M&A 1 (1834):15-16 and Book of Patriarchal Blessings, September 1835.

[27]Orson Pratt, *Account of Several Remarkable Visions*, p. 23. For additional references by early leaders of the Church to the restoration of the Aaronic Priesthood see JD 12:362; 19:152; 22:305; 23:32; 24:342-43; 25:207; 26:106-107; *The Prophet*, (New York), March 8, 1845, p. 3; and *Western Standard* (San Francisco), June 28, 1856, p. 1.

[28]"1832 History" and "1842 History." This quotation has been changed from third to first person.

[When]John the Baptist laid his hands upon my head and ordained me . . .a priest, [I was told that this] office was to preach repentance and baptism for the remission of sins, and also to baptize. But I was informed that this office did not extend to the laying on of hands for the giving of the Holy Ghost; that that office was a greater work and was to be given afterwards . . . .[John the Baptist also told me] that he acted under the direction of Peter, James and John, who held the keys of the priesthood of Melchizedek, which Priesthood, he said, would in due time be conferred on us [Joseph and Oliver].[29]

The Priesthood is everlasting. The Savior, Moses, and Elias gave the keys to Peter, James, and John on the mount, when they were transfigured before him . . . .How have we . . .[obtained] the Priesthood in the last days? It came down, in regular succession. Peter, James, and John had it given to them and they gave it to others.[30]

[The Lord] sent unto [me, Joseph Smith] . . .Peter, James, and John in the wilderness between Harmony, Susquehanny County, and Colesville, Broome County, on the Susquehannah River, declaring themselves as possessing the keys of the kingdom, and of the dispensation of the fulness of times . . .[and] by whom I [was] ordained . . .and confirmed . . .to be apostles, and especial witnesses. [D&C Section 27:12-13; 128:20.]

There are, in the Church, two priesthoods, namely, the Melchizedek and Aaronic, including the Levitical Priesthood.

Why the first is called the Melchizedek Priesthood is because Melchizedek was such a great high priest.

Before his day it was called the Holy Priesthood, after the Order of the Son of God.

But out of respect or reverence to the name of the Supreme Being, to avoid the too frequent repetition of his name, they, the Church, in ancient days, called that priesthood after Melchizedek, or the Melchizedek Priesthood. [See D&C Section 107:1-4.][31]

---

[29]*HC* 1:40-41, 6:249-50; Andrew F. Ehat and Lyndon W. Cook, *The Words of Joseph Smith* (Provo: BYU Religious Studies Center, 1980), p. 327; and *T&S* 3 (August 1, 1842):866.

[30]*T&S* 2 (August 2, 1841):488 and Ehat and Cook, *Words of Joseph Smith*, p. 9.

[31]For additional references by early Latter-day Saints of the restoration of the higher priesthood, see *JD* 4:1, 16-18, 275; 12:359; 13:48, 325; 16:294; 19:152; 20:144-45; 23:32; 25:178, 207, 292; *The Prophet* (New York), March 8, 1845, p. 3; and *Western Standard* (San Francisco) June 28, 1856, p. 1.

Oliver Cowdery

We [Joseph Smith and Oliver Cowdery] received the high and holy priesthood...after...we...were baptized.[32] I...stood in the presence of John, with our departed Joseph, to receive the Lesser Priesthood—and in the presence of Peter, to receive the Greater.[33]

Oliver Cowdery - Interview

Long after the authority to administer in holy things had been taken away, the Lord opened the heavens and sent forth his word for the salvation of Israel. In fulfillment of the sacred Scripture the everlasting Gospel was proclaimed by the mighty angel (Moroni) who, clothed with the authority of his mission, gave glory to God in the highest. This gospel is the "stone taken from the mountain without hands." John the Baptist, holding the keys of the Aaronic Priesthood; Peter, James and John holding the keys of the Melchizedek Priesthood, have also ministered for those who shall be heirs of salvation, and with these ministrations ordained men to the same Priesthoods. These priesthoods, with their authority, are now, and must continue to be, in the body of the Church of Jesus Christ of Latter-day Saints....In connection with Joseph the Seer, [I] was blessed with the above ministrations.[34]

Orson Pratt

A revelation and restoration to the earth of the *everlasting gospel* through the angel Moroni would be of no benefit to the nations, unless some one should be ordained with authority to preach it and administer its ordinances. Moroni might reveal a book containing a beautiful and glorious system of salvation, but no one could obey even its first principles without a legally authorized administrator, ordained to preach, baptize, lay on hands for the gifts of the Holy Ghost, etc. Did Moroni ordain Mr. Smith to the apostleship, and command him to administer ordinances? No, he did not. But why not confer authority by

---

[32]Book of Patriarchal Blessings, September 1835.

[33]Oliver Cowdery to Phineas Young, March 23, 1846, photocopy, Church Archives.

[34]Statement of Oliver Cowdery to Samuel W. Richards, January 13, 1849, cited in the *Deseret Evening News* (Salt Lake City), March 22, 1884.

ordination, as well as reveal the everlasting gospel? Because in all probability he had no right so to do. All angels have not the same authority—they do not all hold the same keys . . .How then did Mr. Smith obtain the office of an apostle, if Moroni had no authority to ordain him to such office? Mr. Smith testifies that Peter, James, and John came to him in the capacity of ministering angels, and by the laying on hands ordained him an apostle, and commanded him to preach, baptize, lay on hands for the gift of the Holy Ghost, and administer all the ordinances of the gospel as they themselves did in ancient days.[35]

We consider the restoration of the Aaronic priesthood [by John the Baptist] to be among some of the most important events of the last dispensation. . . .As this priesthood has not authority to administer the laying on of hands for the gift of the Holy Ghost . . .Peter, James, and John appeared as ministering angels, and conferred the Apostleship upon Joseph Smith and others; after which they were authorized to confirm the Church by the laying on of hands.[36]

Response by Others to the Restoration of the Priesthood

Joseph Smith

Our minds being now enlightened, we began to have the scriptures laid open to our understandings, and the true meaning and intention of their more mysterious passages revealed unto us in a manner which we never could attain to previously, nor ever before had thought of. In the meantime, we were forced to keep secret the circumstances of our having received the Priesthood and our having been baptized, owing to a spirit of

---

[35]Orson Pratt, *Divine Authority, or the Question, Was Joseph Smith Sent of God?* (Liverpool, England: R. James, 1848), p. 4.

[36]Orson Pratt, *Divine Authority of the Book of Mormon*, Number 4 (Liverpool, England: R. James, 1850), p. 59. While John Taylor was serving as a missionary in France in 1850, he participated in a series of debates with ministers of other faiths and was asked during one of these public discussions if "Joseph Smith had declared that Peter, James, and John came down from Heaven to ordain him." Elder Taylor's opponent said that Latter-day Saints testify that "an angel" ordained Joseph Smith and also that "Peter, James, and John" ordained him. Responding to this apparent contradiction, John Taylor said that Joseph Smith had "several visits and ministrations," including being ordained by the angels, Peter, James, and John. (John Taylor, *Three Nights' Public Discussion* [Liverpool: J. Taylor, 1850], pp. 10, 12.)

persecution which had already manifested itself in the neighborhood. We had been threatened with being mobbed, from time to time, and this, too by professors of religion. And their intentions of mobbing us were only counteracted by the influence of my wife's father's family (under Divine providence), who had become very friendly to me, and who were opposed to mobs, and were willing that I should be allowed to continue the work of translation without interruption; and therefore [they] offered and promised us protection from all unlawful proceedings as far as in them [protection] lay.

After a few days, however, feeling it to be our duty, we commenced to reason out of the scriptures with our acquaintances and friends, as we happened to meet with them. About this time, my brother Samuel H. Smith came to visit us. We informed him of what the Lord was about to do for the children of men, and [we reasoned] with him out of the Bible. We also showed him that part of the work which we had translated and labored to persuade him concerning the gospel of Jesus Christ, which was now about to be revealed in its fulness. He was not, however, very easily persuaded of these things, but after much enquiry and explanation he retired to the woods in order that by secret and fervent prayer he might obtain of a merciful God wisdom to enable him to judge for himself. The result was that he obtained revelations for himself sufficient to convince him of the truth of our assertions to him, and, on the fifteenth day [twenty-fifth] of that same month in which we had been baptized and ordained, Oliver Cowdery baptized him; and he returned to his father's house greatly glorifying and praising God, being filled with the Holy Sprit.[37]

[While Oliver and I were working on the translation of the Book of Mormon], an old gentleman, came to visit us of whose name I wish to make honorable mention: Mr. Joseph Knight, Sen. of Colesville, Broome County, New York, who, having heard of the manner in which we were occupying our time, very kindly and considerately brought us a quantity of provisions in order that we might not be interrupted in the work of translation by the want of such necessaries of life; and I would just mention here (as in duty bound) that he several times brought us supplies (a distance of at least thirty miles), which enabled us to continue work which otherwise we must have relinquished for a season.

Being very anxious to know his duty as to this work, I enquired of the Lord for him and obtained as follows:

---

[37]JS-H 1:74-75 and T&S 3 (August 1, 1842):866.

Revelation given to Joseph Knight, Sr. at Harmony, Susquehannah County, Pennsylvania, May 1829 [see D&C Section 12:1, 3, 6-8]. A great and marvelous work is about to come forth among the children of men. . . . .Behold, the field is white already to harvest; therefore, whose desireth to reap let him thrust in his sickle with his might, and reap while the day lasts. . . .

Now, as you have asked, behold, I say unto you, keep my commandments, and seek to bring forth and establish the cause of Zion.

Behold, I speak unto you, and also to all those who have desires to bring forth and establish this work; and no one can assist in this work except he shall be humble and full of love, having faith, hope, and charity, being temperate in all things, whatsoever shall be entrusted to his care.[38]

Joseph Knight

When Joseph began to translate he was poor. . .and had no one to write for him but his wife, and, in the winter, her brother wrote a little for him. Even though his wife, Emma, did write for him she could not do much because she had to take care of the house. His wife's father and family were all against him [Joseph] and would not help him. He and his wife came up to see me [in Colesville, New York,] the first winter of 1828 and told me his case. But I was not in easy circumstances and I did not know what it might amount to, and my wife and family were all against me helping him. But I did give him a few provisions and a few things out of the store: a pair of shoes and three dollars in money to help him a little. . . .

The last of March [1828] I told my wife that I must go down and see Joseph again. She asked, "Why do you go so soon?"

I said, "Come, go and see."

And she went with me. Next morning we went down and found them well and they were glad to see us. Joseph talked to us about his

---

[38]*T&S* 3 (August 15, 1842):884. Joseph Smith included D&C Section 11 (current edition) in his history under the date May 1829 with the introduction that at the request of Hyrum Smith he had received the revelation through the Urim and Thummim.

translating and some revelations he had received. From that time my wife began to believe . . . .

In the spring of 1829 Oliver Cowdery [traveled to Pennsylvania where] he received a revelation concerning the work. Oliver was convinced of the truth of the work and agreed to write for Joseph until the work was finished. Now Joseph and Oliver came up to see me and asked if I could help them buy some provisions, they having no way to buy them. When they arrived I was not there. I was in the Catskills. But when I came home my folks told me what Joseph wanted. I had engaged to go to the Catskills again the next day and I went, but I did buy a barrel of mackrel and some lined paper for writing. When I returned home, I bought some nine or ten bushels of grain and five or six bushels of taters and a pound of tea. I left to see them and they were in want. Joseph and Oliver were gone seeking employment for provisions, but they found none. They returned home and found me there with the provisions and they were glad for they were out. Their family consisted of four, Joseph, and his wife, Oliver, and Samuel Smith. They went back to work and had provisions enough to last until the translation was finished.[39]

The Move to Fayette

Joseph Smith

Shortly after commencing to translate, I became acquainted with Mr. Peter Whitmer of Fayette, Seneca County, New York, and also with some of his family. In the beginning of the month of June, his son, David Whitmer, came to the place where we were residing and brought with him a two horse wagon for the purpose of having us accompany him to his father's place and there remain until we should finish the work. He proposed that we should have our board free of charge and the assistance of one of his brothers to write for me [and] also his own assistance when convenient.

Having much need of such timely aid in an undertaking so arduous and being informed that the people of the neighborhood were anxiously awaiting the opportunity to enquire into these things, we accepted the invitation and accompanied Mr. Whitmer to his father's house.[40]

---

[39]Reminiscences of Joseph Knight, Church Archives. For the sake of clarity, many spelling errors have been corrected in this quote and proper punctuation has been inserted.

[40]*T&S* 3 (August 15, 1842):884-85.

David Whitmer - Interview

After thinking over the matter for a long time [the story of Joseph Smith securing the golden plates that he had heard from people in the area of Palmyra], and talking with [Oliver] Cowdery, who also gave me a history of the finding of the plates, I went home; and after several months, Cowdery told me he was going to Harmony, Pennsylvania, where Joseph Smith had gone with the plates on account of the persecutions of the neighbors, . . .[to] see him [Joseph Smith] about the matter. He did go, and on the way stopped at my father's house and told me that as soon as he found out anything, either truth or untruth, he would let me know. After he got there he became acquainted with Joseph Smith, and shortly after, wrote to me telling me that. . .Joseph had told him his [Oliver's] secret thoughts, and all he had mediatated about going to see him, which no man on earth knew, as he supposed, but himself. . .[He also told me that] he was convinced that Smith had the records, and that he [Joseph Smith] had told him that it was the will of heaven that he [Oliver Cowdery] should be his scribe to assist in the translation of the plates. He went on and Joseph translated from the plates and he wrote it down. Shortly after this, Cowdery wrote me another letter, in which he gave me a few lines of what they translated, and he assured me that he knew of a certainty that he had a record of a people that inhabited this continent, and that the plates they were translating gave a complete history of these people. When Cowdery wrote me these things and told me that he had revealed knowledge concerning the truth of them, I showed these letters to my parents and my brothers and sisters. Soon after I received another letter from Cowdery, telling me to come down into Pennsylvania, and bring him and Joseph to my father's house, giving as a reason therefore that they had received a commandment from God to that effect . . . .

I did not know what to do, I was pressed with my work. I had some twenty acres to plow, so I concluded I would finish plowing and then go. I got up one morning to go to work as usual, and on going to the field, found between five and seven acres of my ground had been plowed during the night.

I don't know who did it; but it was done just as I would have done it myself, and the plow was left standing in the furrow.

This enabled me to start sooner. When I arrived at Harmony, Joseph and Oliver were coming toward me, and met me some distance from the house. Oliver told me that Joseph had informed him when I started from home, where I had stopped the first night, how I read the sign at the tavern, where I stopped the next night, etc., and that I would be there that day before dinner, and this was why they had come out to meet me; all of which was exactly as Joseph had told Oliver, at which I was greatly astonished . . . .

The next day after I got there they packed up the plates, and we proceeded on our journey to my father's house . . . .

When I was returning to Fayette, with Joseph and Oliver, all of us riding in the wagon, Oliver and I on an old fashioned wooden spring seat and Joseph behind us; while traveling along in a clear open place, a very pleasant, nice-looking old man suddenly appeared by the side of our wagon and saluted us with, "good morning, it is very warm," at the same time wiping his face or forehead with his hand. We returned the salutation, and, by a sign from Joseph, I invited him to ride if he was going our way. But he said very pleasantly, "No, I am going to Cumorah." This name was something new to me, I did not know what Cumorah meant. We all gazed at him and at each other, and as I looked around enquiringly of Joseph, the old man instantly disappeared, so that I did not see him again . . . .He [the stranger] was about 5 feet 8 or 9 inches tall and heavy set . . . .He was dressed in a suit of brown woolen clothes, his hair and beard were white. I also remember that he had on his back sort of a knapsack with something, shaped like a book. It was the messenger who had the plates, who had taken them from Joseph just prior to our starting from Harmony . . . .

Joseph . . .said that . . .he had the plates of the Book of Mormon in the knapsack.[41]

Events in Fayette (June 1829)

Joseph Smith

Upon our arrival [in Fayette], we found Mr. Whitmer's family very anxious concerning the work and very friendly towards ourselves. They continued so, boarded and lodged us according to proposal; and John Whitmer, in particular, assisted us very much in writing during the remainder of the work.[42]

---

[41]This is a harmony of different interviews, one by an editor of the *Kansas City Journal* and the other by a Latter-day Saint. See *Kansas City Journal*, June 5, 1881, cited in *M S* 43 (July 4, 1881): 422-23 and *MS* 40 (December 9, 1878): 772. See also Journal of Edward Stevenson, Febrauary 9, 1886, pp. 32-37, Church Archives and Lucy Smith, *Biographical Sketches*, pp. 136-37.

[42]*T&S* 3 (August 15, 1842):885.

David Whitmer - Interview

Soon after our [Joseph, Oliver, and David] arrival home [in Fayette], I saw something which led me to the belief that the plates were placed or concealed in my father's barn. I frankly asked Joseph if my supposition was right, and he told me it was. Sometime after this, my mother was going to milk the cows, when she was met out near the yard by the same old man (judging by her description of him) who said to her: "You have been very faithful and diligent in your labors, but you are tired because of the increase of your toil; it is proper therefore that you should receive a witness that your faith may be strengthened." There upon he showed her the plates. My father and mother had a large family of their own, the addition to it therefore of Joseph, his wife Emma and Oliver very greatly increased the toil and anxiety of my mother. And although she had never complained she had sometimes felt that her labor was too much, or at least she was perhaps beginning to feel so. This circumstance, however, completely removed all such feelings and nerved her up for her increased responsibilities.[43]

Joseph Smith

In the meantime, David, John, and Peter Whitmer Jr. became our zealous friends and assistants in the work....[44] We [also] found the people of Seneca County in general friendly and disposed to enquire into the truth of these strange matters which now began to be noised abroad: many opened their houses to us in order that we might have an opportunity of meeting with our friends for the purposes of instruction and explanation. We met with many, who were willing to hear us and wishful, from time to time, who were to find out the truth as it is in Christ Jesus and apparently willing to obey the gospel when once fairly convinced and satisfied in their own minds. In this same month of June, my brother, Hyrum Smith, David Whitmer, and Peter Whitmer, Jr. were baptized in Seneca Lake: the two former by myself, [and] the latter by

---

[43]*M S* 40 (May 2, 1878):772-73.

[44]*T&S* 3 (August 15, 1842):885. Following the quotation appearing in this work, Joseph Smith included in his history three revelations (D&C sections 14, 15, 16) given to David Whitmer, John Whitmer, Jr., and Peter Whitmer. These men had requested Joseph Smith to inquire of the Lord "concerning them." Joseph Smith further wrote that these revelations were received "through the means of the Urim and Thummim."

Oliver Cowdery. From this time forth many became believers and were baptized, while we continued to instruct and persuade as many as applied for information.[45]

Meantime, we continued to translate at intervals, when not necessitated to attend to the numerous enquirers that now began to visit us; some for the sake of finding the truth, others for the purpose of putting hard questions and trying to confound us. Among the latter class were several learned priests who generally came for the purpose of disputation: however, the Lord continued to pour out upon us his Holy Spirit, and, as often as we had need, he gave us in that moment what to say; so that, although unlearned and inexperienced in religious controversies, yet were able to confound those learned Rabbis of the day, whilst at the same time, we were enabled to convince the honest in heart that we had obtained (through the mercy of God) to the true and everlasting gospel of Jesus Christ, so that almost daily we administered the ordinance of baptism for the remission of sins to such as believed. We now became anxious to have that promise realized to us, which the angel that conferred upon us the Aaronic Priesthood had given us, viz: that, provided we continued faithful, we should also have the Melchizedek Priesthood, which holds the authority of the laying on of hands for the gift of the Holy Ghost.[46] We had for some time made this matter a subject of humble prayer, and at length we got together in the chamber of Mr. Whitmer's house in order more particularly to seek of the Lord what we now so

---

[45]*T&S* 3 (September 1, 1842):897.

[46]*T&S* 3 (September 15, 1842):915. Commenting on the statement in Joseph Smith's history regarding the desire of Joseph and Oliver to have the Melchizedek Priesthood conferred upon them, B. H. Roberts wrote that this reference "is to be regarded as instruction to them as to how they should proceed in the matter of ordaining each other, and calling and ordaining others to the same ministry, after they themselves should have received the keys of the Melchizedek Priesthood. The ordination of each other to be Elders of the Church was deferred until the meeting at which the Church was organized, the 6th of April, 1830 . . . .[One] evidence of this [interpretation] is in the fact that the revelation in Whitmer's chamber about ordaining each other "Elders of the Church," precedes [another] . . . revelation [which was also received in June] . . . making known the calling of the Twelve Apostles. Meantine, as we have seen . . . probably before that very month of June, 1829, had expired, Peter, James and John had come and conferred upon Joseph and Oliver the keys of the Melchizedek Priesthood, the holy apostleship, by which authority they were authorized to organize the Church, ordain each other Elders, and also call and ordain others to the same office." (*HC*, 1:60-61.)

earnestly desired: and here to our unspeakable satisifaction did we realize the truth of the Savior's promise; "Ask, and you shall receive, seek, and you shall find, knock and it shall be opened unto you," for we had not long been engaged in solemn and fervent prayer when the word of the Lord came unto us in the chamber, commanding us that I should ordain Oliver Cowdery to be an elder in the church of Jesus Christ and that he also should ordain me to the same office, and then to ordain others as it should be made known unto us, from time to time. We were, however, commanded to defer this our ordination until such time as it should be practicable to have our brethren who had been and who should be baptized assembled together, when we must have their sanction to our thus proceeding to ordain each other and have them decide by vote whether they are willing to accept us as spiritual teachers or not, when also we were commanded to bless bread and break it with them and to take wine, bless it and drink it with them, [and] afterward proceed to ordain each other according to the commandment, [and] then call out such men as the spirit should dictate and ordain them. Then [we should] attend to the laying on of hands for the gift of the Holy Ghost upon all those whom we had previously baptized, doing all things in the name of the Lord.[47]

The following commandment will further illustrate the nature of our calling to this Priesthood as well as that of others who were yet to be sought after.

> Revelation to Joseph Smith, Jr., Oliver Cowdery, and David Whitmer, making known the calling of twelve apostles in these last days, and also, instructions relative to building up the church of Christ, according to the fulness of the gospel: given in Fayette, New York, June, 1829. [See D&C Section 18:1-2, 9, 14-15, 26-27, 37-39.]

> Now, behold, because of the thing which you, my servant Oliver Cowdery, have desired to know of me, I give unto you these words: Behold, I have manifested unto you, by my Spirit in many instances, that the things which you have written are true; wherefore you know that they are true . . . .

> And now, Oliver Cowdery, I speak unto you, and also unto David Whitmer, by the way of commandment; . . .you are called to cry repentance unto this people. And if it so be that you should labor all your days in crying repentance unto this

---

[47]*T&S* 3 (September 15, 1842):915.

people, and bring, save it be one soul unto me, how great shall be your joy with him in the kingdom of my Father! . . .

And now, behold, there are others who are called to declare my gospel, both unto Gentile and unto Jew; yea, even twelve; and the Twelve shall be my disciples, and they shall take upon them my name; and the Twelve are they who shall desire to take upon them my name with full purpose of heart . . .

And now, behold, I give unto you, Oliver Cowdery, and also unto David Whitmer, that you shall search out the Twelve, who shall have the desires of which I have spoken; and by their desires and their works you shall know them. And when you have found them you shall show these things unto them.[48]

David Whitmer

In June 1829 . . . I was baptized, confirmed, and ordained an elder . . . by Bro. Joseph Smith. Previous to this, Joseph Smith and Oliver Cowdery had baptized, confirmed and ordained each other to the office of an elder.[49]

Translation Completed in Fayette

Joseph Smith

We [Joseph, his wife, and Oliver] resided [in Peter Whitmer's home] until the translation was finished and the copyright secured.[50]

David Whitmer - Interview

I, as well as all of my father's family, Smith's wife, Oliver Cowdery, and Martin Harris, were present during the translation . . . . The translation at my father's occupied about one month, that is from June 1 to July 1, 1829.[51]

---

[48]*T&S* 3 (September 15, 1842):915-16.

[49]David Whitmer, *Address to All Believers*, p. 82.

[50]*T&S* 3 (August 15, 1842):885.

[51]*Kansas City Journal*, June 5, 1881, cited in *MS* 43 (July 4, 1881):423.

Lucy Smith

[After arriving at the Whitmer home, Joseph, Oliver, and others] continued without further interruption until the whole work [of translation] was accomplished. As soon as the Book of Mormon was translated, Joseph despatched a messenger to Mr. Smith, bearing intelligence of the completion of the work, and a request that Mr. Smith and myself should come immediately to Waterloo [a community located near the Whitmer farm]....Accordingly, the next morning, we all set off together, and before sunset met Joseph and Oliver at Mr. Whitmer's.

The evening was spent in reading the manuscript, and it would be superfluous for me to say, to one who has read the foregoing pages, that we rejoiced exceedingly. It then appeared to those of us who did not realize the magnitude of the work, as if the greatest difficulty was then surmounted.[52]

Diedrich Willers, German Reformed Minister of Fayette

In the month of July [June 1829], Joseph Smith made his appearance in Seneca County, in the neighborhood of Waterloo, about 6 miles from my hometown. There a certain David Whitmer claimed to have seen an angel of the Lord, so Smith proceeded to his house, in order to complete the translation of the above work [Book of Mormon] himself. According to the reports, only there could he work—where men who have had association with the other world also reside....

He [Joseph Smith] asserted that the Angel of the Lord appeared to him and made it known that in the neighborhood of Palmyra there were golden plates in the earth, upon which was described the doings of a Jewish prophet's family, associated with many not yet fulfilled prophecies. The Angel indicated that the Lord destined him to translate these things into English from the ancient language, that under these plates were hidden spectacles, without which he could not translate these plates, that by using these spectacles, he [Smith] would be in a position to read these ancient languages, which he had never studied, and that the Holy Ghost would reveal to him the translation in the English language. Therefore, he [Smith] proceeded to Manchester township, Ontario County, and found everything as described, the plates buried next to the spectacles in the earth, and soon he completed the translation of this work.

---

[52]Lucy Smith, *Biographical Sketches*, pp. 137-38.

Upon receiving this report, I hurried immediately to Whitmer's house to see this man, in order to learn the actual source of this story and to find out how it might be possible to nip this work in the bud. However, I received the reply from Whitmer's father that Smith had already departed to take his translation to press.[53]

Summary
Testimonies That Joseph Smith was the Translator of the Book of Mormon

Joseph Smith

Moroni...who deposited the plates, from whence the Book of Mormon was translated, in a hill in Manchester, Ontario County, New York, being dead and raised again therefrom, appeared unto me and told me where they [the plates] were and gave me directions how to obtain them. I obtained them, and the Urim and Thummim with them, by the means of which I translated the plates...by the gift and power of God...and thus came the Book of Mormon.[54]

Emma Smith - Interview

I wrote for Joseph Smith during the work of translation, as did also Reuben Hale [Emma's brother]...and O. Cowdery....The larger part of

---

[53]This early account of the coming forth of the Book of Mormon was based on stories that were being circulated in Fayette, New York, about 1830. It was included in a letter dated June 18, 1830, written by Diedrich Willers and designed to warn others about this new religious movement. Willers was the Reformed (German) minister of Fayette who sometimes preached to members of the Zion church located in West Fayette. Members of the Peter Whitmer family were affiliated with that congregation prior to their becoming members of the restored Church. Willers was openly disturbed because so many members of his church and other Protestants in Fayette had embraced Mormonism. An English translation of this letter which is located in the archives at Cornell University has been reproduced in D. Michael Quinn, "The First Months of Mormonism: A Contemporary View by Rev. Diedrich Willers," *New York History* 54 (July 1973):317-33.

[54]*Elder's Journal* 1 (July 1838):42-43; *T&S* 3 (March 1, 1842):707; and *HC*, 3:28; *HC*, 4:537. Joseph Smith reaffirmed his testimony that he translated the Book of Mormon in a letter sent to James Arlington Bennett, November 13, 1843: "I translated the Book of Mormon from hieroglyphics; the knowledge of which was lost to the world." (See *Reply of Joseph Smith to the Letter of J. A. B. of A--n House* [Liverpool: R. Hedlock & T. Ward, 1844], p. 12.)

this labor was done [in] my presence and where I could see and know what was being done . . . .During no part of it [the work of translation] did Joseph Smith have any mss. or book of any kind from which to read or dictate except the metalic plates which I knew he had . . . .[55] Joseph Smith could neither write nor dictate a coherent and well-worded letter, let alone dictate a book like the Book of Mormon . . . .The Book of Mormon is of divine authenticity—I have not the slightest doubt of it. I am satisifed that no man could have dictated the writing of the manuscripts unless he was inspired; for, when acting as his scribe, your father would dictate to me hour after hour; and when returning after meals, or after interruptions, he would at once begin where he had left off, without either seeing the manuscript or having any portion of it read to him. This was a usual thing for him to do. It would have been improbable that a learned man could do this; and, for one so ignorant and unlearned as he was, it was simply impossible.[56]

Martin Harris, David Whitmer, and Oliver Cowdery

We . . .know that they [the plates which contained the record from which the Book of Mormon was translated] have been translated by the gift and power of God, for his voice hath declared it unto us; wherefore we know of a surety that the work is true.[57]

---

[55]Joseph Smith III to James T. Cobb, February 14, 1879, Letterbook 2:85-88, RLDS Archives. This information was related by Emma to her son, Joseph, and recorded by him. The quote has been changed from third to first person and punctuation (commas) has been changed for sake of clarity. Emma also told her son that she "never saw or knew Sidney Rigdon until long after the Book of Mormon was translated." Katherine Smith Salisbury, Joseph Smith's sister, also testified that during the translation of the Book of Mormon she was acquainted with the people who visited her family in Manchester, New York, and remembered meeting Sidney Rigdon for the first time when he arrived at her father's place after the family had moved to a farm near Waterloo months after the publication of the Book of Mormon. ("Testimony of Katherine Salisbury," *Saints' Herald* 28 [June 1, 1881]:169.)

[56]Statement of Emma Smith to her son, Joseph Smith III, February 1879, cited in *The Saints' Herald* 26 (October 1, 1879):289-90. See also Joseph Smith III, "Last Testimony of Sister Emma," *Saints' Advocate* 2 (October 1879):52.

[57]"The Testimony of Three Witnesses," published in the first edition of the Book of Mormon (Palmyra: E. B. Brandin, 1830) and in all subsequent editions. For the background of this testimony and additional remarks of these three men regarding this experience, see Chapter 6 of this work.

Martin Harris - Interview

Joseph Smith was the first to handle the. . .tablets of gold. . .and I. . .the second. At one time. . .[I held] the plates on my knee an hour-and-a-half, whilest in conversation with Joseph, when we went to bury them in the woods, that the enemy might not obtain them. . . .There was also found in the chest [that contained the Book of Mormon plates] the Urim and Thummim, by the means of which the writing upon the plates was translated, but not until after the most learned men had exhausted their knowledge of letters in the vain effort to decipher the characters.[58]

Martin Harris

I do firmly believe and do know that Joseph Smith was a prophet of God; for without I know he could not have translated. . .the plates containing the Book of Mormon. . .No man ever heard me in any way deny the truth of the Book of Mormon.[59]

David Whitmer

I testify to the world that I am an eye-witness to the translation of the greater part of the Book of Mormon. Part of it was translated in my father's house in Fayette, Seneca County, New York. . . .No man could read it [the characters on the plates], but God gave to an unlearned boy the gift to translate. . . .Brother Joseph would read. . .the English to Oliver Cowdery, who was his principle scribe. . . .Thus the Book of Mormon was translated by the gift and power of God, and not by any power of man.[60]

---

[58]David B. Dille, "Additional Testimony of Martin Harris," *MS* 21 (August 20, 1859):545 and *Iowa State Register* (Des Moines) August 26, 1870, p. 4. (See Appendix E)

[59]Martin Harris to H. B. Emerson, November 28, 1860 and January 1871, cited in *The True Latter Day Saints' Herald*, 22 (1875):630.

[60]David Whitmer, *An Address to All Believers in Christ* (Richmond, Missouri: David Whitmer, 1887), pp. 11-12. Since David Whitmer and Martin Harris probably did not actually witness Joseph Smith translating the record, I have omitted from their writings their opinions concerning the precise process of translation. All that Joseph Smith and Oliver Cowdery said on this subject was that the plates were translated by the gift and power of God by means of the Urim and Thummim.

Neither Joseph Smith, Oliver Cowdery, Martin Harris or myself ever met Sydney Rigdon until after the Book of Mormon was in print. I know this of my own personal knowledge, being with Joseph Smith, in Seneca County, New York, in the winter of 1830, when Sydney Rigdon and Edward Partridge came from Kirtland, Ohio, to see Joseph Smith and where Rigdon and Partridge saw Joseph Smith for the first time in their lives. The Spaulding manuscript story is a myth; there being no direct testimony on record in regard to Rigdon's connection with the manuscript of Solomon Spaulding . . . .There is also no similarity whatever between it [the manuscript of Solomon Spaulding that had been discovered and placed in the library of Oberlin College] and the Book of Mormon.[61]

Oliver Cowdery

Through him [Joseph Smith] the Lord revealed his will to the church: he was ministered unto by the angel, and by his direction he obtained the Records of the Nephites and translated [them] by the gift and power of God.

Day after day I continued, uninterrupted, to write from his [Joseph Smith's] mouth, as he translated, with the Urim and Thummim, or, as the Nephites would have said, "Interpreters," the history, or record, called "The Book of Mormon."[62]

Oliver Cowdery - Interview

I wrote with my own pen the entire book of Mormon (save a few pages) as it fell from the lips of the Prophet as he translated it by the gift and power of God by means of the Urim and Thummim or as it is called by the book holy Interpreters. I beheld with my eye and handled with my hands the gold plates from which it was translated. I also beheld the Interpreters. That book is true. Sidney Rigdon did not write it. Mr. Spaulding did not write it. I wrote it myself as it fell from the lips of the Prophet. It contains the everlasting gospel and came in fulfillment of the revelations of John where he says [that] he saw an angel come with the everlasting gospel to preach to every nation, tongue and people.[63]

---

[61]Ibid., p. 11.

[62]*M&A* 1 (October 1834):14.

[63]Journal of Reuben Miller, 1848 and *MS* 21 (August 20, 1859):544.

William Smith

The statements . . .concerning the strange vision[s] shown to Joseph Smith, are true; and the translation of the record as found by the [my] brother [Joseph] as stated, is also true, and in no other way did Joseph Smith compile, or compose the Book of Mormon only as stated by the gift and power of God.[64]

Lucy Smith

Joseph, after repenting of his sins and humbling himself before God, was visited by an holy angel whose countenance was as lightning and whose garments were white above all whiteness, who gave unto him commandments which inspired him from on high; and who gave unto him, by the means of which was before prepared, that he should translate this book . . . .[65] I want you to remember that God himself has given to Joseph that he is able to translate . . .for as God lives I have written the truth.[66]

---

[64]William Smith, *On Mormonism* (Lamoni, Iowa: Herald, 1883), p. 28.

[65]Lucy Smith to Solomon Mack, January 6, 1831, Church Archives.

[66]Lucy Smith to Mary Pierce, January 23, 1829, in possession of Brent F. Ashowrth, Provo, Utah.

CHAPTER SIX

Eleven Special Witnesses

In the mouth of two or three witnesses shall every word be established. (2 Corinthians 13:1.)
Wherefore, the Lord God will proceed to bring forth the words of the book; and in the mouth of as many witnesses as seemeth him good will he establish his word. (2 Nephi 27:14.)

There are many incredible statements in the writings of the Prophet Joseph Smith. These include his testimonies that he was instructed in 1820 by God the Eternal Father and His Son, Jesus Christ; that he received numerous visitations from angelic messenger after 1823; that he was directed by a heavenly being to a prominent hill where he located a set of golden plates buried in a stone box; and that he translated these plates by the gift and power of God. Moreover, he testified that he received (in company with Oliver Cowdery) God's authority to baptize, confirm, ordain, and reestablish Christ's church upon the earth by the laying of hands from John the Baptist and Peter, James, and John.

The uncommon aspects of the restoration movement do not cease with these startling pronouncements. In the summer of 1829, eleven men examined the Book of Mormon plates and wrote testimonies that are unparalleled in the annals of religious history. Three men declared with words of soberness that they not only saw the plates from which the Book of Mormon was translated and the engravings thereon, but that they were shown this record by a heavenly being and heard a voice from heaven

131

which verified the correct translation of the book.[1] A day or two after the Three Witnesses saw the plates during a heavenly vision, eight other men walked into a grove where they were shown the plates by Joseph Smith. These men, in the presence of one another, examined the golden plates meticulously. They hefted them, they saw the curious writings on the metal record, and they turned the thin leaves or pages which the Prophet had translated, one by one.[2]

After the eleven witnesses had examined the golden plates, they wrote an account of their experience and signed their names to the document.[3] Since three of the witnesses saw the plates during a vision, beheld an angel, and were instructed by the voice of God, and eight men examined the plates under different circumstances, the eleven special witnesses endorsed two separate accounts of their experiences. Both of these testimonies were published in the first edition of the Book of Mormon which was available for sale in March 1830, less than one year after the eleven had examined the record. The testimonies of these eleven men, with their names attached, have been republished in all subsequent editions of the Book of Mormon. These testimonies were also printed in many newspapers across the land, and were recopied or referred to periodically in the writings of these witnesses and many of their contemporaries.[4]

The testimonies of the eleven witnesses of the Book of Mormon plates are without parallel in religious history and are a powerful external evidence of the divine calling of Joseph Smith. Ordinarily, the testimony of eleven men would be sufficient to establish the reality of an historical event. All were eye-witnesses of the record. All saw the plates during the daylight hours. All examined the plates in such close proximity as to see

---

[1]*The Book of Mormon* (Palmyra: E. B. Grandin, 1830). The testimonies of the witnesses to the Book of Mormon are currently printed in the forepart of this book, but in the first edition they appeared at the end.

[2]Ibid.

[3]"Report of Elders Orson Pratt and Joseph F. Smith," *MS* 40 (December 9, 1878): 773.

[4]Some of the earliest reprintings of the testimonies of the eleven witnesses appeared in American newspapers, such as the *Rochester Daily Advertiser and Telegraph* (New York), April 2, 1830; *Loraine Gazette* (Elyria, Ohio), May 21, 1830, p. 2; and the *Republican Advocate* (Wooster, Ohio), May 22, 1830, p. 3. See also *T&S* 3 (September 1, 1842): 898-99 and David Whitmer, *Address to All Believers in Christ*, p. 18.

the curious inscriptions on the record. All became active members of the religious community organized by the Prophet Joseph Smith. All devoted their time and energy and sacrificed their material means to advance the restoration movement. Because of their refusal to deny that which they had declared in defense of the Prophet and of the Book of Mormon, they all experienced economic distress and financial loss. Some were forced to leave their homes and move to new communities. All experienced humiliation, defaming criticism, social ostracism, and other forms of persecution. Most were driven by ruthless mobs from their homes and one (Hyrum Smith) was killed by a mob at the time the Prophet was martyred. There is no reliable evidence that any of the eleven men at any time denied his testimony as published in the Book of Mormon. All of their wives and children and close associates knew that they bore an unwavering affirmation of the authenticity of the Book of Mormon. After establishing their homes in different parts of the young nation, four of the men (Oliver Cowdery, Martin Harris, David Whitmer, and Samuel Smith) lost contact at one time or another with all the other witnesses, so that if they had been involved in a fraudulent plot they were granted opportunities to expose it without fear of reprisal. None, however, did.[5]

The witnesses were members of five families. The Three Witnesses, Oliver Cowdery, David Whitmer, and Martin Harris, were from three family groups and the Eight Witnesses also belonged to three families (with members of the Whitmer family being represented in both sets of witnesses). Three of the eight were Smiths: Joseph Smith's father, Joseph Smith, Sr., and his two brothers Hyrum and Samuel. Four were Whitmers: David's brothers, Christian, Jacob, Peter, and John. The other witness was Hiram Page.

At the time of the viewing of the Book of Mormon plates, all eleven witnesses were men of maturity, competent observers, and trustworthy

---

[5]According to Luke Johnson, an early convert of the Church, at a conference held in Orange, Cuyahoga County, Ohio, during the early 1830s, the "eleven witnesses to the Book of Mormon, with uplifted hands, bore their solemn testimony to the truth of that book, as did also the Prophet Joseph Smith" (Luke Johnson, "History of Luke Johnson, *Deseret News* (Salt Lake City), May 26, 1858, p. 57.). The best summary of the life and testimonies of the witness to the Book of Mormon is Richard L. Anderson, *Investigating the Book of Mormon Witnesses* (Salt Lake City: Deseret Book Co., 1981). This work was based on a series of articles which Anderson wrote for publication in *The Improvement Era* (August 1968 to August 1969). Additional biographical sketches of the eleven witnesses appear in Andrew Jenson's *Latter-day Saint Biographical Encyclopedia, 4 vols. (Salt Lake City: The Andrew Jenson History Co., 1901.)*

individuals who believed in living a life which harmonized with the teachings of Christ. The average age of these witnesses in 1829 was thirty, the youngest, Peter Whitmer, Jr., being nineteen and the oldest, Joseph Smith, Sr., being fifty-nine. There is no evidence that any of these witnesses had in 1829 (or before or after that date) any serious emotional or physical handicap that would have impaired their ability to judge accurately that which they observed. Records further indicate that the witnesses believed in the divinity of Christ. Before uniting with the restoration movement, the Whitmers were active members of a German Reformed church.[6] Joseph Smith, Sr., helped organize a Universalist church in Vermont, and Hyrum and Samuel Smith belonged to the Presbyterian church during the 1820s.[7] All of the witnesses were baptized and became active members of the Church organized by the Prophet.[8]

Although few Americans in 1829 accepted Joseph Smith's unusual claims, all of the witnesses had expressed genuine interest in the Prophet's work. Some had served as scribes and others had listened sympathetically as Joseph Smith informed them of the religious patterns of ancient America and other themes unfolded in the Book of Mormon.[9]

---

[6]Before joining the restored Church, members of the Peter Whitmer family were affiliated with the Zion's Church, a Reformed (German) Church located in West Fayette served by Rev. Diedrich Willers.) See *Manual of the Churches of Seneca County with Sketches of their Pastors* [Seneca Falls, New York: Courier Printing Co., 1896], p. 102 and *Diedrich Willers: Local Historian of the Centennial Years 1879-1904* [n.p., n. d.], p. 89.) Prior to joining the Church members of this family were given political responsibilities by their neighbors. In 1828 and 1829 Christian Whitmer was elected constable and Peter Whitmer an overseer of the highways in Fayette township. (Records of the town of Fayette, 1802-1845, Waterloo Historical Society, pp. 170, 172, 176. See also Larry C. Porter, "A Study of the Origins of the Church of Jesus Christ of Latter-day Saints in the States of New York and Pennsylvania, 1816-1831" [Ph.D. diss., Brigham Young University, 1971], pp. 227-29.)

[7]Richard L. Anderson, *Joseph Smith's New England Heritage* (Salt Lake City: Deseret Book Co., 1972), pp. 105-06 and Milton V. Backman, Jr., *Joseph Smith's First Vision: Confirming Evidences and Contemporary Accounts*, 2nd ed. enlarged (Salt Lake City: Bookcraft, 1980), pp. 67-69, 182-83.

[8]All of the six original members of the church were witnesses to the Book of Mormon. These six were Joseph Smith, Jr., Oliver Cowdery, David Whitmer, Hyrum Smith, Samuel Smith, and Peter Whitmer, Jr. Other witnesses were batpized shortly after the organization of the Church (*HC*, 1:76, 79, 81, 166.)

[9]Martin Harris, Oliver Cowdery, and John Whitmer served as scribes during the translation of the Book of Mormon. (*HC*, 1:20, 32-33 and Jenson, *Biographical Encyclopedia* 1:251.)

After the Three Witnesses had seen the plates, Joseph Smith invited members of his family, four brothers of David Whitmer, and Hiram Page to be special witnesses of the restoration. At that time (the summer of 1829), the Whitmers were visiting the Smiths in Manchester, New York.

All of the Three Witnesses and three of the Eight Witnesses (John and Jacob Whitmer and Hiram Page) eventually rejected the leadership of Joseph Smith. A number of forces combined to create an internal crisis within the restored Church in 1837 and 1838 that led to the apostasy of many leaders. Economic failures, a visible pride and selfishness of some members, the unfolding of new doctrines by the Prophet, and the failure of some members to pattern their life after the revelatory writings of Joseph Smith (such as complying with provisions of the health code known as the Word of Wisdom) were included among these debilitating influences. Between the fall of 1837 and the summer of 1838, four of the witnesses were excommunicated (Martin Harris, David Whitmer, Oliver Cowdry, and John Whitmer) and two others (Jacob Whitmer and Hiram Page) became alienated and never returned to active participation. Two of the six men (Oliver Cowdery and Martin Harris) admitted that they had transgressed, repented of their mistakes, and were rebaptized into The Church of Jesus Christ of Latter-day Saints during the administration of President Brigham Young. Although these six witnesses criticized the Prophet in 1837 and 1838 for some of his actions, not one of the six denied viewing the plates nor rejected the authenticity of the Book of Mormon. Their testimony, therefore, regarding the Book of Mormon is strengthened because of the consistency of their affirmations even after denouncing the Prophet. Moreoever, all of the Three Witnesses and some of the eight made it a point to reaffirm their testimonies regarding the truthfulness of the Book of Mormon on their death beds.[10]

The witness who was interviewed on more occasions than any other individual who examined the plates was David Whitmer. David was the last of the eleven witnesses to die and, following his excommunication in 1838, lived among non-members in Missouri for more than fifty years. During this half century, he served as a city councilman and mayor of Richmond and earned a living by farming and operating a transportation business (furnishing customers with horses and carriages). While living in Richmond, he was constantly interviewed by members and non-members alike. Many elders of the Church who were traveling east on missions stopped in Richmond specifically to visit him, desiring to hear from David's own lips his account of seeing the angel, the plates, and

---

[10]Anderson, *Investigating the Book of Mormon Witnesses*, pp. 38, 63, 69-70, 89-90, 110, 118, 127-28 and *HC*, 3:3, 7, 18-19.

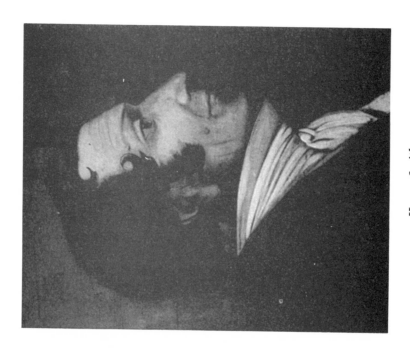

Hyrum Smith

David Whitmer

Viewing of the plates
by the Eight Witnesses

hearing a voice from heaven.[11] During one of these interviews held in 1883, David Whitmer said that he had been "visited by thousands of people, believers and unbelievers, men and ladies of all degrees." He said that he had been interviewed as many as fifteen times in a single day, and that never he had failed to bear his testimony to those questioning him. "They will know some day," he predicted, "that my testimony is true."[12]

An opportune occasion for David Whitmer to have denied his testimony occurred in 1833. While Latter-day Saints were being persecuted in Jackson County, Missouri, an armed mob threatened his life. After placing a loaded rifle next to David's chest, one of the mobsters told Whitmer that if he did not deny his testimony, he would shoot. This same mobster offered him a reward for renouncing his testimony. He said that by complying with his demands he would not only save his life, but that he would allow him to remain in the county and retain his property. Instead of repudiating his conviction in the authenticity of the Book of Mormon, David Whitmer raised his hands before the angry crowd and declared that the Book of Mormon was "the word of God." "The testimony I bore [to] the mob," David recalled, "made them tremble before me."[13]

Although there is no reliable evidence that David Whitmer repudiated his testimony as published in the Book of Mormon, a few interviewers assumed that he was contradicting his published declaration when he told them that he saw the plates with his spiritual rather than his natural eyes. Explaining what he meant by this statement, David Whitmer wrote in 1887:

> Of course we were in the spirit when we had the view, for no man can behold the face of an angel, except in a spiritual view, but we were in the body also, and everything was as natural to us, as it is at any time. Martin Harris...called it

---

[11]Anderson, *Investigating the Book of Mormon Witnesses*, pp. 84-90.

[12]Edward L. Hart, *Mormon in Motion: The Life and Journals of James H. Hart, 1825-1906* (Windsor Books, 1978), p. 216.

[13]Ibid; *Western Standard* (San Francisco, California), February 7, 1857; Heman C. Smith to *Saints' Herald*, June 28, 1884, cited in *Saints' Herald* 31 (1884):442; and John P. Greene, *Facts Relating to the Expulsion of the Mormons...from the State of Missouri* (Cincinnati, Ohio: R. P. Brooks, 1839), p. 17.

"being in vision".....A bright light enveloped us where we were...and there in a vision, or in the spirit, we saw and heard just as it is stated in my testimony in the Book of Mormon.[14]

Some skeptics who did not endorse David Whitmer's published testimony suggested that he must have been deceived. When a military officer informed Whitmer that he must have been mentally disturbed or suffered an hallucination which caused him to think that he saw an angel, plates, and other objects, Whitmer replied emphatically that he "was not under any hallucination," nor was he "deceived." "I saw with these eyes, and I heard with these ears!" he asserted. "I know whereof I speak."[15]

In partial response to accusations that he had denied his testimony and that he suffered some type of mental disturbance, David Whitmer published a pamphlet in 1887 entitled *An Address to All Believers in Christ* in which he emphasized that he and the other witnesses who examined the plates had never denied their testimonies as published in the Book of Mormon. Moreover, he insisted, "It was no delusion."[16]

One contemporary who wrote about the consistency of the testimonies of the witnesses of the Book of Mormon was Edward Stevenson. Edward joined the Church during the early 1830s, when he was a teenager living with his parents in Pontiac, Michigan. In 1834 he heard Joseph Smith, Oliver Cowdery, Martin Harris, David Whitmer, Hyrum Smith, and Joseph Smith, Sr., bear witness of the truthfulness of their tes-

---

[14]David Whitmer to A. Metcalf, April 2, 1887, cited in A. Metcalf, *Ten years Before the Mast* (Malad, Indiana: New Haven, Conn. Research Publication, 1967), pp. 73-74. Joseph Smith taught that during visions, individuals were quickened by the spirit and saw with their spiritual eyes. (D&C 67:10-11.)

[15]Memoirs of Joseph Smith, III, cited in Mary Audentia Smith Anderson, ed., *Joseph Smith III and the Restoration* (Independence, Mo.: Herald House, 1952), pp. 311-312.

[16]David Whitmer, *Address to All Believers in Christ*, pp. 8-9. In addition to the testimonies of the witnesses that they were not deceived, another evidence that these men did not experience a form of hallucination is that they examined the plates at different times under different circumstances. The eight were shown the plates by Joseph Smith and the three by an angel during two different visions.

timonies regarding their having examined the Book of Mormon plates.[17] On other occasions during the 1830s, he heard the Three Witnesses testify concerning the authenticity of the Book of Mormon. In 1870, 1877, and 1886, he heard David Whitmer explain his experience of examining the plates in the presence of a heavenly messenger.[18] Meanwhile, Edward Stevenson became a personal friend of Martin Harris. Stevenson ultimately encouraged Martin to move to Utah, and he traveled west with him in 1870. After arriving in the Salt Lake Valley, Edward Stevenson rebaptized Martin Harris and listened as Martin bore his testimony to hundreds of Saints in public meetings and to many others in private conversations.[19] Edward Stevenson, therefore, heard all three of the Three Witnesses bear their testimonies at different times during their lives and wrote in letters, journals, and articles the reaffirmations of all these men regarding the angel, the plates, and the voice from heaven. He also was acquainted with some of the Eight Witnesses and heard these men at different times bear witness to the reality of the Book of Mormon plates.[20]

Since most interviewers of the eleven witnesses were not trained in the techniques of reporting, some undoubtedly did not quote with precise accuracy that which had been related to them. With the passage of time and the constant retelling of the same experience, the witnesses in some instances also might have erred in describing every detail of their experience. Nevertheless, the fact that more than one hundred detailed descriptions of their testimonies harmonize with the statements published in the first edition of the Book of Mormon is solid evidence that the witnesses

---

[17]Joseph Grant Stevenson, *The Stevenson Family History; Consisting of Biographical Sketches of the Joseph Stevenson Family which came to America in 1828, Including Sketches of Lives of Their Wives and Husbands*, 2d ed. (Provo: Joseph Grant Stevenson, 1955), pp. 27-28; Edward Stevenson, *Reminiscences of Joseph, the Prophet, and the Coming Forth of the Book of Mormon* (Salt Lake City: Edward Stevenson, 1893), pp. 5, 46; Edward Stevenson, "Incidents of My Early Days in the Church," *Juvenile Instructor* 29 (September 1, 1894): 551-52. Edward Stevenson was ordained a seventy on May 1, 1845 and was set apart as one of the First Seven Presidents of Seventies on October 9, 1894.

[18]Edward Stevenson, *Reminiscences of Joseph, the Prophet*, p. 23; Joseph Grant Stevenson, *The Stevenson Family History*, p. 180.

[19]Joseph Grant Stevenson, *The Stevenson Family History*, pp. 152-68 and *Deseret News* (Salt Lake City), August 19, 1870, p. 3 and September 17, 1888, p. 2.

[20]Joseph Grant Stevenson, *The Stevenson Family History*, pp. 28-29 and Edward Stevenson, "Incidents of My Early Days in the Church, p. 551.

constantly told others the same basic affirmation regarding the plates. (See Appendix E and F.)[21]

The eleven witnesses also exhibited their conviction in the authenticity of the Book of Mormon by preaching the restored gospel to others. Without generally receiving any financial support from the Church, most witnesses served as full-time missionaries. While laboring in this capacity, they not only experienced the joy of seeing others accept the restored gospel and baptizing them into the Church, but they endured fatigue, hunger, physical pain, and public humiliation. In 1830, six months after the Church had been organized, two of the witnesses, Oliver Cowdery and Peter Whitmer, Jr., were called, along with two other elders, to preach the gospel to Indians living in the Missouri frontier.[22] If the witnesses to the Book of Mormon had been involved in a plot to deceive mankind, it is inconceivable that they would have undertaken such an extensive journey at their own expense to teach Americans who were unpopular and oppressed. One of the elders, Parley P. Pratt, who participated in this first extended mission in the history of the Church, aptly described the suffering of these missionaries as they crossed the sparsely settled state of Missouri in the winter of 1831:

> We traveled for whole days, from morning till night, without a house or fire, wading in snow to the knees at every step . . . We carried on our backs our changes of clothing, several books, and corn bread and raw pork. We often ate our frozen bread and pork by the way, when the bread would be so frozen that we could not bite or penetrate any part of it but the outside crust.[23]

All of the Smiths who handled the plates also served as full-time missionaries. In August 1830, in company with his son, Don Carlos, Joseph Smith, Sr., labored as a missionary in St. Lawrence County, New York. During this mission, he bore testimony to the truthfulness of the restored gospel to his father and brothers and sisters who lived in that

---

[21]Anderson, *Investigating the Book of Mormon Witnesses*, pp. 89-90. An examination of the charges that the witnesses denied their testimonies is also found in Anderson's work. (Ibid., pp. 153-62.)

[22]*HC*, 1:118-25 and Parley P. Pratt, *Autobiography of Parley Parker Pratt*, ed. Parley P. Pratt (Salt Lake City: Deseret Book Co., 1976), pp. 47-60.

[23]Parley P. Pratt, *Autobiography*, p. 52.

county, and most of his family joined the Church. In 1836 he traveled with his brother John about 2,400 miles in the northeastern states preaching, baptizing, and bestowing patriarchal blessings on several hundred members.[24] Meanwhile, Hyrum Smith was accepting calls to serve as a missionary. In the fall of 1830 he labored as a missionary with Newel Knight and Orson Pratt. In the summer of 1831 he preached to settlers living between northeastern Ohio and western Missouri. During the winter of 1831-1832, he preached in New York and Ohio and in 1836 he served as a missionary in Salem, Massachusetts.[25]

Samuel Smith was another witness who was actively involved in missionary service. On June 30, 1830, after being set apart by his brother, Joseph, Samuel commenced missionary labors by preaching in western New York. In December of that same year he was called to preach in northeastern Ohio. In June 1831 he was called by revelation to labor in Missouri as a missionary in company with Reynolds Cahoon. After returning to Kirtland, Ohio, Samuel continued his missionary labors in Ohio. In January 1832, he was called to serve another mission in the eastern states, where, for approximately one year, he traveled with Orson Hyde in New York and New England, preaching, teaching, and baptizing. After his marriage to Mary Bailey in August 1834, he devoted more time to farming and less to missionary activity, but he continued to serve by holding various positions of responsibility in the Church. After fleeing from his home in Kirtland and being driven from his home in Far West, Missouri, Samuel moved with other exiled Saints to Illinios. His missionary service continued after he had settled in Nauvoo. In April 1841, he accepted a call to preach in Illinois, where he labored during the summer and fall of that year.[26]

David Whitmer and Martin Harris also served the Church by participating in different types of missionary activity. During the winter of 1831-1832, David Whitmer preached in Ohio; and during the summer of 1831, at the call of the Prophet, Martin Harris traveled west to Missouri as one of Joseph Smith's companions. In 1834 Martin Harris again traveled from Ohio to Missouri with the Prophet as a member of Zion's Camp. This army of Latter-day Saints journeyed west in an attempt to aid members

---

[24]*HC* 4:190-91.

[25]Pearson H. Corbett, *Hyrum Smith, Patriarch* (Salt Lake City: Deseret Book Co., 1963), pp. 78, 88, 93-99, 157.

[26]*HC*, 7:216-21.

who, in November 1833, had been driven by mobs from their homes in Jackson County, Missouri.[27]

Members of the restored Church demonstrated their conviction in the integrity of the witnesses by sustaining these men in positions of leadership and responsibility. David Whitmer served as president of the Church in Missouri with John Whitmer as one of his counselors. Oliver Cowdery and Hyrum Smith served as assistant presidents of the Church in Ohio. Joseph Smith, Sr., was called to serve as Patriarch to the Church, giving blessings to hundreds of Saints. (Following his death, Hyrum assumed this responsibility.) Christian and Peter Whitmer, Jr., served on the Missouri High Council—a judicial, decision-making, and advisory body—and Martin Harris and Samuel Smith served on the High council organized in Kirtland, Ohio. In many instances, these men held these ecclesiastical positions, sacrificing their time and talents, without receiving financial remuneration.[28]

All of the members of the Smith family who were witnesses to the Book of Mormon died while they were actively involved in church service. Immediately following their deaths in the 1840s in Nauvoo, Illinois, members referred to some of their most noteworthy character traits. Joseph Smith, Sr., who was respectfully referred to as "Father Smith," was considered "one of the most benevolent of men." During his funeral, one of his friends, Elder Robert B. Thompson declared:

If ever there was a man who had claims on the affections of the community, it was our beloved but now deceased Pat-

---

[27]*M&A* 1 (January 1835):62 and *HC*, 1:188; 2:184. Ezra Booth, an early convert to the church who apostatized during the summer of 1831, wrote a series of letters immediately after leaving the Church in which he verified the preaching of the Three Witnesses and their bearing their testimonies in Ohio in 1831. In one of these letters published in the *Ohio Star* (Ravenna) and later reprinted in Howe's *Mormonism Unvailed*, Booth wrote:

You have probably read the testimony of the three witnesses appended to the Book of Mormon. These witnesses testify, that an angel appeared to them, and presented them the golden plates, and the voice of God declared it to be a Divine Record. To this they frequently testify, in the presence of large congregations. (*Ohio Star* [Ravenna], October 27, 1831, p. 3 and Howe, *Mormonism Unvailed*, pp. 86-7.)

[28]*HC*, 1:166; 2:32, 124, 126, 165, 379-80, 510; 4:229.

riarch . . .for truly we can say with the king of Israel, "A prince and a great man has fallen in Israel." A man endeared to us by every feeling calculated to entwine around and adhere to the human heart, by almost indissoluble bonds. A man faithful to his God and to the Church in every situation and under all circumstances through which he was called to pass . . . .He . . .was chosen by the Almighty to be one of the witnesses to the Book of Mormon. From that time, his only aim was the promotion of truth—his soul was taken up with the things of the Kingdom; his bowels yearned over the children of men; and it was more than his meat and drink to do the will of his Father, who is in heaven.[29]

Following the martyrdom of Joseph and Hyrum Smith, John Taylor, who witnessed the "brutal" murders of June 27, 1844, wrote that these men sealed their testimonies of the truthfulness of the Book of Mormon with their blood. Hyrum Smith, he added, "was forty-four years old in February 1844, and Joseph Smith was thirty-eight in December, 1843; and henceforward their names will be classed among the martyrs of religion . . .In life they were not divided, and in death they were not separated, . . .and glory is their eternal reward. From age to age shall their names go down to posterity as gems for the sanctified."[30]

One month following the death of Joseph and Hyrum, Samuel H. Smith, aged thirty-six, died of "bilious fever." In the obituary notice published in the local Mormon paper, Times and Seasons, Samuel Smith was praised for his "steadfastness as one of the witnesses to the Book of Mormon." He was also referred to as a "man of God," who had "many saintly traits of virtue, knowledge, temperance, patience, godliness, brotherly kindness and charity."[31]

After becoming close friends or acquaintances with various witnesses to the Book of Mormon, many non-Mormons also declared that the witnesses they knew were men of integrity. Not one individual who had more than a fleeting acquaintance with these men wrote that they were dishonest, lacked sincerity, or were incompetent judges of events. Instead of denouncing their characters, many critics of the Church who knew the witnesses declared that they were trustworthy individuals. In 1830, for example, Martin Harris traveled to Geneva, New York, in an

---

[29]HC, 4:191-93. Italics were not included in the initial printing.

[30]D&C 135:3-6.

[31]HC, 7:222.

attempt to secure a loan of thirteen hundred dollars from Charles Butler, a financier and philantropist who founded the Union Theological Seminary. Butler wrote that Harris brought a letter of introduction to him from Mr. Jessup (probably Henry Jessup), a leading elder in the Presbyterian Church. Butler depended on Jessup's recommendations respecting character and financial status for all seeking loans who lived in the area of Palmyra. According to Butler, Jessup introduced Martin Harris as a "very worthy and substantial farmer, possessing a very excellent farm which would furnish a very ample security for the amount of money which he wished to obtain." Although Butler was favorably impressed with Harris' credentials, the financier decided not to grant him a loan when he learned that the money was to be used for the publication of a "Mormon Bible."[32]

In addition to Henry Jessup, othrs living in Palmyra judged Martin Harris to be honest and responsible. In 1829, the *Palmyra Freeman* reported that one of the few individuals who believed in the story of the "Golden Bible" was Martin Harris, "an honest and industrious farmer" of Palmyra.[33] While traveling in western New York in 1831, James Gordon Bennett, a journalist for the New York *Courier and Enquirer* learned from those he interviewed that Martin Harris had a reptuation of being a "respectable . . . hard working . . . substantial farmer" and was known for his "sobriety."[34] When Martin Harris left Palmyra to gather with the Latter-day Saints in Ohio, the *Wayne Sentinel* reported that Harris was one of the earliest settlers of that town and "has ever borne the character of an honorable and upright" citizen.[35] And after publishing the testimony of the Three Witnesses in his history of Mormonism, Pomeroy Tucker wrote, "How to reconcile the act of Harris in signing his name to such a statement, in view of the character of honesty which had always been conceded to him, could never be easily explained."[36]

---

[32]A portion of a typescript of this letter is located in the Charles Butler Collection, Library of Congress.

[33]"Golden Bible," *Rochester Advertiser and Telegraph*, August 31, 1829, reprinting an article published in the *Palmyra Freeman*.

[34]Leonard J. Arrington, "James Gordon Bennett's 1831 Report on 'The Mormonites,'" *BYU Studies* 10 (Spring 1970):355, 358 and *Hillsborough Gazette* (Ohio), October, 29, 1831.

[35]*Wayne Sentinel*, May 27, 1831.

[36]Tucker, *Origin, Rise and Progress of Mormonism*, pp. 69-71. For additional references that Martin Harris was "considered an honest, industrious citizen by his neighbors," see E. D. Howe, *Mormonism Unvailed*, p. 13 and the *Palmyra Courier*, May 24, 1872.

After leaving the Church in 1838, Oliver Cowdery established warm friendships with a number of non-members. Samuel Murdock, an attorney who became "intimately acquainted" with Cowdery while he was residing in Kirtland, wrote that he was indebted to him for his "special kindness" and "the many lessons of instruction" he received from him. Murdock concluded that Oliver Cowdery was one of the most "amiable, generous, and kindhearted" individuals he had ever known.[37] Judge William Lang, Oliver Cowdery's law partner in Tiffin, Ohio, wrote that he was granted many opportunities "to study and love his noble and true manhood." According to Lang, Cowdery was "an able lawyer and a great adovcate . . .He was modest and reserved, never spoke ill of any one, [and] never complained."[38] Shortly after Oliver Cowdery moved from Tiffin, *The Seneca Advertiser* reported that Cowdery had been nominated as the democratic candidate for the House of Representatives in Wisconsin. During his seven year residency in Tiffin, the article continued,

> our esteemed friend . . .earned himself an enviable distinction at the Bar of this place and of this Judicial circuit, as a sound and able lawyer, and as a citizen none could have been more esteemed. His honesty, integrity, and industry were worthy the imitation of all, whilst his unquestioned legal abilities reflected credit as well upon himself as upon the professin of which he was a member.[39]

Following the death of Oliver Cowdery, the Ray County Missouri Bar Association formally declared that the law "profession has lost an accomplished member, and the community a valuable and worthy citizen."[40] And *The Seneca Advertiser* declared that they were "pained to learn . . .of the death of . . .(their) much esteemed friend and former fellow citizen, Oliver Cowdery . . . .He was a man of more than ordinary

---

[37]Samuel Murdock to Editor of *Dubuque Daily Times*, April 13, 1893, cited in R. Etzenhouser, *From Palmyra, New York, 1830, to Independence, Missouri, 1894* (Independence, Mo.: Ensign Publishing House, 1894), pp. 338-41.

[38]W. Lang, *History of Seneca County* (Springfield, Ohio: Transcript Printing Co., 1880), pp. 364-65.

[39]*The Seneca Advertiser* (Tiffin, Ohio), May 5, 1848, p. 2.

[40]Circuit Court Journal, Ray County, Missouri, March 5, 1850. For additional character references on Oliver Cowdery and his activities after he left the Church, see Anderson, *Investigating the Book of Mormon Witnesses*, pp. 38-44.

ability, and during his residence among us had endeared himself to all who knew him in the private and social walks of life."[41]

Non-Mormons also certified that John and David Whitmer were "truthful, honest and law abiding citizens." After living in Richmond, Missouri, for forty-three years, David Whitmer secured the signatures of twenty-two leading citizens of that town, including the mayor, attorneys, judges, bankers, merchants, and public servants who verified that they had "been long and intimately acquainted with him" and knew "him to be a man of the highest integrity, and of undoubted truth and veracity."[42] A few days following his death, the *Richmond Democrat* published an article which apparently expressed the views of many of the friends of David Whitmer regarding his character and his testimony regarding the Book of Mormon.

> No man ever lived here, who had among our people, more friends and fewer enemies. Honest, conscientious and upright in all his dealings, just in his estimate of men, and open, manly and frank in his treatment of all, he made lasting friends who loved him to the end . . .
>
> Skeptics may laugh and scoff if they will, but no man can listen to Mr. Whitmer as he talks of his interview with the angel of the Lord, without being most forcibly convinced that he has heard an honest man tell what he honestly believes to be true.[43]

---

[41]*The Seneca Advertiser* (Tiffin, Ohio), November 1, 1850, p. 2.

[42]Anderson, *Investigating the Book of Mormon Witnesses*, pp. 72-76, 131-33. The statement regarding the character of David Whitmer signed by twenty-two leading citizens of Richmond, Missouri, was published in the *Richmond Conservator*, March 25, 1881, and in a pamphlet written by David Whitmer, *Address to All Believers in Christ*, pp. 9-10. A photocopy of the document is located in the Church Archives and in Ebbie L. V. Richardson, "David Whitmer: A Witness to the Divine Authenticity of the Book of Mormon" (Master's thesis, Brigham Young University, 1952.) See also Appendix F.

[43]*Richmond Democrat*, January 26, 1888, and reprinted February 2, 1888, in the same newspaper. See also *Richmond Conservator*, January 26, 1888. The *Richmond Conservator* reported that David Whitmer had lived in Richmond for forty-six years "without stain or blemish." He enjoys the "confidence and esteem of his fellow men," this report added and is considered "a good citizen." (*Richmond Conservator*, August 22, 1881.)

Because more than one hundred detailed personal statements or descriptions of interviews with the Three Witnesses have been preserved (and additional testimonies of the Eight Witnesses also exist), the testimony of the Book of Mormon witnesses is better documented than any other declaration of direct revelation in the world's history.[44] The striking harmony of reports spanning a variety of times and circumstances, coupled with numerous character references that portray the witnesses as men of integrity, is compelling evidence of the truthfulness of the testimonies published in the Book of Mormon. These numerous personal statements and interviews also serve as evidence that amidst persecution, economic trials, public criticism, and apostasy from the Church the eleven never deviated from their conviction that they carefully examined the metallic plates and that the Book of Mormon was a product of the translation of this record. Even though six of the eleven rejected the leadership of Joseph Smith in the late 1830s, there is no reliable evidence that any of the witnesses at any time deviated from their conviction in the authenticity of the Book of Mormon. The published testimonies of the eleven witnesses, therefore, enable us to better understand a unique event in the ecclesiastical history of mankind and substantiate Joseph Smith's testimony that eleven men did indeed examine the ancient record which he translated "by the gift and power of God."

The combined testimonies of Joseph Smith and the eleven witnesses included in this chapter are based on countless sources. In some instances harmonies have been created by blending primary and secondary sources. Secondary sources are generally cited only when a number of interviewers reported the same basic concepts.

A Prophecy of Special Witnesses

Joseph Smith

In the course of the work of translation, we ascertained that three special witnesses were to be provided by the Lord, to whom he would grant that they would see the plates from which this work (the Book of Mormon) should be translated and that these witnesses should bear record of the same. [This] will be found [in the] Book of Mormon, first edition [which reads as follows:]

---

[44]Anderson, *Investigating the Book of Mormon Witnesses*, p. 79.

Wherefore, at that day when the book shall be delivered unto the man of whom I have spoken, the book shall be hid from the eyes of the world, that the eyes of none shall behold it, save it be that three witnesses shall behold it, by the power of God, besides him to whom the book shall be delivered; and they shall testify to the truth of the book, and the things therein. And there is none other which shall view it, save it be a few, according to the will of God, to bear testimony of his word unto the children of men . . .Wherefore, the Lord will proceed to bring forth the words of the book; and in the mouth of as many witnesses as seemeth him good will he establish his word.[45]

Three Witnesses Identified by Revelation
Revelation given March 1829 [see D&C Section
5:1-3, 15-16, 18, 26-28, 32.]

Behold, I say unto you, that as my servant Martin Harris has desired a witness at my hand, that you, my servant Joseph Smith, Jr., have got the plates of which you have testified and borne record that you have received of me. And now, behold, this shall you say unto him—he who spake unto you, said unto you: I the Lord, am God, and have given these things unto you, my servant Joseph Smith, Jr., and have commanded you that you shall stand as a witness of these things; and I have caused you that you should enter into a covenant with me, that you should not show them except to those persons to whom I command you . . .And the testimony of three witnesses will I send forth of my word. And behold, whosoever believeth on my words, them will I visit with the manifestation of my Spirit . . . .And their testimony shall also go forth unto the condemnation of this generation if they harden their hearts against them . . .And I the Lord command him, my servant Martin Harris, that he shall say no more unto them concerning these things, except he shall say: I have seen them, and they have been shown unto me by the power of God; and these are the words which he shall say. But if he deny this he will break the covenant which he has before covenanted with me, and

---

[45]*T&S* 3 (September 1, 1842):897 and *Book of Mormon* (1830), pp. 110-11, located in 2 Nephi 27:12-14 in the current edition of that work.

behold, he is condemned. And now, except he humble himself and acknowledge unto me the things that he has done which are wrong, and covenant with me that he will keep my commandments, and exercise faith in me, behold, I say unto him, he shall have no such views, for I will grant unto him no views of the things of which I have spoken...I foresee that if my servant Martin Harris humbleth not himself and receive a witness from my hand, that he will fall unto transgression.

Almost immediately after we had made this dicovery [that three special witnesses would view the plates by the power of God], it occurred to Oliver Cowdery, David Whitmer, and the aforementioned Martin Harris (who had come to inquire after our progress in the work) that they would have me inquire of the Lord to know if they might not obtain of him to be these three special witnesses. Finally, they became so very solicitous and teased me so much that at length I complied and through the Urim and Thummim I obtained of the Lord for them the following Revelation:

Revelation to Oliver Cowdery, David Whitmer and Martin Harris, at Fayette, Seneca County, N.Y., June 1829; given previus to their viewing the plates containing the Book of Mormon. [See D&C Section 17:1-6.]

Behold, I say unto you, that you must rely upon my word, which if you do with full purpose of heart, you shall have a view of the plates, and also of the breastplate, the sword of Laban, the Urim and Thummim which were given to the brother of Jared upon the mount, when he talked with the Lord face to face, and the miraculous directors which were given to Lehi while in the wilderness, on the borders of the Red Sea. And it is by your faith that you shall obtain a view of them, even by that faith which was had by the prophets of old.

And after that you have obtained faith, and have seen them with your eyes, you shall testify of them, by the power of God; and this you shall do that my servant Joseph Smith, Jr., may not be destroyed, that I may bring about my righteous purposes unto the children of men in this work. And ye shall testify that you have seen them, even as my servant Joseph Smith, Jr., has seen them; for it is by my power that he has seen them, and it is because he had faith. And he has translated the book, even that part which I have commanded him.[46]

---

[46]*T&S* 3 (September 1, 1842): 897.

Lucy Smith

The next morning [the morning following the arrival of Joseph's father and mother and his friend, Martin Harris, at the Whitmer home], after attending to the usual services, namely, reading, singing and praying, Joseph arose from his knees, and approaching Martin Harris with a solemnity that thrills through my veins to this day, when it occurs to my recollection, said, "Martin Harris, you have got to humble yourself before your God this day, that you may obtain a forgiveness of your sins. If you do, it is the will of God that you should look upon the plates, in company with Oliver Cowdery and David Whitmer."[47]

The Vision of the Three Special Witnesses

Joseph Smith

Not many days after the above commandment was given [D&C 17], we four, viz.: Martin Harris, David Whitmer, Oliver Cowdery, and myself agreed to retire into the woods and try to obtain by fervent and humble prayer the fulfillment of the promises given in the revelation: that they should have a view of the plates & etc. We accordingly made choice of a piece of woods convenient to Mr. Whitmer's house to which we retired, and, having knelt down, we began to pray in much faith to Almighty God to bestow upon us a realization of these promises. According to previous arrangements, I commenced by vocal prayer to our heavenly Father and was followed by each of the rest in succession; we did not yet, however, obtain any answer or manifestation of the divine favor in our behalf. We again observed the same order of prayer: each calling on and praying fervently to God in rotation, but with the same result as before. Upon this, our second failure, Martin Harris proposed that he would withdraw himself from us, believing, as he expressed himself, that his presence was the cause of our not obtining what we wished for. He accordingly withdrew from us, and we kelt down again and had not been many minutes engaged in prayer when presently we beheld a light above us in the air of exceeding brightness. Behold, an angel stood before us; in his hands he held the plates which we had been praying for these [Cowdery and Whitmer] to have a view of: he turned over the leaves one by one, so that we could see them and discover the engravings thereon distinctly. He addressed himself to David Whitmer

---

[47]Lucy Smith, *Biographical Sketches*, p. 138.

and said, "David, blessed is the Lord and he that keeps his command-ments." Immediately afterwards, we heard a voice from out of the bright light above us saying, "These plates have been revealed by the power of God, and they have been translated by the power of God; the translation of them which you have seen is correct, and I command you to bear record of what you now see and hear."

I now left David and Oliver and went in pursuit of Martin Harris, whom I found at a considerable distance, fervently engaged in prayer. He soon told me, however, that he had not yet prevailed with the Lord and earnestly requested me to join him in prayer that he also might realize the same blessings which we had just received. We accordingly joined in prayer and ultimately obtained our desires, for before we had yet finished, the same vision was opened to our view, at least it was again to me, and I once more beheld and heard the same things. At the same moment, Martin Harris cried out, apparently in ecstasy of joy, "Tis enough; mine eyes have beheld," and jumping up, he shouted hosanna, blessing God, and otherwise rejoiced exceedingly.

Having thus, through the mercy of God, obtained these manifesta-tions, it now remained for these three individuals to fulfill the command-ment which they had received, viz.: to bear record of these things, in order to accomplish which, they drew up and subscribed the following document:—[48]

The Testimony of Three Witnesses.

Be it known unto all nations, kindreds, tongues, and people, unto whom this work shall come; that we, through the grace of God the Father, and our Lord Jesus Christ, have seen the plates which contain this record, which is a record of the people of Nephi, and also of the Lamanites, their brethren. and also of the people of Jared, who came from the tower of which hath been spoken. And we also know that they have been translated by the gift and power of God, for his voice hath declared it unto us; wherefore we know of a surety that the work is true. And we also testify that we have seen the en-gravings which are upon the plates; and they have been shown unto us by the power of God, and not of man. And we declare with words of soberness, that an angel of God came down

---

[48]*T&S* 3 (September 1, 1842): 897-98.

from heaven, and he brought and laid before our eyes, that we beheld and saw the plates, and the engravings thereon; and we know that it is by the grace of God the Father, and our Lord Jesus Christ, that we beheld and bear record that these things are true. And it is marvelous in our eyes. Nevertheless, the voice of the Lord commanded us that we should bear record of it; wherefore, to be obedient unto the commandments of God, we bear testimony of these things. And we know that if we are faithful in Christ we shall rid our garments of the blood of all men, and be found spotless before the judgment seat of Christ, and shall dwell with him eternally in the heavens. And the honor be to the Father, and to the Son, and to the Holy Ghost, which is one God. Amen.

Oliver Cowdery
David Whitmer
Martin Harris

Testimonies of the Three Witnesses

David Whitmer - A Harmony of Primary and Secondary Sources

In June 1829, the Lord called Oliver Cowdery, Martin Harris, and myself as the three witnesses to behold the vision of the Angel, as recorded in the fore part of the Book of Mormon and to bear testimony to the world that the Book of Mormon is true.[49] [I saw] the plates . . .about 11:00 a.m. . . .in the latter part of June 1829. Joseph, Oliver Cowdery and myself were together, and the angel showed them to us . . .as I supposed to fulfill the words of the book itself.[50] The angel was dressed in white and spoke and called me by name and said, ''Blessed is he that keepeth His commandments.[51] [As] the angel stood before us, he turned the leaves

---

[49]David Whitmer, *Address to All Believers in Christ*, p. 82.

[50]''Report of Elders Orson Pratt and Joseph F. Smith,'' *MS* 40 (1878): 771; *Kansas City Journal*, June 5, 1881, p. 1; and Journal of Edward Stevenson, December 22, 1877, Church Archives. (See also Appendix F.)

[51]William H. Kelley to *Saints' Herald*, January 16, 1882, cited in *Saints' Herald* 29 (1882): 68.

one by one . . .[of] that part of the book which was not sealed.[52] Martin Harris, the other witness, saw them the same day, and the eight witnesses . . .saw them [the] next day . . .or the day after.[53] The plates . . .appeared to be of gold, about six by nine inches in size, about as thick as parchment, a great many in number, and bound together like the leaves of a book by massive rings passing through the back edges. The engravings upon them were very plain and of very curious appearance . . . .We not only saw the plates of the Book of Mormon, but he [the angel] also showed us the brass plates of the Book of Ether and many others.[54]

They [the plates] were shown to us in this way. Joseph and Oliver and I were sitting on a log, when we were overshadowed by a light more glorious than that of the sun . . .It extended away round us, I cannot tell how far, but in the midst of this light . . .there appeared as it were, a table with many records or plates upon it, besides the plates of the Book of Mormon, also the Sword of Laban, the directors—i.e., the ball which Lehi had, and the Interpreters.[55] The Interpreters . . .which I saw . . .in the holy vision . . .looked like whitish stones put in the rim of a bow . . .like spectacles, only much larger.[56] The heavenly messenger brought the several plates and laid them on the table before our eyes.[57] I saw them just as plain as I see this bed . . .and the angel told us we must bear testimony to the world . . . .I [also] heard the voice of the Lord, distinctly as I ever heard anything in my life, declaring that the records of the plates of the Book of

---

[52]Wilhelm Poulson to *Deseret News* (Salt Lake City), August 13, 1878, cited in *Deseret Evening News* (Salt Lake City), August 16, 1878.

[53]*Kansas City Journal*, June 5, 1881, p. 1 and "Report of Elders Orson Pratt and Joseph F. Smith," p. 771.

[54]*Kansas City Journal*, June 5, 1881, p. 1 and "Report of Elders Orson Pratt and Joseph F. Smith, p. 771. See also M. J. Hubble's account of an interview with David Whitmer, Richmond, Missouri, November 13, 1896, University of Missouri, Western Historical Manuscripts Library, Columbia, Missouri.

[55]*Kansas City Journal*, June 5, 1881, p. 1; "Reports of Elders Orson Pratt and Joseph F. Smith," p. 771; and P. Wilhelm Poulson to *Deseret News* (Salt Lake City), August 13, 1878.

[56]Interview notes of Zenas H. Gurley, January 14, 1885, cited in *Autumn Leaves* 5 (1892): 452.

[57]James H. Hart to *Deseret News* (Salt Lake City, August 23, 1883, cited in *Deseret Evening News* (Salt Lake City), September 4, 1883.

Mormon were translated by the gift and power of God.[58] Our testimony as recorded in the Book of Mormon is absolutely true, just as it is there written.[59]

It is recorded in the American Cyclopaedia and the Encyclopaedia Britannica, that I, David Whitmer, have denied my testimony as one of the three witnesses to the divinity of the Book of Mormon; and that the other two witnesses, Oliver Cowdery and Martin Harris, denied their testimony to that Book. I will say once more to all mankind, that I have never at any time denied that testimony or any part thereof. I also testify to the world, that neither Oliver Cowdery or Martin Harris ever at any time denied their testimony. They both died reaffirming the truth of the divine authenticity of the Book of Mormon.[60]

I wish now, standing as it were, in the very sunset of life, and in the fear of God, once [and] for all to make this public statement:

That I have never at any time denied that testimony or any part thereof, which has so long since been published with that Book, as one of the three witnesses. Those who know me best, well know that I have always adhered to that testimony. And that no man may be misled or doubt my present views in regard to the same, I do again affirm the truth of all of my statements, as then made and published.

"He that hath an ear to hear, let him hear;" it was no delusion! What is written is written, and he that readeth let him understand.[61]

Beware how you hastily condemn that book which I know to be the word of God; for his own voice and an angel from heaven declared the

---

[58]"Report of Elders Orson Pratt and Joseph F. Smith," p. 772; *Kansas City Journal*, June 5, 1881, p. 1; and David Whitmer to Susie Gates, February 11, 1887, Whitmer Papers, RLDS Church Library Archives.

[59]"Report of Elders Orson Pratt and Joseph F. Smith," p. 772; *Kansas City Journal*, June 5, 1881, p. 1; and David Whitmer, *Address to All Believers in Christ*, pp. 8-9, 43.

[60]David Whitmer, *Address to All Believers in Christ*, p. 8.

[61]Ibid., pp. 8-9. In the summer of 1838, Thomas B. Marsh asked David Whitmer if it were "true that he had seen the angel, according to his testimony as one of the witnesses of the Book of Mormon." He replied, "As sure as there is a God in heaven, he saw the angel according to his testimony in that book." (Thomas B. Marsh, "History of Thos. Baldwin Marsh," *Deseret News* [Salt Lake City], March 24, 1858, p. 18.) A similar testimony was recorded by James H. Moyle, "A Visit to David Whitmer," *Instructor* 80 (September 1945): 401. Moyle served as Assistant Secretary of Treasury during two administrations.

truth of it unto me, and to two other witnesses who testified on their death-bed that it was true.[62]

And if these things are not true, then there is no truth; and if there is no truth, there is no God; and if there is no God, there is no existence. But I know there is a God, for I have heard His voice and witnessed the manifestation of his power.[63]

Oliver Cowdery - Interview

In company with the Prophet Joseph Smith and David Whitmer, [I] . . .beheld the plates, the leaves being turned over by the angel, whose voice I heard, and . . .we were commanded as witnesses to bear a faithful testimony to the world of the vision that we were favored to behold, and that the translation from the plates in the Book of Mormon was accepted of the Lord, and that it should go forth to the world and no power on earth should stop its progress.[64]

Martin Harris

I now solemnly state that as I was praying unto the Lord that I might behold the ancient record, lo there appeared to view a holy angel, and before him a table, and upon the table the holy spectacles or Urim and Thummim, and other ancient relics of the Nephites, and lo, the Angel did take up the plates, and turn them over so as we could plainly see the engravings thereon, and lo there came a voice from heaven saying "I am the Lord," and that the plates were translated by God and not by men, and also that we should bear record of it to all the world, and thus the vision was taken from us . . . .[65] No man ever heard me in any way deny the truth of the Book of Mormon [or] the administration of the angel that

---

[62]David Whitmer, *Address to All Believers in Christ*, p. 43.

[63]James H. Hart to *Deseret News* (Salt lake City), August 23, 1883, cited in *Deseret Evening News* (Salt Lake City), September 4, 1883.

[64]This quotation from the writings of Edward Stevenson has been changed from the third to the first person and was preceeded by the statement, "I have often heard him [Oliver Cowdery] bear a faithful testimony to the restoration of the gospel by the visitation of an angel." (Edward Stevenson, "The Three Witnesses to the Book of Mormon," *MS* 48 [July 5, 1886]:420-32.)

[65]Martin Harris to Walter Conrad, January 13, 1873, in possession of Brent F. Ashworth, Provo, Utah.

showed me the plates. The Lord has shown me these things by his Spirit.[66]

Martin Harris - Interview

The Prophet Joseph Smith, Oliver Cowdery, and David Whitmer and myself went into the woods to pray that we might have the privilege of seeing the golden plates. We bowed our heads in prayer, but we seemed to be praying with no results. The Prophet was the spokesman. He prayed with no results twice, then I withdrew from them, telling them that it was on my account that their prayer was not answered.[67] After they had been visited by the angel, the Prophet then came over to me where I was praying, and I asked the Prophet to pray with me so that I might have the privilege also of seeing the golden plates; and after praying,[68] I saw the angel descend from heaven.[69] The angel stood on the opposite side of the table on which were the plates . . . took the plates in his hand and turned them over . . . one by one.[70] I [also] saw the Urim and Thummim,

---

[66]Martin Harris to H. B. Emerson, November 23, 1870 and Martin Harris to H. B. Emerson, January 1871, cited in *The True Latter Day Saints' Herald* 22 (1875): 630.

[67]Affidavit of John E. Godfrey, photocopy, BYU.

[68]Ibid. and Ole A. Jensen, "Martin Harris Testimony of the Book of Mormon," typescript, BYU.

[69]*Iowa State Register* (Des Moines), August 26, 1870, p. 4 (See Appendix E); Simon Smith to Joseph Smith (son of the Prophet), December 29, 1880, cited in *The Saints' Herald* 28 (1881):390; and William Pilkington, "The Dying Testimony of Martin Harris," p. 5, photocopy included in Wayne Cutler Gunnell, "Martin Harris: Witness and Benefactor to the Book of Mormon" Master's thesis, Brigham Young Univesity, 1955, pp. 104-11. For more than one year William Pilkington worked for Martin Harris' son and lived on his farm at a time Martin Harris was residing there. On many occasions, Pilkington heard Harris bear his testimony and following Harris' death wrote an account of what he learned from this witness of the Book of Mormon.

[70]Edward Stevenson, "The Three Witnesses to the Book of Mormon," p. 390; Affidavit of John E. Godfrey; and Ole A. Jensen, "Martin Harris Testimony of the Book of Mormon." During an interview with Edward Stevenson and G. D. Keaton, Martin Harris illustrated what he meant when he said the angel turned the leaves of the plates, by placing a book in his hands and turned the pages of the volume, one by one. (Edward Stevenson, "The Three Witnesses to the Book of Mormon," p. 390.)

the Breastplate, and the Sword of Laban.[71] The angel declared that the Book of Mormon was correctly translated by the power of God and not of man, and that it contained the fulness of the gospel of Jesus Christ to the Nephites, who were a branch of the lost sheep of the House of Israel and had come from the land of Jerusalem to America.[72] When he [the angel] had finished his message, I saw him ascend up into heaven. Then . . .I heard the voice of God declare that everything the angel had told us was true and that the Book of Mormon was translated correctly.[73] I was [then] commanded by God's voice to testify to the whole world what I had seen and heard.[74] Following the vision, I cried out in . . .ecstasy.[75]

[I have] never failed to bear testimony to the divine authenticity of the Book of Mormon.[76] I know of a surety that the work is true.[77] It is not a matter of belief . . .but of knowledge.[78] Just as surely as the sun is shining on us and gives us light, and the sun and stars give us light by night, just

---

[71]William Pilkington, "The Dying Testimony of Martin Harris," p. 5.

[72]Edward Stevenson, "The Three Witnesses to the Book of Mormon," p. 390.

[73]*Iowa State Register* (Des Moines), August 26, 1870, p. 4; Affidavit of John E. Godfrey, photocopy, BYU; and Ole A. Jensen, "Martin Harris Testimony of the Book of Mormon," typescript, BYU.

[74]Edward Stevenson, "The Three Witnesses to the Book of Mormon," p. 390; Affidavit of John E. Godfrey; and Pilkington, "The Dying Testimony of Martin Harris," p. 5. Some interviewers of Martin Harris reported that Harris informed them that he handled the plates. Possibly Harris was referring to handling the record when he was assisting the Prophet with the translation. He also might have handled the plates, "plate after plate," during the vision in which he was shown the plates by a heavenly messenger. (David B. Dille, "Additional Testimony of Martin Harris," p. 545; Simon Smith to Joseph Smith, December 29, 1880; and Letter of Edward Stevenson, cited in *Deseret Evening News* [Salt Lake City], August 19, 1870, p. 3.)

[75]Pilkington, "The Dying Testimony of Martin Harris," p. 5 and Ole A. Jensen, "Martin Harris Testimony of the Book of Mormon."

[76]James McKnight, "Correspondence," *MS* 24 (April 19, 1862):251; Edward Stevenson, "Incidents in the Life of Martin Harris," *MS* 44 (February 6, 1882): 86; Autobiography of John Thompson, p. 2, typescript, BYU; *Deseret Evening News* (Salt Lake City), August 19, 1870, p. 3; Pilkington, "The Dying Testimony of Martin Harris," p. 5; and David Whitmer, *Address to All Believers in Christ*, p. 8.

[77]*Iowa State Register* (Des Moines), Agust 26, 1870, p. 4.

[78]Stevenson, "Incidents in the Life of Martin Harris," p. 86.

as surely as the breath of life sustains us, so surely do I know that Joseph Smith was a true prophet of God, chosen of God to open the last dispensation of the fulness of times; so surely do I know that the Book of Mormon was divinely translated. I saw the plates; I saw the angel; I heard the voice of God. I know that the Book of Mormon is true, and that Joseph Smith was a true prophet of God. I might as well doubt my own existence as to doubt the divine authenticity of the Book of Mormon or the divine calling of Joseph Smith.[79]

[My] testimony [which] has accompanied every copy of the Book [of Mormon], that an angel of God came down from heaven, and he brought and laid before our eyes, that we beheld and saw the plates, and the engravings thereon . . .has not varied . . .in 41 years.[80]

Historical Setting of the Vision of the Three Witnesses

Lucy Smith

Joseph, Martin, Oliver, and David, repaired to a grove, a short distance from the house, where they commenced calling upon the Lord, and continued in earnest supplication, until he permitted an angel to come down from his presence, and declare to them, that all which Joseph had testified of concerning the plates was true.

When they returned to the house it was between three and four o'clock P.M. Mrs. [Mary] Whitmer, Mr. Smith, and myself, were sitting in a bedroom at the time. On coming in, Joseph threw himself down beside me, and exclaimed, "Father, mother, you do not know how happy I am; the Lord has now caused the plates to be shown to three more besides myself. They have seen an angel, who has testified to them, and they will have to bear witness to the truth of what I have said, for now they know for themselves, that I do not go about to deceive the people, and I feel as if I was relieved of a burden which was almost too heavy for me to bear, and it rejoices my soul, that I am not any longer to be entirely alone in the world." Upon this, Martin Harris came in: he seemed almost overcome with joy, and testified boldly to what he had both seen and heard. And so did David and Oliver, adding, that no tongue could express the joy of

---

[79]William Harrison Homer, "The Passing of Martin Harris," *The Improvement Era* 29 (1926): 470.

[80]Stevenson, "Incidents in the Life of Martin Harris," p. 470.

their hearts, and the greatness of the things which they had both seen and heard.

Their written testimony . . .is contained in the Book of Mormon.[81]

Eight Examine the Plates

Joseph Smith

Soon after these things had transpired [the Three Witnesses examining the plates], the following additional testimony was obtained:[82] . . .

The Testimony of Eight Witnesses.

Be it known unto all nations, kindreds, tongues, and people, unto whom this work shall come: that Joseph Smith, Jr., the translator of this work, has shown unto us the plates of which hath been spoken, which have the appearance of gold; and as many of the leaves as the said Smith has translated, we did handle with our hands; and we also saw the engravings thereon, all of which has the appearance of ancient work, and of curious workmanship. And this we bear record with words of soberness, that the said Smith has shown unto us, for we have seen and hefted, and know of a surety, that the said Smith has got the plates of which we have spoken. And we give our names unto the world, to witness unto the world that which we have seen. And we lie not, God bearing witness of it.

> Christian Whitmer,
> Jacob Whitmer,
> Peter Whitmer, Jr.
> John Whitmer,
> Hiram Page,
> Joseph smith, Sr.
> Hyrum Smith,
> Samuel H. Smith

---

[81]Lucy Smith, *Biographical Sketches*, pp. 138-39.

[82]*T&S* 3 (September 1, 1842): 898-99.

Historical Setting of the Experience of the Eight

Lucy Smith

The following day [the day after the Three Witnesses had viewed the plates] we returned [to our home in Manchester], a cheerful, happy company. In a few days we were followed by Joseph, Oliver, and the Whitmers, who came to make us a visit, and make some arrangements about getting the book printed. Soon after they came, all the male part of the company, with my husband, Samuel, and Hyrum, retired to a place where the family were in the habit of offering up their secret devotions to God. They went to this place, because it had been revealed to Joseph that the plates would be carried thither by one of the ancient Nephites. Here it was, that those eight witnesses, whose names are recorded in the Book of Mormon, looked upon them and handled them.

After these [eight] witnesses returned to the house, the angel again made his appearance to Joseph, at which time Joseph delivered up the plates into the angel's hands. The ensuing evening, we held a meeting, in which all the witnesses bore testimony to the facts, as stated above; and all of our family, even to Don Carlos, who was but fourteen years of age, testified of the truth of the Latter-day Dispensation—that it was then ushered in.[83]

Testimonies of the Eight Witnesses

John Whitmer

David Whitmer, Oliver Cowdery, and Martin Harris, were the three witnesses whose names are attached to the Book of Mormon according to the prediction of the book, who knew and saw, for a surety, into whose presence the angel of God came and showed them the plates, the ball, the directors, etc. And also other witnesses even eight, viz., Christian Whitmer, Jacob Whitmer, John Whitmer, Peter Whitmer, Jr., Hiram Page, Joseph Smith, Hyrum Smith, and Samuel H. Smith, are the men to whom Joseph Smith, Junior, showed the plates. These witnesses' names go forth also of the truth of this work in the last days, to the convincing or condemning of this generation in the last day.[84]

---

[83]Lucy Smith, *Biographical Sketches*, pp. 140-41.

[84]John Whitmer's History, p. 25, photocopy, Church Archives.

To say that the Book of Mormon is a revelation from God, I have no hesitance; but with all confidence have signed my name to it as such . . . .I desire to testify to all that will come to the knowledge of this address; that I have most assuredly seen the plates from whence the Book of Mormon is translated, and that I have handled these plates, and know of a surety that Joseph Smith, Jr. has translated the Book of Mormon by the gift and power of God . . . .I know that the Bible, Book of Mormon and book of Doctrine and Covenants of the church of the Latter Day Saints, contain the revealed will of heaven.[85]

Hyrum Smith

Having given my testimony to the world of the truth of the Book of Mormon . . .I thought that it might be strengthening to my beloved brethren, to give them a short account of my sufferings, for the truth's sake, and the state of my mind and feelings, while under circumstances of the most trying and afflicting nature. Prior to my settlement in Missouri [I] endured almost all manner of abuse, which was poured out upon the church of Latter Day Saints, from its commencement . . .After enduring many privations and much fatigue, . . .I arrived with my family in Far West. [In the fall of 1838, I was imprisoned with my brethren] for about six months . . .and suffered much for want of proper food, and from the nauseous cell in which I was confined . . . .How inadequate is language to express the feelings of my mind, . . .knowing that I was innocent of crime, and that I had been dragged from my family at a time, when my assistance was most needed; that I had been abused and thrust into a dungeon, and confined for months on account of my faith, and the "testimony of Jesus Christ." However I thank God that I felt a determination to die, rather than deny *the things which my eyes had seen, which my hands had handled, and which I had bore testimony to* . . . .I can assure my beloved brethren that I was enabled to bear as strong a testimony, when nothing but death presented itself, as ever I did in my life . . . .I yet feel a determination to do the will of God, in spite of persecutions, imprisonments or death.[86]

---

[85]*M&A* 2 (March 1836): 286-87. During a conference held in the early 1830s in Ohio, John Whitmer declared that he had "seen, hefted, and handled [the plates] with his own hands." Commenting on this talk, Oliver Cowdery stated that "no man possessed of common reason and common sense, can doubt, or will be so vain as to dispute" John Whitmer's testimony (*M&A* 1 [June 1835]: 143. See also "Visit of E. C. Brandt to John Whitmer," Whitmer Papers, RLDS Church Library Archives.)

[86]"Hyrum Smith to the Saints scattered abroad," *T&S* 1 (December 1839): 20-23.

Samuel H. Smith - Interview

The Book of Mormon, or, as it is called by some, the Golden Bible . . .is a revelation from God . . . .I [am] one of the witnesses . . . .I know the book to be a revelation from God, translated by the gift and power of the Holy Ghost, and that my brother Joseph Smith, Jr., is a Prophet, Seer and Revelator . . . .If you will read this book with a prayerful heart, and ask God to give you a witness, you will know of the truth of this work.[87]

The Last Testimonies

Testimony of Christian and Peter Whitmer, Jr., Reported by Oliver Cowdery

Among those who have gone home to rest, we mention the names of our two brothers-in-law, Christian and Peter Whitmer, Jr. the former died on the 27th of November 1835, and othe other the 22nd of September last [1836], in Clay County, Missouri. By many in this church, our brothers were personally known: they were the first to embrace the new covenant, on hearing it, and during a constant scene of persecution and perplexity, to their last moments, maintained its truth—they were both included in the list of the eight witnesses in the Book of Mormon.[88]

Oliver Cowdery's Final Testimony Reported by David Whitmer and John C. Whitmer, Son of Jacob Whitmer

I was present at the deathbed of Oliver Cowdery in 1850 . . . .Oliver died the happiest man I ever saw . . . .His last words were, "Brother David, be true to your testimony to the Book of Mormon, for we know that it is of God and that it is verily true." After shaking hands with the family and kissing his wife and daughter, he said, "Now I lay me down for the last time, I am going to my Savior," and died immediately, with a smile on his face. Many witnesses yet live in Richmond, who will testify to the truth of these facts, as well as to the good character of Oliver Cowdery.[89]

---

[87]This testimony was spoken during a conversation in 1830 between Samuel H. Smith and Phineas Howe Young (brother of Brigham Young) and was recorded in Phineas Young's autobiography. (*MS* 25 [June 6, 1863]: 360-61.)

[88]*M&A* 3 (December 1836): 426.

[89]David Whitmer, *Address to All Believers in Christ*, p. 8 and Andrew Jenson, Edward Stevenson, and Joseph B. Black, "Historical Landmarks," *Deseret News* (Salt Lake City), September 17, 1888, p. 2. See also Jenson, *Biographical Encyclopedia*, 1:246-51; John Whitmer's letter dated March 3, 1876, Whitmer Papers, RLDS Church Library Archives; and David Whitmer to E. L. Kelley, March 3, 1884, Whitmer Papers, RLDS Church Archives.

Martin Harris' Last Testimony Reported by William H. Homer

July 10, 1875, marked the end. I stood by the bedside holding the patient's right hand and my mother at the foot of the bed. Martin had been unconscious for a number of days. When we first entered the room the old gentleman appeared to be sleeping. He soon woke up and asked for a drink of water. I put my arm under the old gentleman, raised him, and my mother held the glass to his lips. He drank freely, and then he looked up at me and recognized me. He said, "I know you. You are my friend." He said, "Yes, I did see the plates on which the Book of Mormon was written; I did see the angel; I did hear the voice of God; and I do know that Joseph Smith is a Prophet of God, holding the keys of the Holy Priesthood."

This was the end.[90]

Final Testimonies of Jacob and John Whitmer Reported by Jacob's son, John C. Whitmer

My father, Jacob Whitmer, was always faithful and true to his testimony to the Book of Mormon, and confirmed it on his deathbed. Of my Uncle John [Whitmer] I will say that I was with him a short time before he died at Far West, Missouri, when he confirmed to me what he had done so many times previously that he knew the Book of Mormon was true.[91]

The Dying Testimony of Hiram Page and Other Witnesses Reported by Philander Page, son of Hiram

I knew my father to be true and faithful to his testimony of the divinity of the Book of Mormon until the very last. Whenever he had an opportunity to bear his testimony to this effect, he would always do so, and seemed to rejoice exceedingly in having been privileged to see the plates and thus become one of the Eight Witnesses. I can also testify that Jacob, John and David Whitmer and Oliver Cowdery died in full faith in the divinity of the Book of Mormon. I was with all these witnesses on their deathbeds and heard each of them bear his last testimony.[92]

---

[90]Homer, "The Passing of Martin Harris," p. 470. See also a biographical sketch of Martin Harris written by Martin Harris, Jr. in "Excerpt from the Adventure," copy located in RLDS Church Library-Archives.

[91]Andrew Jenson, Edward Stevenson, and Joseph B. Black, "Historical Landmarks," *Deseret News* (Salt Lake City), September 17, 1888, p. 2.

[92]Andrew Jenson, *Biographical Encyclopedia*, 1:278.

David Whitmer's Last Testimonies Reported by Angus M. Cannon and the Richmond Democrat

My friend [speaking to Angus M. Cannon on January 7, 1888], if God ever uttered a truth the testimony I now bear is true. I did see the angel of God and beheld the glory of the Lord and He declared that Record [to be] true.[93]

On Sunday evening at 5:30, Jan. 22, 1888, Mr. Whitmer called his family and some friends to his bedside, and addressing himself to the attending physician, said:

"Dr. Buchanan, I want you to say whether or not I am in my right mind, before I give my dying testimony."

The doctor answered: "Yes, you are in your right mind, for I have just had a conversation with you."

He [David Whitmer] then addressed himself to all around his bedside in these words: "Now you must all be faithful in Christ. I want to say to you all, the Bible and the Record of the Nephites (Book of Mormon) is [are] true, so you can say you have heard me bear my testimony on my deathbed. All be faithful in Christ, and your reward will be according to your works. God bless you all. My trust is in Christ forever, world[s] without end.—Amen.[94]

The Plates Returned to the Angel

Joseph Smith

By the wisdom of God, they [the plates] remained safe in my hands, until I had accomplished by them what was required at my hand. When, according to arrangements, the messenger called for them, I delivered them up to him; and he has them in his charge until this day, being the second day of May, one thousand eight hundred and thirty-eight.[95]

---

[93]Journal of Angus M. Cannon, January 7, 1888, Church Archives.

[94]*Richmond Democrat*, February 2, 1888. See also *Richmond Conservator*, January 26, 1888 and *The Kansas City Times*, January 26, 1888.

[95]*T&S* 3 (May 2, 1842): 772.

Martin Harris

The plates from which the Book of Mormon was translated...were returned to the angel, Moroni, from whom they were received, to be brought forth again in the due time of the Lord; for they contain many things pertaining to the gathering of Israel, which gathering will take place in this generation and shall be testified of among all nations, according to the old Prophets; as the Lord will set his ensign to the people, and gather the outcasts of Israel.[96]

Conclusion

Orson Pratt

The Lord would not permit the Book of Mormon to go forth to this generation without giving further evidence of its truth than that of its translation. Consequently three other men,...Oliver Cowdery, David Whitmer and Martin Harris, had a testimony concerning the divine authenticity of this work, not by seeing the plates, merely; that would not have been sufficient. What was their testimony? They have left it on record, and it is printed and bound with the Book of Mormon to be sent forth to all nations, peoples and tongues under the whole heavens....[97]

Now is there any chance for deception here? An angel...sent forth from God,...clothed in glory and brightness! An angel...[taking] these plates and turn[ing] them over leaf after leaf and show[ing] the engravings thereon [to Joseph Smith and the three witnesses][98]....It would be impossible for four men...to be deceived in seeing an angel descend from heaven,...hearing his voice...seeing the plates [and] the engravings upon them, and ...hearing the voice of the Lord out of heaven.

If these men, whose testimonies are attached to the Book of Mormon were not deceived, it must be admitted...[that] there are only two among the nations, have called up him [in western Missouri] from time to time, and they all bear the same testimony—that Mr. David Whitmer, still, in the most solemn manner, declares that he saw the angel and that he saw the plates in his hands....

---

[96]Martin Harris to H. B. Emerson, January 1871.

[97]Orson Pratt in *JD*, 12:358.

[98]Ibid., 14:262.

If these men, whose testimonies are attached to the Book of Mormon were not deceived, it must be admitted...[that] there are only two alternatives—that they were impostors, or else the Book of Mormon is a divine revelation from heaven.

Now let us inquire what grounds there are to suppose that they were impostors?...Did either of these three men, or did the translator of the Book of Mormon, ever deny the truth...[or] the divinity of the Book of Mormon? Never, no never. Whatever the circumstances they were placed in, however much they were mobbed and ridiculed, however much they suffered by the persecution of their enemies, their testimony all the time was—"We saw the angel of God, we beheld him in his glory, we saw the plates in his hands, and the engravings thereon, and we know that the Book of Mormon is true"....

Oliver Cowdery did not live his faith as he should have done, and he was excommunicated from this Church during Joseph's lifetime. Did he still continue to hold fast to his testimony? He did. Never was he known to swerve from it to the least degree; and after being out of the Church several years, he returned...and...acknowledged his sins, and humbly asked the church to forgive him, bearing his testimony to the sacred things recorded in the Book of Mormon....He was rebaptized a member of the Church, and soon after departed this life.

Martin Harris did not follow...this people [when they migrated west in the late 1830's and 1840's]; but we often heard of him, and whenever we did so we heard of him telling, in public and private of the great vision that God had shown to him concerning the divinity of the Book of Mormon. A few years ago he came to this Territory...and was rebaptized...[and] continue[d] to bear testimony. In his last testimony, he bore record concerning the divinity of the work.

One more witness remains who saw that angel and the plates,...David Whitmer....Many of the elders of this Church, in going to and fro among the nations, have called upon him [in western Missouri] from time to time, and they all bear the same testimony—that Mr. David Whitmer, still, in the most solemn manner, declares that he saw the angel and that he saw the plates....[99]

Have any persons ever seen the plates of the Book of Mormon, besides the four witnesses [referring to Joseph Smith and the Three Witnesses]? Yes: there are eight other witnesses, who send forth their

---

[99]Ibid., 18:158-60.

printed testimony, in connection with the Book of Mormon, unto all nations, kindreds, tongues, and people. They testify that they saw and handled the plates, and examined the engravings upon them, and that they had "the appearance of the ancient work and of curious workmanship." They close their testimony with the following words: "And we give our names unto the world, to witness unto the world that which we have seen; and we lie not, God bearing witness of it." Here, then, are twelve witnesses of the existence of the plates. Neither of these witnesses have ever denied their testimony to this day. Some of these witnesses have died—some have been martyred for their testimony; and others are still living. Is there a person on the earth, that can prove that these twelve witnesses did not see the plates? No, there is not. The existence of the plates, filled with engravings, is proved by twelve eye witnesses: while the correctness of their translation is proved by four eye witnesses, not only of the plates, but of the angel. Therefore, the evidences which this generation have of the Divine Authenticity of the Book of Mormon, and of the existence of the plates, are far greater than the evidences which they have for the truth of any of the books of the Bible. Hence, if they would be condemned for rejecting the Bible, how much more will they be condemned for rejecting the Book of Mormon which was confirmed, in its very origin, by so many witnesses?[100]

---

[100]Orson Pratt, *Divine Authenticity of the Book of Mormon*, No. 4 (Liverpool: R. James, 1850), p. 57.

CHAPTER SEVEN

The Prophet, The Book, and The Church

July 1829–April 1830

"And in the days of these kings shall the God of heaven set up a kingdom, which shall never be destroyed . . . . And this gospel of the kingdom shall be preached in all the world for a witness unto all nations; and then shall the end come." (Daniel 2:44 and Matt. 24:14.)

The decade stretching from the spring of 1820 to 1830 was a period of preparation. It began with the call of a prophet and culminated with the translation and publication of an ancient history and the organization of a church. Early in the spring of 1830, ten years following the First Vision, the first edition of the Book of Mormon was available for distribution and Christ's church was formally organized. Responding to latter-day revelations, Joseph Smith established an organization designed to prepare people for the Second Coming of Christ and for an eternal, celestial life with God. This "marvelous work and a wonder" was so important that all who embraced it were challenged with the responsibility of warning their neighbor and carrying the message of salvation and exaltation to all the world.

Following the restoration of the priesthood and the organization of the Church, God manifested his power among the converts. Members prophesied, devils were cast out, the sick were healed, and all who received the gift of the Holy Ghost rejoiced. This manifestation of the power of God, which has continued to this day, is another evidence of the divine calling of the Propeh Joseph Smith. Although there have been many "faith healers" in the history of mankind, Joseph Smith was different from miracle workers in that he conferred the power and authority which he possessed on others.

Joseph Smith's challenges in bringing forth the Book of Mormon did not end with the completion of the translation. Securing a copyright was not difficult (Joseph Smith deposited the title page with R. R. Lansing, clerk of the Northern District Court of New York on June 11, 1829.)[1], locating a publisher was. Recognizing the advantages of having the work printed in Palmyra village where members of the Prophet's family could supervise the publication, Joseph Smith requested E. B. Grandin, publisher of the *Wayne Sentinel*, to print and bind the work. Because Grandin had heard negative stories about the "golden Bible," he initially refused to print the Book of Mormon.[2] Following Grandin's rejection, Joseph Smith traveled to Rochester, New York, where he sought assistance from Thurlow Weed, a politician and publisher of the Rochester *Telegraph*. According to a reminiscence written by Weed, Joseph Smith informed him that "he had been directed in a vision to a place in the woods near Palmyra, where he resided, and that he found a 'golden Bible,' from which he was directed to copy the book that he wanted published." Although Weed told the Mormon prophet that he would not print the volume, this publisher recalled that shortly following this first visit, Joseph Smith, accompanied by Martin Harris, again called on him. Harris, continued Weed, was "a substantial farmer residing near Palmyra, who had adopted the Mormon faith and . . .offered to become security for the expense of printing." Although Weed was assured that he would be

---

[1]A reproduction of the copyright of the Book of Mormon is located in the first edition of The Book of Mormon.

[2]Mary M. Allen to "the Librarian of the Palmyra Library," March 1964, E. B. Grandin file, King's Daughters' Library, Palmyra, New York, cited in Larry C. Porter, "A Study of the Origins of the Church of Jesus Christ of Latter-day Saints in the States of New York and Pennsylvania, 1816-1831" (Ph.D. diss., Brigham Young University, 1971), p. 86. See also Pomery Tucker, *Origin, Rise, and Progress of Mormonism* (New York: D. Appleton and Co., 1867), pp. 50-51.

paid for his services, he again declined to publish the book for he "thought" that Joseph Smith was "either crazed or a very shallow imposter."[3]

Following Weed's refusal, Joseph Smith sought assistance from Elihu F. Marshall, another publisher living in Rochester, who "gave his terms for the printing and binding of the book with his acceptance of the profered mode of security for the payment."[4] Before signing an agreement with Marshall, the Prophet returned to Palmyra and asked Grandin to reconsider his request. Since the work would be printed without his assistance, and this proposal was strictly a business arrangement, Grandin reluctantly agreed to print and bind 5,000 copies for $3,000, taking as security the bond and mortgage of Martin Harris. According to a mortgage dated August 26, 1829, Martin Harris agreed to pay Grandin $3,000 within eighteen months. The contract further specified that if Harris failed to meet his financial commitment his land was to be sold at public auction to satisfy the obligation.[5]

The Book of Mormon was printed and later sold in the Grandin printing establishment. The printing office was located on the third floor of a building nestled among other stores in downtown Palmyra. The binding was accomplished on the second floor; and the book was sold in the Palmyra bookstore, located on the first floor.[6]

The manuscript which was written on foolscap paper and delivered in stages to the publisher had been recopied from the original by Oliver Cowdery and other scribes. These two manuscripts (the original and the printer's copy) help us better understand some of the procedures employed in bringing forth the Book of Mormon and provide another evidence of the reliability of Joseph Smith's histories. The original manus-

---

[3]Harriet A. Weed, ed., *Autobiography of Thurlow Weed* (Boston: Houghton, Mifflin and Co., 1884), pp. 358-59.

[4]Pomeroy Tucker, *Origin, Rise and Progress of Mormonism*, p. 52.

[5]Ibid., pp. 52-53; Wayne County, New York, Book of Mortgages, Book 3, p. 325, microfilm copy located in the Genealogical Society of The Church of Jesus Christ of Latter-day Saints, Salt Lake City, Utah (hereafter cited as Church Genealogical Society); and Porter, "Origins of the Church in New York and Pennsulvania," p. 86.

[6]The following announcement appeared in the *Wayne Sentinel* (Palmyra, New York), March 26, 1830: "The above work, containing about 600 pages, Large Duodecimo, is now for sale, wholsesale and retail, at the Palmyra Bookstore, By E. B. Grandin."

cript remained in Joseph Smith's possession until October 1841. On the second of that month, Joseph placed this manuscript in the cornerstone of a hotel which was under construction in Nauvoo, called the Nauyoo House.[7] Forty years later, in 1882, Lewis C. Bidamon, who had married Emma, the Prophet's widow, removed this document from its depository. After obtaining the manuscript, Bidamon found that many had been soaked and ruined. Other pages were destroyed as Bidamon distributed them to different people. Eventually, 72½ leaves were given to the Church and were deposited in the archives in Salt Lake City. These surviving fragments comprise about 145 pages of the original text.[8]

The second copy, the manuscript delivered to the printer, was preserved by Oliver Cowdery and following his death was protected by David Whitmer, Oliver's brother-in-law. Following Whitmer's death, his heirs held the manuscript and in 1903 gave these sheets to the Reorganized Church of Jesus Christ of Latter Day Saints where they are deposited today in their archives. With the exception of a few missing words on the first page of this manuscript, the printers copy is complete, containing 464 numbered and several unnumbered pages. When Oliver Cowdery and others recopied the manuscript they corrected some of the errors that scribes had made in the initial recording. Since nearly all of the changes on this second manuscript are corrections in spelling and capitalization, the printer's copy is like the original manuscript (the pages that have survived) in that it contains no punctuation and paragraphing. The printer, therefore, was responsible for the punctuation and paragraphing that appeared in the first edition of the Book of Mormon.[9]

---

[7]Warren Foote wrote in his autobiography that he was present on this cool and clear day in October when Joseph Smith placed the manuscript of the Book of Mormon in a square hole that had been chiseled in the southeast cornerstone of the Nauvoo House. After this and other items had been placed in that depository another stone was placed over the hole and cemented in place. (Autobiography of Warren Foote, October 2, 1841, Church Archives.) Ebenezer Robinson, who was acquainted with the handwriting of Oliver Cowdery, wrote that when he examined the original Book of Mormon manuscript which was deposited in the cornerstone of the Nauvoo House he recognized Oliver Cowdery's handwriting on that document. (Ebenezer Robinson, "Items of Personal History of the Editor [Taken from the *Return*]," p. 98, typescript, BYU.)

[8]Stan Larson, "A Most Sacred Possession," *Ensign* (September 1977):88-89. The text of the original manuscript of the Book of Mormon which has been preserved contains information that is found in the current edition of the Book of Mormon from 1 Nephi 2:2 to 2 Nephi 1:30 and from Alma 22:22 to Helaman 3:22.

[9]Richard P. Howard, *Restoration Scriptures: A Study of their Textual Development* (Independence, Mo.: Herald Publishing House, 1969), pp. 34-35, 39.

The original manuscript of the Book of Mormon suggests that this religious history was dictated to scribes who wrote word for word that which was related to them. The fact that there are few alterations in the text is evidence that there was no rewriting of the history as it was dictated. A number of grammatical errors (some of which would not be considered grammatical errors in Hebrew and other languages) and spelling errors (sometimes caused by the omission of a letter) were not corrected in the original manuscript. These errors help one "appreciate the great difficulty of writing carefully a longhand transcription from dictation" and indicate that some of the scribes were not good spellers.[10] Although there are few scribal corrections in the pages of the original manuscript, some of the changes also suggest that the work was dictated. In one instance, for example, a scribe recorded the word "no" and then corrected it to read "know," which sounds the same but has a different meaning. The lack of punctuation, paragraphing, and capitalization of proper nouns in the original manuscript indicate that "the pressure on the scribe, writing longhand from dictation, was such as to preclude his attention to such grammatical considerations."[11] In the writings of Oliver Cowdery, when he was not serving as a scribe for the Prophet, Oliver capitalized words and consistently created sentences with punctuation marks. The fact that the portion of the original manuscript which has been preserved is in the handwriting of Oliver Cowdery and John Whitmer also indicates that when Oliver Cowdery commenced writing for the prophet he began by recording information that followed the 116 pages that had been lost and that the last portion of the Book of Mormon to be translated (the section translated in the Whitmer home) was what is today the first section of the Book of Mormon, the portion taken from the Small plates of Nephi.[12]

During the printing of the Book of Mormon, a few chapters were published in serial form in the Palmyra *Reflector*. An ex-justice of the peace, Abner Cole, editor and proprietor of the *Reflector*, gained access to Grandin's printing establishment on Sundays and evenings and commenced publishing this paper on September 2, 1829, on the same press that was being used to print the Book of Mormon.[13] Beginning with the

[10]Ibid., p. 36.

[11]Ibid., p. 36 and Larson, "A Most Sacred Possession," pp. 90-91.

[12]Stan Larson, "A Study of Some Textual Variations in the Book of Mormon Comparing the Original and the Printer's Manscripts and the 1830, the 1837, and the 1840 Edition" (Master's thesis, Brigham Young University, 1974), pp. 9, 19-21.

[13]*The Reflector* (Palmyra, New York), January 2, 1830, p. 9; January 13, 1830, p. 17; January 22, 1830, pp. 27-28; and Lucy Smith, *History of Joseph Smith*, pp. 148-49.

THE REFLECTOR.

BY O. DOGBERRY, Esq.]   PALMYRA: JANUARY 2, 1830.   [NEW SERIES—NO. 3.

[From the Book of Mormon.]

THE FIRST BOOK OF NEPHI.

HIS REIGN AND MINISTRY.

CHAPTER I.

I, Nephi, having been born of goodly parents, therefore I was taught somewhat in all the learning of my father; and having seen many afflictions in the course of my days—nevertheless, having been highly favored of the Lord in all my days; yea, having had a great knowledge of the goodness and the mysteries of God, therefore I make a record of my proceedings in my days; yea, I make a record in the language of my father, which consists of the learning of the Jews and the language of the Egyptians. And I know that the record which I make, to be true; and I make it with mine own hand; and I make it according to my knowledge.

For it came to pass, in the commencement of the first year of the reign of Zedekiah, king of Judah, (my father Lehi having dwelt at Jerusalem in all his days;) and in that same year there came many prophets, prophesying to the people, that they must repent, or the great city Jerusalem must be destroyed. Wherefore it came to pass, that my father Lehi, as he went forth, prayed unto the Lord, yea, even with all his heart, in behalf of his people.

And it came to pass, as he prayed to the Lord, there came a pillar of fire and dwelt upon a rock before him; and he saw and heard much; and because of the things which he saw and heard, he did quake and tremble exceedingly.

And it came to pass that he returned to his own house at Jerusalem; and he cast himself upon his bed, being overcome with the spirit and the things which he had seen; and being surrounded with numberless concourses of angels in the attitude of singing and praising their God.

And it came to pass that he saw one descending out of the midst of Heaven, and he beheld that his lustre was above that to the sun at noon-day; and he also saw twelve others following him, and their brightness did exceed that of the stars in the firmament; and they came down and went forth upon the face of the earth; and the first came and stood before my father, and gave unto him a Book, and bade him that he should read.

And it came to pass that as he read, he was filled with the spirit of the Lord, and he read saying, Wo, wo unto Jerusalem! for I have seen thine abominations; yea, and many things did my father read concerning Jerusalem—that it should be destroyed, and the inhabitants thereof, many should perish by the sword, and many should be carried away captive into Babylon.

And it came to pass that when my father had read and saw many great and marvellous things, he did exclaim many things unto the Lord; such as, Great and marvellous are thy works, O Lord God Almighty! Thy throne is high in the Heavens, and thy power, and goodness, and mercy is over all the inhabitants of the earth; and because thou art merciful, thou wilt not suffer those who come unto thee that they shall perish! And after this man read the language of my father in the praising of his God; for his soul did rejoice, and his whole heart was filled, because of the things which he had seen; yea, which the Lord had shewn unto him. And now I, Nephi, do not make a full account of the things which my father hath written, for he hath written many things which he saw in visions and in dreams; and he also hath written many things which

Behold I make an abridgment of the record of my father, upon plates which I have made with mine own hands; wherefore, after that I have abridged the record of my father, then will I make an account of mine own life.

Therefore, I would that ye should know that after the Lord had shewn so many marvellous things unto my father Lehi, yea, concerning the destruction of Jerusalem, behold he went forth among the people, and began to prophesy and to declare unto them concerning the things which he had both seen and heard.

And it came to pass that the Jews did mock him because of the things which he testified of them; for he truly testified of their wickedness and their abominations; and he testified that the things which he saw and heard, and also the things which he read in the Book, manifested plainly of the coming of a Messiah, and also the redemption of the world.

And when the Jews heard these things, they were angry with him; yea, even as with the prophets of old, whom they had cast out and stoned and slain; and they also sought his life, that they might take it away. But behold, I, Nephi, will shew unto you that the tender mercies of the Lord is over all them whom he hath chosen, because of their faith, to make them mighty even unto the power of deliverance.

For behold it came to pass that the Lord spake unto my father, yea, even in a dream, and saith unto him, Blessed art thou Lehi, because of the things which thou hast done; and because thou hast been faithful, and declared unto this people the things which I commanded thee, behold they seek to take away thy life.

And it came to pass that the Lord commanded my father, that he should take his family and depart into the wilderness. And it came to pass that he was obedient

Printer's Copy of the Book of Mormon
1 Nephi 2:1–17

January 2, 1830, issue and continuing in the 13 and 22 issues, Esquire Cole printed selections from 1 Nephi and Alma (1 Nephi 1:1-20; 2:1-15 and Alma 43:22-20 in the current edition of the Book of Mormon or 1 Nephi parpagraphs 1-16 and Alma 20 paragraphs 5-9 in the first edition.) Undoubtedly Cole used printed sheets that he found in Grandin's office for his articles rather than the original manuscript, for the text was reproduced exactly (with the exception of a few printing errors) as it later appeared in the first edition of the Book of Mormon.[14]

After learning of Cole's illegal actions, the Prophet traveled from his home in Harmony, Pennsylvania, to Palmyra, New York, and threatened to sue this editor. The problem was eventually resolved through arbitration, and, with some misgivings, Cole accepted the decision that he should stop violating the copyright.[15]

Meanwhile, Cole published a series of articles in the *Reflector* on the Book of Mormon. At first he denounced the publication, but his tone mellowed while he was printing the work in his paper. In one of the first commentaries published on this book, Cole wrote:

> The Book, when it shall come forth before the public must stand or fall, according to the whims and fancies of its readers. How it will stand the test of criticism, we are not prepared to say, not having as yet examined many of its pages.—We are, however, prepared to state that from part of the first chapter, now before us, and which we this day publish, we cannot discover anything treasonable, or which will have a tendency to subvert our liberties. As to its religious character, we have as yet no means of determining, and if we had, we should be quite loth [sic] to meddle with the tender consciences of our neighbors.[16]

---

[14]*The Reflector* (Palmyra, New York), January 2, 1830, p. 9; January 13, 1830, p. 17; and January 22, 1830, pp. 27-28.

[15]Lucy Smith, *Biographical Sketches*, pp. 148-50. Lucy Smith incorrectly recorded in her history that the name of the newspaper which included selections from the Book of Mormon was "Dogberry Paper on Winter Hill." In some issues of the *Reflector* there was a statement that the paper was being published at the "Bowery on Wintergreen Hill," a title that was inserted after the caption, "Obediah Dogberry, Esquire." Wintergreen Hill (also called Walton Hill) is located directly north of the main business district of Palmyra. (Porter, "Origins of the Church in New York and Pennsylvania," pp. 90-92.)

[16]*The Reflector* (Palmyra, New York), January 2, 1830, p. 13.

Following Joseph Smith's insistance that Cole discontinue printing selections from the Book of Mormon, Cole returned to a negative outlook of this book and denounced the Prophet for interfering with his publishing adventure.[17]

Although Esquire Cole undoubtedly hoped to increase the circulation of his paper by publishing selections from the Book of Mormon, many citizens who might have read selections from this work as it appeared in the newspaper, decided that they would not buy the book after it had been published. This boycott nearly stopped the publication of the book. Fearing that he would not be paid for his services, Grandin complained to Joseph. The Prophet succeeded in assuring Grandin that the contract which he had made with him would be honored. The work continued, and the book was released for public sale on March 26, 1830.[18]

In order to raise the money owed Grandin, Martin Harris sold 151 acres of his farm to Thomas Lakey of Palmyra on April 7, 1831, receiving $3,000 for this property. Consequently, Martin Harris, one of the Three Witnesses to the Book of Mormon, exemplified his conviction in the divine mission of Joseph Smith and in the authenticity of the Book of Mormon by first mortgaging and then selling a portion of his farm.[19]

A few days after the Book of Mormon was available for sale in Palmyra, about fifty persons crowded into the log-cabin farmhouse of Peter Whitmer, Sr. in Fayette, New York. On April 6, 1830, these settlers from Fayette, Manchester, Colesville, and other New York towns witnessed the formal organization of the Church of Christ, a church whose official name was given by an 1838 revelation as The Church of Jesus Christ of Latter-day Saints.[20] The visions, revelations, and authority which Joseph Smith had received, prepared the young prophet to reestablish on the earth the purity of the New Testament Church, and the book which was now available to members of this Church and to others in quest of religious truth, contained the fulness of the gospel of Christ. It was now the responsibility of members of this Church to warn others,

---

[17]Russell R. Rich, "The Dogberry Papers and the Book of Mormon," *BYU Studies* 10 (Spring 1970):316-20.

[18]Lucy Smith, *Biographical Sketches*, pp. 150-51 and *Wayne Sentinel* (Palmyra), March 22, 1830.

[19]Wayne County, New York, Book of Deeds, Book 10, pp. 515-16, microfilm, Church Genealogical Society.

[20]D&C 115:4. Throughout this work, I have used the current punctuation of the name of the Chuch.

informing them of the restoration and in turn becoming modern witnesses for Christ.[21]

Publication of the Book of Mormon

Joseph Smith

Meantime, our translation drawing to a close, we went to Palmyra, Wayne County, New York, secured the copyright, and agreed with Mr. Egbert B. Grandin to print five thousand copies for the sum of three thousand dollars.

I wish also to mention here that the title page of the Book of Mormon is a literal translation, taken from the very last leaf, on the left hand side of the collection or book of plates, which contained the record which has been translated, the language of the whole running the same as all Hebrew writing in general; and that said title page is not by any means a modern composition, either of mine or of any other man who has lived or does live in this generation. Therefore, in order to correct an error which generally exists concerning it, I give below that part of the title page of the English version of the Book of Mormon, which is a genuine and literal translation of the title page of the original Book of Mormon, as recorded on the plates.

THE BOOK OF MORMON
An account written by the hand of Mormon, upon plates,
taken from the plates of Nephi.

"Wherefore, it is an abridgement of the record of the people of Nephi, and also of the Lamanites—Written to the Lamanites, who are a remnant of the house of Israel; and also to Jew and Gentile—Written by way of commandment, and also by the spirit of prohecy and of revelation—Written and sealed up, and hid up unto the Lord, that they might not be destroyed—to come forth by the gift and power of God unto the interpretation thereof—Sealed by the hand of Moroni, and hid up unto the Lord, to come forth in due time by the way of Gentile—the interpretation thereof by the gift of God.

An abridgement taken from the book of Ether also, which is a record of the people of Jared, who were scattered at the time the Lord con-

---

[21]D&C 4:4; 6:3; 11:3; 12:3.

founded the language of the people, when they were building a tower to get to heaven—Which is to show unto the remnant of the House of Israel what great things the Lord hath done for their fathers; and that they may know the covenants of the Lord, that they are not cast off forever—and also to the convincing of the Jew and Gentile that Jesus is the Christ, the Eternal God, manifesting himself unto all nations—And now, if there are faults they are the mistakes of men; wherefore, condemn not the things of God, that ye may be found spotless at the judgement-seat of Christ."

The remainder of the title page is of course, modern.[22]

Pomeroy Tucker

In June [probably should be July or August], 1829, Smith the prophet, his brother Hyrum, Cowdery the scribe, and Harris the believer, applied to Mr. Egbert B. Grandin, the publisher of the *Wayne Sentinel* at Palmyra (now deceased), for his price to do the work of one edition of three thousand copies. Harris offered to pay or secure payment if a bargain should be made. Only a few sheets of the manuscript, as a specimen, with the title-page, were exhibited at this time, though the whole number of folios was stated, whereby could be made a calculation of the cost. Mr. Grandin at once expressed his disinclination to entertain the proposal to print at any price, believing the whole affair to be a wicked imposture and a scheme to defraud Mr. Harris, who was his friend, and whom he advised accordingly. This admonition was kindly but firmly resisted by Harris. . . . Further interviews followed, Grandin being earnestly importuned to reconsider his opinion and determination. He was assured by Harris, that if he refused to do the work, it would be procured elsewhere. And the subject was temporarily dropped, except that Grandin complied with Harris' request for an approximate estimate of the cost of the proposed edition . . . .

[After learning that arrangement had been made with Elihu F. Marshall to print the book] Mr. Grandin, on taking the advice of several discreet, fair-minded neighbors, finally reconsidered his course of policy, and entered into contract for the printing and binding of five thousand copies of the Book of Mormon at the price of $3,000, taking Harris's bond and mortgage as offered in security for payment.[23]

---

[22]T&S 3 (October 15, 1842):943.

[23]Tucker, *Origin, Rise, and Progress of Mormonism*, pp. 50-53.

Lucy Smith

[After] making a contract with . . .E. B. Grandin [and] . . .before [returning] . . .to Pennsylvania, where he had left his wife, he [Joseph Smith] received a commandment, which was, in substance, as follows:—

First, that Oliver Cowdery should transcribe the whole manuscript. Second, that he should take but one copy at a time to the office, so that if one copy should get destroyed, there would still be a copy remaining. Third, that in going to and from the office, he should always have a guard to attend him, for the purpose of protecting the manuscript. Fourth, that a guard should be kept constantly on the watch, both night and day, about the house, to protect the manuscript from malicious persons, who would infest the house for the purpose of destroying the manuscript. All these things were strictly attended to, as the Lord commanded Joseph. After giving these instructions, Joseph returned to Pennsylvania.[24]

Pomeroy Tucker

In the beginning of the printing the Mormons professed to hold their manuscripts as "sacred," and insisted upon maintaining constant vigilance for their safety during the progress of the work, each morning carrying to the printing-office the instalment required for the day, and withdrawing the same at evening. No alteration from copy in any manner was to be made. These things were "strictly commanded," as they said. Mr. John H. Gilbert, as printer, had the chief operative trust of the typesetting and press-work of the job. After the first day's trial he found the manuscripts in so very imperfect a condition, especially in regard to grammar, that he became unwilling further to obey the "command," and so announced to Smith and his party; when, finally, upon much friendly expostulation, he was given a limited discretion in correcting, which was exercised in the particulars of syntax, orthography, punctuation, capitalizing, paragraphing, etc . . . .Very soon, too—after some ten days— the constant vigilance by the Mormons over the manuscripts was relaxed by reason of the confidence they came to repose in the printers.[25]

John H. Gilbert, Printer

But one copy of the manuscript was furnished the printer . . .As quick as Mr. Grandin got his type and got things all ready to commence the

---

[24]Lucy Smith, *Biographical Sketches*, pp. 53-54.

[25]Tucker, *Origin, Rise, and Progress of Mormonism*, pp. 53-54.

work, Hyrum Smith brought to the office 24 pages of manuscript on foolscap paper, closely written and legible . . . . This was about the middle of August, 1829, and the printing was completed in March, 1830. It was some weeks after this before the binder [Luther Howard] was able to deliver any copies.

I cannot say whether the entire work of "translation" was completed at the time the printing was commenced or not, but think it was. [Before the contract was signed] a few pages of the manuscript were submitted as a specimen of the whole, and it was said there would be about 500 pages . . . .

Martin Harris, Hyrum Smith and Oliver Cowdery, were very frequent visitors to the office during the printing of the Mormon Bible. The manuscript was supposed to be in the handwriting of Cowdery. Every Chapter, if I remember correctly, was one solid paragraph, without a punctation mark, from beginnig to end. Names of persons and places were generally capitalized, but sentences had no end . . . . I punctuated it to make it read as I supposed the Author intended, and but very little punctuation was altered in proofreading . . . . [Some nights I took the manuscript] home with me and read it, and punctuated it with a lead pencil . . . . Cowdery held and looked over the manuscript when most of the proofs were read. Martin Harris once or twice, and Hyrum Smith once, Grandin supposing these men could read their own writing as well, if not better, than anyone else; and if there are any discrepancies between the Palmyra edition and the manuscript these men should be held responsible.[26]

Lucy Smith

The work of printing still continued with litle or no interruption, until one Sunday afternoon, when Hyrum became very uneasy as to the security of the work left at the printing office, and requested Oliver to accompany him thither, to see if all was right. Oliver hesitated for a moment, as to the propriety of going on Sunday, but finally consented, and they set off together.

On arriving at the printing establishment, they found it occupied by an individual by the name of Cole, an ex-justice of the peace, who was

---

[26]John H. Gilbert to James T. Cobb, February 10, 1879, New York Public Library, New York City, New York, and cited in Porter, "Origins of the Church in New York and Pennsylvania," pp. 88-89; and "Memorandum, made by John H. Gilbert, Esq., Sept. 9th, 1893," in possession of John B. Nesbitt, Palmyra, New York. A typescript copy is in the BYU Library.

busily employed in printing a newspaper. Hyrum was much surprised at finding him there, and remarked, "How is it, Mr. Cole, that you are so hard at work on Sunday?"

Mr. Cole replied, that he could not have the press, in the day time during the week, and was obliged to do his printing at night, and on Sundays.

Upon reading the prospectus of his paper, they found that he had agreed with his subscribers to publish one form of "Joe Smith's Gold Bible" each week, and thereby furnish them with the principal portion of the book in such a way that they would not be obliged to pay the Smiths for it. His paper was entitled, DOGBERRY PAPER ON WINTER HILL. In this, he had thrown together a parcel of the most vulgar, disgusting prose, and the meanest, and most low-lived doggrel, in juxtaposition with a portion of the Book of Mormon, which he had pilfered. At this perversion of common sense and moral feeling, Hyrum was shocked, as well as indignant at the dishonest course which Mr. Cole had taken, in order to possess himself of the work.

"Mr. Cole," said he, "what right have you to print the Book of Mormon in this manner? Do you not know that we have secured the copyright?"

"It is none of your business," answered Cole, "I have hired the press, and will print what I please, so help yourself."

"Mr. Cole," rejoined Hyrum, "that manuscript is sacred, and I forbid your printing any more of it."

"Smith," exclaimed Cole, in a tone of anger, "I don't care a d--n for you: that d--d gold bible is going into my paper, in spite of all you can do."

Hyrum endeavoured to dissuade him from his purpose, but finding him inexorable, left him to issue his paper, . . .he had already issued six or eight numbers, and by taking them ten or twenty miles into the country, had managed to keep them out of our sight.

On returning from the office, they asked my husband what course was best for them to pursue, relative to Mr. Cole. He told them that he considered it a matter with which Joseph ought to be made acquainted. Accordingly, he set out himself for Pennsylvania, and returned with Joseph the ensuing Sunday. The weather was so extremely cold, that they came near perishing before they arrived at home, nevertheless, as soon as Joseph made himself partially comfortable, he went to the printing office, where he found Cole employed, as on the Sunday previous. "How do you do, Mr. Cole," said Joseph, "You seem hard at work."

"How do you do, Mr. Smith," answered Cole, dryly.

Joseph examined his DOGBERRY PAPER, and then said firmly, "Mr. Cole, that book, [the Book of Mormon] and the right of publishing it, belongs to me, and I forbid you meddling with it any further."

At this Mr. Cole threw off his coat, rolled up his sleeves, and came towards Joseph, smacking his fists together with vengeance, and roaring out, "do you want to fight, sir? do you want to fight? I will publish just what I please. Now, if you want to fight, just come on."

Joseph could not help smiling at his grotesque appearance, for his behaviour was too ridiculous to excite indignation. "Now, Mr. Cole," said he, "you had better keep your coat on—it is cold, and I am not going to fight you, nevertheless, I assure you, sir, that you have got to stop printing my book, for I know my rights, and shall maintain them."

"Sir," bawled out the wrathy gentleman, "if you think you are the best man, just pull off your coat and try it."

"Mr. Cole," said Joseph, in a low, significant tone, "there is law, and you will find that out, if you do not understand it, but I shall not fight you, sir."

At this, the ex-justice began to cool off a little, and finally concluded to submit to an arbitration, which decided that he should stop his proceedings forthwith, so that he made us no further trouble.

Joseph, after disposing of this affair, returned to Pennsylvania, but not long to remain there, for when the inhabitants of the surrounding country perceived that the work still progressed, they became uneasy, and again called a large meeting. At this time, they gathered their forces together, far and near, and organizing themselves into a committee of the whole, they resolved, as before, never to purchase one of our books, when they should be printed. They then appointed a commitee to wait upon E. B. Grandin, and inform him of the resolutions which they had passed, and also to explain to him the evil consequences which would result to him therefrom. The men who were appointed to do this errand, fulfilled their mission to the letter, and urged upon Mr. Grandin the necessity of his putting a stop to the printing, as the Smiths had lost all their property, and consequently would be unable to pay him for his work, except by the sale of the books. And this they would never be able to do, for the people would not purchase them. This information caused Mr. Grandin to stop printing, and we were again compelled to send for Joseph. These trips, back and forth, exhausted nearly all our means, yet they seemed unavoidable.

When Joseph came, he went immediately with Martin Harris to Grandin, and succeeded in removing his fears, so that he went on with the work, until the books wre printed, which was in the spring of eighteen hundred and thirty.[27]

Pomeroy Tucker

The contract [with Grandin regarding publishing the Book of Mormon] was faithfully and satisfactorily fulfilled by both parties, and the book in its entire edition as bargained for was completed and delivered early in the summer [should be spring] of 1830 . . .

Meanwhile, Harris and his wife had separated by mutual arrangement, on account of her persistent unbelief in Mormonism and refusal to be a party to the mortgage. The family estate was divided, Harris giving her about eighty acres of the farm, with a comfortable house and other property as her share of the assets; and she occupied this property until the time of her death. The main farm and homestead, about one hundred and fifty acres of land, was retained by himself, the mortgage covering only this portion . . . .The farm mortgaged was sold by Harris in 1831 at private sale, not by foreclosure, and a sufficiency of the avails [proceeds] went to pay Grandin . . .$3,000.[28]

Conversion and Early Missionary Activity of Solomon Chamberlain

Solomon Chamberlain

In the year 1816 . . .the Lord showed me in a vision that there were no people on the earth that were right, and that faith was gone from the earth, excepting a few, and that all churches were corrupt. I further saw in the vision that he would soon raise up a church that would be after the apostolic order, that there would be in it the same powers and gifts that were in the days of Christ, and that I should live to see the day, and that there would [be] a book come forth, like unto the Bible, and the people would be guided by it, as well as the Bible . . . .

[About 1830] I had occasion to go on a visit into Upper Canada. . . .When the boat came to Palmyra, I felt as if some Genii or good spirit told me to leave the boat. This was a few miles from where the record (Book of Mormon) was found. After leaving the boat, the Spirit manifested to me to travel a south course. I did so for about 3 miles. I had not as

---

[27]Lucy Smith, *Biographical Sketches*, pp. 148-51. See also footnote 15.

[28]Tucker, *Origin, Rise, and Progress of Mormonism*, pp. 54-55.

yet heard of the Gold Bible (so called) nor any of the Smith family. I was a stranger in that part of the country . . . .About sundown . . .my guide directed me to put up for the night, which I did to a farm house. In the morning the people of the house asked me if I had heard of the Gold Bible; when they said Gold Bible, there was a power like electricity [that] went from the top of my head to the end of my toes. This was the first time I ever heard of the Gold Bible. I was now within a half a mile of the Smith family where Joseph [had] lived. From the time I left the boat until now, I was wholly led by the Spirit or my Genii. I soon made my way across lots to Father Smiths and found Hyrum walking the floor as I entered the door. I said, "Peace be to this house."

He [Hyrum Smith] looked at me as one astonished and said, "I hope it will be peace."

I then said, "Is there anyone here that believes in visions and revelations?"

He said, "Yes, we are a visionary house."

I said, "Then I will give you one of my pamphlets, which was visonary and of my own experience."

They then called the people together which consisted of 5 or 6 men who were out at the door. Father Smith was one and some of the Whitmer's. They then sat down and read my pamphlet. Hyrum read first, but was so affected, he could not read it. He then gave it to a man, which I learned was Christian Whitmer. He finished reading it. I then opened my mouth and began to preach to them in the words that the angel had made known to me in the vision, that all churches and denominations on the earth had become corrupt and [that] no church of God [was] on the earth but that he would shortly raise up a church that would never be confounded or brought down, and be like unto the apostolic church. They wondered greatly who had been telling me these things, for said they, we have the same things written down in our house, taken from the Gold record that you are preaching to us . . . .

I then said, "If you are a visionary house, I wish you would make known some of your discoveries, for I think I can bear them."

They then made known to me that they had obtained a gold record and [had] just finished translating it. Now the Lord revealed to me by the gift and power of the Holy Ghost that this was the work I had been looking for. I stayed 2 days and they instructed me in the manuscripts of the Book of Mormon.

After I had been there 2 days, I went with Hyrum and some others to Palmyra printing office where they began to print the Book of Mormon, and as soon as they had printed 64 pages, I took them with their leave and pursued my journey to Canada, and I preached all that I knew concerning

Mormonism to all, both high and low, rich and poor, and thus you see this was the first, that ever printed Mormonism was preached to this genera-tion. I did not see anyone in traveling 7 or 800 miles that had ever heard of the Gold Bible (so called). I exhorted all people to prepare for the great work of God that was now about to come forth.[29]

Organization of the Church

Joseph Smith

[After receiving the priesthood,] we obtained of Him the following, by the spirit of prophecy and revelation; which not only gave us much information, but also pointed out to us the precise day upon which, according to His will and commandment, we should proceed to organize His Church once more here upon the earth.[30]

[A Revelation on Church Government (see D&C Section 20:1-17)]

---

[29]Autobiography of Solomon Chamberlain, pp. 3-11, photocopy, Church Archives. This account has been edited by the insertion of punctuation and correction of a few spelling errors and verb tenses. See also Larry C. Porter, "Solomon Chamberlain—Early Missionary," *BYU Studies* 12 (Spring 1972):314-18.

[30]*T&S* 3 (October 1, 1842):928-29. In the initial publication of Joseph Smith's history there was no caption introducing this revelation. However, the inscription that introduced this revelation when it was originally printed in *The Evening and The Morning Star* (Independence, Missouri, June 1832) read: "The Articles and Covenants of the Church of Christ." In the Book of Commandments (1833) this revelation was introduced with the statement: "The Articles and Covenants of the church of Christ, given in Fayette, New York, June 1830," and in the first edition of the Doctrine and Covenants (1835) there was no explanatory caption. Probably this revelation, which became known as the "Articles and Covenants of the Church" or the "Constitution of the Church," is based on a series of revelations received by the Prophet. The combined revelations were then read to the mem-bership on June 9, 1830 "at the first conference of the Church in Fayette, New York." Since members unanimously approved this revelation (or series of revela-tions) on June 9, 1830, section 20 (in our current edition of the Doctrine and Covenants) became the first revelation canonized by the Church. (Robert J. Woodford, "The Historical Development of the Doctrine and Covenants," 2 vols., Ph.D. dissertation, Brigham Young University, 1;286-93 and Lyndon W. Cook, *The Revelations of the Prophet Joseph Smith* [Provo: Seventy's Mission Bookstore, 1981], p. 31.)

The rise of the Church of Christ in these last days, being one thousand eight hundred and thirty years since the coming of our Lord and Savior Jesus Christ in the flesh, it being regularly organized and established agreeable to the laws of our country, by the will and commandments of God, in the fourth month, and on the sixth day of the month which is called April—Which commandments were given to Joseph Smith, Jr., who was called of God, and ordained an apostle of Jesus Christ, to be the first elder of this church; and to Oliver Cowdery, who was also called of God, an apostle of Jesus Christ, to be the second elder of this church, and ordained under his hand; and this according to the grace of our Lord and Savior Jesus Christ, to whom be all glory, both now and forever. Amen. After it was truly manifested unto this first elder that he had received a remission of his sins, he was entangled again in the vanities of the world; but after repenting, and humbling himself sincerely, through faith, God ministered unto him by an holy angel, whose countenance was as lightning, and whose garments were pure and white above all other whiteness; and gave unto him commandments which inspired him; and gave him power from on high, by the means which were before prepared, to translate the Book of Mormon; which contains a record of a fallen people, and the fulness of the gospel of Jesus Christ to the Gentiles and to the Jews also; which was given by inspiration, and is confirmed to others by the ministering of angels, and is declared unto the world by them—proving to the world that the holy scriptures are true, and that God does inspire men and call them to his holy work in this age and generation, as well as in generations of old; thereby showing that he is the same God yesterday, today, and forever.

The Formal Organization: April 6, 1830

Joseph Smith

Whilst the Book of Mormon was in the hands of the printer, we still continued to bear testimony and give information, as far as we had opportunity; and also made known to our brethren, that we had received commandment to organize the Church, and accordingly we met together for that purpose, at the house of the above mentioned Mr. [Peter]

Whitmer, [Sr.] (being six in number) on Tuesday, the sixth day of April, A. D. one thousand eight hundred and thirty.

Having opened the meeting by solemn prayer to our Heavenly Father we proceeded (according to previous commandment) to call on our brethren to know whether they accepted us as their teachers in the things of the kingdom of God, and whether they were satisfied that we should proceed and be organized as a church according to said commandment which we had received. To these they consented by an unanimous vote. I then laid my hands upon Oliver Cowdery and ordained him an elder of the "Church of Jesus Christ of Latter-Day Saints;" after which he ordained me also to the office of an elder of said Church. We then took bread, blessed and brake it with them; also wine, blessed it, and drank it with them. We then laid our hands on each individual member of the Church present that they might receive the gift of the Holy Ghost, and be confirmed members of the Church of Christ. The Holy Ghost was poured out upon us to a very great degree—some prophesied, whilst we all praised the Lord and rejoiced exceedingly. Whilst yet together, I received the following commandment:[31]

Revelation to Joseph Smith, Jr. given April 6, 1830. [See D&C Section 21:1-5, 9-12.]

Behold, there shall be a record kept among you; and in it thou shalt be called a seer, a translator, a prophet, an apostle of Jesus Christ, an elder of the church through the will of God the Father, and the grace of your Lord Jesus Christ, being inspired of the Holy Ghost to lay the foundation thereof, and to build it up unto the most holy faith. Which church was organized and established in the year of your Lord eighteen hundred and thirty, in the fourth month, and on the sixth day of the month which is called April.

Wherefore, meaning the church, thou shalt give heed unto all his words and commandments which he shall give unto you as he receiveth them, walking in all holiness before me; for his word ye shall receive, as if from mine own mouth, in all patience and faith. . . .

For, behold, I will bless all those who labor in my vineyard with a mighty blessing, and they shall believe on his words, which are given him through me by the Comforter, which manifesteth that Jesus was crucified by sinful men for the sins

---

[31]*T&S* 3 (October 15, 1842):944-45.

of the world, yea, for the remission of sins unto the contrite heart. Wherefore it behooveth me that he [Joseph Smith] should be ordained by you, Oliver Cowdery mine apostle; this being an ordinance unto you, that you are an elder under his hand, he being the first unto you, that you might be an elder unto this church of Christ, bearing my name—And the first preacher of this church unto the church, and before the world, yea, before the Gentiles; yea, and thus saith the Lord God, lo, lo! to the Jews also. Amen.

We now proceeded to call out and ordain some others of the brethren to different offices of the priesthood, according as the Spirit manifested unto us; and after a happy time spent in witnessing and feeling for ourselves the powers and the blessings of the Holy Ghost, through the grace of God bestowed upon us, we dismissed with the pleasing knowledge that we were now individually members of, and acknowledged of God, "The Church of Jesus Christ," organized in accordance with commandments and revelations given by him to ourselves in the last days, as well as according to the order of the Church as recorded in the New Testament.

Several persons who had attended the above meeting and got convinced of the truth, came forward shortly after, and were received into the Church; among the rest, my own father and mother were baptized, to my great joy and consolation; and about the same time Martin Harris and A. [Orrin Porter] Rockwell.[32]

Manifestations of the Power of God

Joseph Smith

[Following the organization of the Church, others] were called and ordained by the Spirit of revelation and prophecy, and began to preach as the Spirit gave them utterance, and though weak, yet were they strengthened by the power of God, and many were brought to repentance, were immersed in the water, and were filled with the Holy Ghost by the laying on of hands. They saw visions and prophesied, devils were cast out, and the sick healed by the laying on of hands. From that time the work rolled forth with astonishing rapidity.[33]

---

[32]*T&S* 4 (November 15, 1842):12.

[33]*T&S* 3 (March 1, 1842):708.

The First Miracle

Joseph Smith

During this month of April, I went on a visit to the residence of Mr. Joseph Knight, of Colesville, Broome County, New York, with whom and his family I had been previously acquainted, and of whose name I have above mentioned as having been so kind and thoughtful towards us, while translating the Book of Mormon. Mr. Knight and his family were Universalists, but were willing to reason with me upon my religious views and were as usual friendly and hospitable. We held several meetings in the neighborhood; we had many friends and some enemies. Our meetings were well attended, and many began to pray fervently to Almighty God that he would give them wisdom to understand the truth. Amongst those who attended our meetings regularly was Newel Knight, son to Joseph Knight. He and I had many serious conversations on the important subject of man's eternal salvation. We had got into the habit of praying much at our meetings, and Newel had said that he would try and take up his cross and pray vocally during meeting; but when we again met together, he rather excused himself; I tried to prevail upon him making use of the figure, supposing that he should get into a mud-hole would he not try to help himself out? And [I said] that we were willing now to help him out of the mud-hole. He replied that provided he had got into a mud-hole through carelessness, he would rather wait and get out himself than have others help him; and so he would wait until he should get into the woods by himself, and there he would pray. Accordingly, he deferred praying until next morning, when he retired into the woods; where (according to his own account afterwards) he made several attempts to pray but could scarcely do so, feeling that he had not done his duty, but that he should have prayed in the presence of others. He began to feel uneasy, and continued to feel worse both in mind and body, until, upon reaching his own house, his appearance was such as to alarm his wife very much. He requested her to go and bring me to him. I went and found him suffering very much in his mind, and his body acted upon in a very strange manner. His visage and limbs distorted and twisted in every shape and appearance possible to imagine; and finally he was caught up off the floor of the apartment and tossed about most fearfully.

His situation was soon made known to his neighbors and relatives, and in a short time as many as eight or nine grown persons had got together to witness the scene. After he had thus suffered for a time, I succeeded in getting hold of him by the hand, when almost immediately he spoke to me, and, with great earnestness, requested of me that I should cast the devil out of him, saying that he knew he was in him and that he also knew that I could cast him out. I replied, "If you know that I can it shall be done;" and then almost unconsciously I rebuked the devil and commanded him in the name of Jesus Christ to depart from him; when immediately Newel spoke out and said that he saw the devil leave him and vanish from his sight.

This was the first miracle which was done in this Church, or by any member of it, and it was done not by man nor by the power of man, but it was done by God, and by the power of godliness; therefore, let the honor and the praise, the dominion and the glory be ascribed to the Father, Son, and Holy Spirit for ever and ever. Amen.[34]

The scene was now entirely changed, for as soon as the devil had departed from our friend, his countenance became natural, his distortions of body ceased, and almost immediately the spirit of the Lord descended upon him, and the visions of eternity were opened to his view.—He afterwards related his experience as follows:

> I now began to feel a most pleasing sensation resting upon me, and immediately the visions of heaven were opened to my view. I felt myself attracted upward, and remained for some time enwrapt in contemplation, insomuch that I knew not what was going on in the room. By and by I felt some weight pressing upon my shoulder and the side of my head, which served to recall me to a sense of my situation, and I found that the spirit of the Lord had actually caught me up off the floor, and that my shoulder and head were pressing against the beams.

All this was witnessed by many, to their great astonishment and satisfaction, when they saw the devil thus cast out, and the power of God and his Holy Spirit thus made manifest. So soon as consciousness returned, his bodily weakness was such that we were obliged to lay him upon his bed and wait upon him for some time. As may be expected, such a scene as this contributed much to make believers of those who witnessed it, and finally the greater part of them became members of the Church.

Soon after this occurrence I returned to Fayette, Seneca County. The Book of Mormon, ('The stick of Joseph in the hands of Ephraim') [Ezekiel 37:16-20.] had now been published for some time, and as the ancient

---

[34]*T&S* 4 (November 15, 1842):12-13.

prophet had predicted of it: "It was accounted as a strange thing." No small stir was created by its appearance. Great opposition and much persecution followed the believers of its authenticity; but it had now come to pass that truth had sprung out of the earth; and righteousness had looked down from heaven [Psalm 85:11.]—so we feared not our opponents, knowing that we had both truth and righteousness on our side; that we had both the Father and the Son, because we had the doctrines of Christ, and abided in them; and therefore we continued to preach, and to give information to all who were willing to hear.[35]

Confirmation of the First Miracle and Other Manifestations of God's Power

Newel Knight

[Shortly after the first miracle occurred, Newel Knight was called to testify in court concerning this incident. Joseph Smith had been arrested in Colesville, New York, probably for disturbing the peace, and Newel Knight recorded in his autobiography his response to questions he was asked during this trial by one of the attorneys.]

Question.—"Did the prisoner, Joseph Smith, Jun., cast the devil out of you?"

Answer.—"No, sir."

Question.—"Why, have you not had the devil cast out of you?"

A.—"Yes, sir."

Q.—"And had not Joseph Smith some hand in it being done?"

A.—"Yes, sir."

Q.—"And did he not cast him out of you?"

A.—"No, sir, it was done by the power of God, and Joseph Smith was the instrument in the hands of God on this occaion. He commanded him to come out of me in the name of Jesus Christ."

Q.—"And are you sure it was the devil?"

A.—"Yes, sir."

Q.—"Did you see him after he was cast out of you?"

A.—"Yes, sir, I saw him."

Q.—"Pray, what did he look like?"

(Here one of the lawyers on the part of the defense told me I need not answer that question). I replied:

---

[35]*T&S* 4 (December 1, 1842):22.

"I believe, I need not answer you that question, but I will do it if I am allowed to ask you one, and you can answer it. Do you, Mr. Seymour, understand the things of the Spirit?"

"No," answered Mr. Seymour, "I do not pretend to such big things."

"Well, then," I replied, "it will be of no use for me to tell you what the devil looked like, for it was a spiritual sight and spiritually discerned, and, of course, you would not understand it were I to tell you of it."

The lawyer dropped his head, while the loud laugh of the audience proclaimed his discomfiture . . . .[36]

[The recipient of the first miracle, Newel Knight, received the priesthood shortly after being baptized and confirmed and after receiving this authority became an instrument in God's hand in performing miracles.[37] The following selections by Newel Knight illustrate that the power which had been bestowed upon Joseph Smith and Oliver Cowdery was in turn bestowed upon others.]

After the close of the meeting [held on October 14, 1830] Brother Hyrum [Smith] and myself intended going to spend the night with one of the brethren who lived a short distance from my uncle's, but as were ready to start, the Spirit whispered to me that I should tarry there at my uncle's all night. I did so, and retired to bed, where I rested till midnight when my uncle came to my room and desired me to get up, saying he feared his wife [Electa Peck] was about to die. This surprised me, as she was quite well when I went to bed. I dressed myself, and having asked my Heavenly Father to give me wisdom, and power to rebuke the destroyer from the habitation, I went to the room where my aunt lay. She was in a most fearful condition; her eyes were closed, and she appeared to be in the last agonies of death. Presently she opened her eyes, and bade her husband and children farewell, telling them she must die for the redemption of this generation, as Jesus Christ had died for the generation in His day. Her whole frame shook, and she appeared to be racked with the most exquisite pain and torment; her hands and feet were cold, and the blood setled in her fingers; while her husband and children stood weep-

---

[36]"Newel Knight's Journal," *Scraps of Biography. Tenth Book of the Faith-Promoting Series* (Salt Lake City: Juvenile Instructor Office, 1883), pp, 59-60. Newel Knight also included in his journal the account of this miracle written by Joseph Smith with the following introduction: "In order that my children may know how the Lord has dealt with me I will make this extract from Joseph Smith's history." (Ibid., pp. 50-52.)

[37]Jenson, *Biographical Encyclopedia*, 2:773-74.

ing around her bed. This was a scene new to me, and I felt she was suffering under the power of Satan—that was the same spirit that had bound and overpowered me at the time Joseph cast him out. I now cried unto the Lord for strength and wisdom that we might prevail over this wicked and delusive power. Just at this time my uncle cried aloud to me saying: "O, Brother Newel, cannot something be done?" I felt the Holy Spirit of the Lord rest upon me as he said this, and I immediately stepped forward, took her by the hand, and commanded Satan, in the name of the Lord Jesus Christ, to depart. I told my aunt she would not die, but that she should live to see her children grown up; that Satan had deceived her, and put a lying spirit in her mouth; that Christ had made the only and last atonement for all who would believe on His name; and that there should be no more shedding of blood for sin. She believed and stretched forth her hand, and cried unto me, and Satan departed from her . . . .[38]

[In April 1831, during a migration of Latter-day Saints from New York to Ohio] my aunt, Electa Peck, fell and broke her shoulder in a most shocking manner; a surgeon was called to relieve her sufferings, which were very great. My aunt dreamed that I returned and laid my hands upon her, prayed for her, and she was made whole, and pursued her journey with the company. She related this dream to the surgeon who replied, "If you are able to travel in many weeks it will be a miracle, and I will be a Mormon too."

I arrived at the place, where the company had stopped, late in the evening; but, on learning of the accident, I went to see my aunt, and immediately on my entering the room she said, "O, Brother Newel, if you will lay your hands upon me, I shall be well and able to go on the journey with you." I stepped up to the bed, and, in the name of the Lord Jesus Christ, rebuked the pain with which she was suffering, and commanded her to be made whole; and it was done; for the next morning she arose, dressed herself, and pursued the journey with us.[39]

Summary

Diedrich Willers, German Reformed Minister of Fayette

Since last year [1830] all of the neighboring congregations have been frequently and earnestly warned to beware of this so-called Golden Book

---

[38]"Newel Knight's Journal," pp. 66-67.

[39]Ibid., p. 69.

[Book of Mormon] and not to buy any. The above-named Smith, however, found his followers . . . . Already in this region more [copies of the Book of Mormon] have been sold than one would have expected . . . . The author has already been frequently challenged to demonstrate his inspiration, as did the Apostles, through genuine miracles. Naturally he cannot perform such. His followers, however, claim that through their preachers devils have been cast out recently . . . .

The effects of this book (Book of Mormon) already extend upon members of various Christian persuasions. Some members of the Lutheran, Reformed, Presbyterian, and Baptist congregations have given this book their approval, have been baptized by immersion, and formed their own sect. Because they baptize by immersion they are winning over many members of the Baptist Church (including General as well as Particular Baptists), first because of their teachings about the universal grace of God and lastly because of their agreement in attitude toward the proper subject of holy baptism.

This upstart sect calls itself The True Followers of Christ; however, because they believe in the Book of Mormon, they bear the name Mormonites. For the past several Sundays many people of both sexes have been immersed by them, and so many during the week that their numbers in the region hereabouts may amount to at least 100 persons. They have their own preachers whom I know, Oliver Cowdery by description and David Whitmer (the so-called Angel-viewer) personally. Their sect, however, numbers still other preachers, unknown to me.[40]

Conclusions

Orson Pratt

In the year 1830, a large edition of the "Book of Mormon" first appeared in print. And, as some began to peruse its sacred pages, the spirit of the Lord bore record to them that it was true; and they were obedient to this requirements, by coming forth, humbly repenting before the Lord, and being immersed in water, for the remission of sins, after which, by

---

[40]Letter of Diedrich Willers, June 18, 1830, Cornell University, translated and published in D. Michael Quinn, "The First Months of Mormonism: A Contemporary View by Rev. Diedrich Willers," *New York History* 54 (July 1973):324-33. This letter contains one of the earliest accounts of the birth of Mormonism and was written by Rev. Willers to warn others about the rise of this new faith.

the commandment of God hands were laid upon them in the name of the Lord, for the gift of the Holy Spirit.

And on the sixth of April, in the year of our Lord one thousand eight hundred and thirty, the "Church of Jesus Christ of Latter-day Saints" was organized in the town of Fayette, Seneca County, State of New York, North America. Some few were called and ordained by the spirit of revelation and prophecy, and began to preach and bear testimony, as the spirit gave them utterance; and, although they were the weak things of the earth, yet they were strengthened by the Holy Ghost, and gave forth their testimony in great power, by which means many were brought to repentance, and came forward with broken hearts and contrite spirits, and were immersed in water confessing their sins, and were filled with the Holy Ghost by the laying on of hands; and saw visions and prophesied. Devils were cast out, and the sick were healed by the prayer of faith, and the laying on of hands. Thus was the word confirmed unto the faithful by the signs following. Thus the Lord raised up witnesses to bear testimony of his name, and lay the foundation of his kingdom in the last days. And thus the hearts of the saints were comforted and filled with great joy.[41]

Lucy Smith

By searching the prophecies contained in the Old Testament we find . . . that God will set his hand the second time to recover his people the house of Israel. He has now commenced that work; he hath sent forth a revelation in these last days, and this revelation is called the Book of Mormon. It contains the fulness of the Gospel to the Gentiles, and is sent forth to show unto the remnant of the house of Israel what great things God hath done for their fathers; that they may know of the covenants of the Lord and that they are not cast off forever; and also of the convincing of both Jew and Gentile that Jesus is the Christ, the Eternal God and manifests himself unto all nations . . . .

There are many in these parts who profess to know God and to be his humble followers, but when this thing [the Book of Mormon] is offered them they say we have Bible enough and want no more; but such are in the gall of bitterness and in the bonds of iniquity and understand not the

---

[41]Orson Pratt, *Remarkable Visions* (Liverpool: R. James, 1848), p. 12. In the first edition of this work, Orson Pratt incorrectly wrote that the Chuch was organized in Manchester, New York, but corrected this error in the second edition, changing "Manchester" to "Fayette."

Bible which they love, for all the holy prophets spoke plainly of the gathering of the house of Israel and of the coming forth of this work, and God says he will give us line upon line, precept upon precept, here a little and there a little; there are more nations than one and if God would not reveal himself alike unto all nations he would be partial. We need not suppose that we have all his words in our Bible, neither need we think that because he has spoken once he cannot speak again.

God, seeing our situation, had compassion upon us and has sent us this revelation that the stumbling block might be removed, that whosoever would might enter. He [has] now established his Church upon the earth as it was in the days of the Apostles. He is now sending forth his servants for to prune his vineyard for the last time . . .the work spreading very fast . . .

I must now now close my letter by entreating you [her brother, Solomon Mack] as one that feels for your soul, to seek an interest in Christ and when you have an opportunity to receive this work do not reject it, but read it and examine for yourselves.⁴²

* * * * * *

Eyewitness accounts of the restoration form a powerful array of evidence supporting the reliability of Joseph Smith's testimony concerning the restoration of the everlasting gospel. The Book of Mormon also is a unique witness of the restoration, and is available for careful examination and prayerful study. Although there are many external evidences of the divine calling of Joseph Smith and of the authenticity of the Book of Mormon, evidences do not produce spiritual conversions.

The New Testament declares that "No man can say that Jesus is the Lord, but by the Holy Ghost." (1 Corinthians 12:3.) As Joseph Smith's sister, Katharine Salisbury, read the Book of Mormon she was convinced that without God's guidance her brother could not have brought forth such a work. Nevertheless, her genuine conversion occurred as she read that book with a prayerful heart. "I can testify to the fact of the coming forth of the Book of Mormon," she affirmed, "and also to its truth, and the truth of the everlasting gospel as contained therein . . .Many times when I have read its sacred pages, I have wept like a child, while the Spirit has borne witness with my spirit of its truth."⁴³

---

⁴²Lucy Smith to Solomon Mack, January 6, 1831, Church Archives.

⁴³Katharine Salisbury to "Dear Sisters," March 10, 1886, cited in *The Saints' Herald* 33 (May 1, 1886):260.

While living in Illinois in 1831, Charles C. Rich learned from one of his friends that a new book had been translated from plates of gold found in New York state "by the gift and power of the Holy Ghost", and that a new church had been organized under the direction of a latter-day Prophet. When he first learned about this new book, he said that a peculiar sensation penetrated his whole system and he was filled with joy. At the time he did not understand why he had received such an impression, but later said that he knew it was the "spirit of God testifying" to him "of the truth of the Prophet and the Book of Mormon."[44] In August of that year, two Mormon missionaries preached in his neighborhood and gave him a copy of the Book of Mormon. Recalling some of his reflections while investigating the restored Church, Charles C. Rich declared:

> In the first instructions we received from the Elders, we were told we must repent of our sins and be baptized, in order to receive the Holy Spirit, and that we had no claims upon the Lord for his Spirit, until we had complied with the requirements made of us. I remember very well my feelings upon this subject before I obeyed the Gospel. I studied carefully, anxiously, and prayerfully, that I might know if it were the Church of Jesus Christ. I did not want to run any risk in the matter, and remain in uncertainty. I was willing to do anything that would give me a knowledge of the truth. I was willing to receive it through the ministration of an angel, through direct revelation, or by any other way, but I did not want to be deceived. Every time I reflected carefully upon the subject, I came to this point—the conditions upon which the promises have been made are, repentance, baptism, and imposition of hands. The spirit would then whisper, you have not been baptized, you have not obeyed the Gospel; but when I had complied with the law, then I had a perfect claim to the blesings and the promises, and did receive them, and obtained a perfect knowledge of the truth, and could then bear a testimony of it to all the world.[45]

---

[44]"History of Morris Phelps," p. 2, typescript, Church Archives.

[45]Charles C. Rich in *JD* 19:250.

On April 1, 1832, Charles C. Rich, along with his father, mother, and sixteen year old sister, Minerva, was baptized and confirmed a member of The Church of Jesus Christ of Latter-day Saints.[46]

On December 29, 1833, Wilford Woodruff, a farmer living in upstate New York, listened as two traveling missionaries unfolded to him the message of the restoration. "The spirit of the Lord rested upon me," he wrote and bore witness of the divine authenticity of the Book of Mormon and of the mission of the Prophet Joseph Smith. Immediately after securing a copy of this new witness for Christ he commenced reading, and as he studied the spirit again bore witness that the record which it contained was true." Two days after meeting the Mormon elders, he and his brother, Azmon, and two young ladies who had been healed the day before, stepped from a three foot bank of snow into a body of icy water and were baptized.[47]

Another leader who was a close associate of the Prophet and was converted after reading the Book of Mormon, unfolded to others a key which would enable inquirers to gain a witness of the authenticity of the Book of Mormon and the divine calling of Joseph Smith. In a sermon delivered by Orson Pratt, this missionary, who probably baptized more individuals than any other Latter-day Saint, declared

> [Although] God condescended to raise up . . .twelve witnesses . . .immediately before he organized this Church . . .there [are] other witnesses and evidences concerning the correctness and divinity of this book [Book of Mormon] that are far greater than those I have named. There is a promise to all the human family, that is far better than the ministrations of angels to others . . . .The very message itself in the book, and in the New Testament, and in the modern revelations that are given through the prophet, told me, told you, told all the people upon the face of this earth, how they also might obtain a knowledge of the truth of this Book of

---

[46]Leonard J. Arrington, *Charles C. Rich: Mormon General and Western Frontiersman* (Provo: Brigham Young University Press, 1974), p. 17.

[47]Matthias F. Cowley, *Wilford Woodruff* (Salt Lake City: Bookcraft, 1964), pp. 32-35.

Mormon and of this work. How?...The Lord has promised that...if the people of all nations of the earth will repent, turn unto him and obey his commandments that they should receive the Holy Ghost. Will that give us a knowledge as clear, as definite, as pointed as could be revealed by the ministration of angels? Yes....If I would...exercise...faith,...would obey the commandments, would be obedient to the principles, and then I received for myself the testimony, I should...[not] be dependent upon David Whitmer, Martin Harris nor Oliver Cowdry, Joseph Smith, nor any of the twelve witnesses that saw the plates, nor any other man....I could then say,..."Lord,...thou hast fulfilled thy promise"...[And] from that [time] forth, I could be a witness myself.[48]

---

[48]Orson Pratt in *JD* 21:175-76.

HARMONY OF EIGHT CONTEMPORARY ACCOUNTS OF THE FIRST VISION

(The dates in the first set of parentheses refer to the approximate date when Joseph Smith wrote the account and the letters in the second set of parentheses refer to four other accounts written or published by contemporaries before 1844, namely Orson Pratt's *Several Remarkable Visions* (1840) (identified as "P"); Orson Hyde's *A Cry From the Wilderness* (1842) (identified as "H"); an account written by a non-Mormon and printed in the New York *Spectator*, September 23, 1843 (identified as "S"); and an account recorded in the diary of Alexander Neibaur (identified as "N").

The Historical Setting

Joseph's quest for forgiveness of his sins, his concern for his soul and/or his preparation for future estate	(1832, 1835, 1842) (P, H)
Joseph's concern for mankind in general	(1832) (P, H)
Joseph's investigation of various faiths	(1832, 1835, 1838, 1842) (P, H)

Joseph's concern because faiths proclaimed conflicting doctrines	(1838, 1842) (P, H)
Joseph's desire to know which church to join or his desire to join Christ's church	(1832, 1835, 1838, 1842) (P, H, S)
Joseph's quest continued for several years	(1832)
Unusual religious excitement in the area	(1838) (N)
Contention among the faiths	(1838, 1842) (P, H)
Joseph's searching the Scriptures (Bible)	(1832, 1835, 1838, 1842) (P, H, S, N)
Joseph reading James 1:5	(1835, 1838, 1842) (P, H, S, N)
Joseph seeking an answer through prayer	(1832, 1835, 1838, 1842) (P, H, S, N)
Vision occurred when he was about fourteen or fifteen	(1832, 1835, 1838, 1842) (P, H, S, N)
Vision occurred in the spring of 1820	(1838)

The Vision (Truths revealed and descriptions of what Joseph beheld)

God hears and answers prayers and intervenes in the affairs of men	(1832, 1835, 1838, 1842) (P, H, S, N)
The power of evil is real and strong	(1835, 1838) (P, H)
The power of God is stronger than the influence of evil	(1835, 1838) (P, H)
Joseph was enrapt in a pillar of light and/or filled with unspeakable joy (or the spirit of God)	(1832, 1835, 1838) (P, H)
Joseph beheld two personages	(1835, 1838, 1842) (P, H, S, N)
The two personages resembled each other in features and likeness	(1835, 1838, 1842) (P, H)
The two personages were identified as the Father and the Son (Joseph learned that man was created in the image of God).	(1838) (S)
Joseph saw many angels	(1835)

The Message

Jesus Christ is the Son of God	(1835, 1838) (S)
The Lord was crucified for the world and all who believe in him will have eternal life	(1832)
The Second Coming of Christ is imminent	(1832)
Joseph was forgiven of his transgressions	(1832, 1835) (P, N)
God's true church was not upon the earth in 1820	(1832, 1838, 1842) (P, H, N)
Professors of religion taught incorrect doctrines	(1832, 1838, 1842) (P, H, N)
Professors of religion denied the power of God	(1838)
The fulness of the gospel would be revealed to Joseph	(1842) (P, H)
Joseph learned many other truths	(1838)

Aftermath

Joseph rejoiced for he was filled with peace and love	(1832) (P, H)
Joseph's unsuccessful attempt to convince ministers and others outside his family of his vision	(1838) (N)
Joseph persecuted after reporting his vision	(1832, 1838) (S)

HARMONY OF SEVEN CONTEMPORARY ACCOUNTS OF MORONI'S VISITATIONS (SEPTEMBER 21-22, 1823)

[The dates in the first set of parentheses refer to the approximate date when Joseph Smith wrote the account, and the letters in the second set refer to three other accounts written by close associates of the Prophet, namely Oliver Cowdery's letters published in the *Latter-day Saints' Messenger and Advocate* (Kirtland, Ohio) in 1834-1835 (identified as "C"); Orson Pratt's *Several Remarkable Visions* (1840) (identified as "P"); and Lucy Mack Smith's *Biographical Sketches of Josph Smith, the Prophet, and his Progenitors for many Generations* (1853) (identified as "LS"). Since Lucy Smith included in her biography of her son (Joseph) the Prophet's account that was written in 1838 and published in the *Times and Seasons* (Nauvoo, Illinois) in 1842, this harmony only includes statements by Lucy that are not direct quotations from Joseph Smith's 1838 history.]

Descriptions of That Which Joseph Learned and Beheld

Moroni was a heavenly messenger   (1835, 1838) (C, P)
   who had a tangible body (a re-

surrected body). The angel was a   (C, P)
little larger than most men of
Joseph's time.

The vision commenced about mid-   (C)
night.

Joseph was told that his sins were   (1832) (C, P)
forgiven.

Joseph learned that he was a cho-   (1838, 1842) (C, P)
sen instrument to bring about
some of the purposes of God.

Joseph learned that his name   (1838) (C, P)
should be known for good and
evil among all nations.

Joseph learned about the composi-   (1832, 1835, 1838, 1842) (C, P)
tion of the Book of Mormon.
The Book of Mormon contains   (1838) (C, P)
the fulness of the gospel as delivered by Christ to the ancient
inhabitants of America.

Joseph learned that the Book of   (1832, 1835, 1838) (C)
Mormon plates were deposited
in a hill near his home.

Joseph learned that two transpa-   (1838, 1842) (P)
rent stones in silver bows were
deposited with the plates and
these stones, fastened to a
breastplate, constituted the
Urim and Thummim.

The Urim and Thummim was to aid   (1835, 1838) (C, P)
Joseph in translating the record.

Joseph was told to show the plates   (1835, 1838) (C)
and Urim and Thummim only to
those identified by revelation.

The messenger appeared three times that night, repeating his instructions of the first visitation during the other visions. (1832, 1835, 1838, 1842) (C, P)

Joseph was warned that Satan would try to tempt him. (1838) (C)

The visions occupied most of the night. (1835, 1838) (C)

Moroni quoted a series of Biblical prophecies, informing Joesph of the characteristics and imminence of the Second Coming, including (1835, 1838, 1842) (C, P)

Malachi 3 (1838)
Malachi 4 (1835, 1838)
Isaiah 11 (1838) (C)
Acts 3:22-23 (Joseph learned that the prophet mentioned here was Christ.) (1838)
Joel 2:28-32

He learned that the fulness of the Gentiles was soon to "come in." (1838) (C)

Moroni quoted many other scriptures and commented on many of the Biblical passages. (1838) (C)

Joseph learned that the basic Bible message was correct, but that there were mis-translations in the Bible. (Malachi 4 was quoted with some variations from the King James Version.) (1838)

The angel appeared a fourth time in the field. (1832, 1835, 1838) (C, P, LS)

The angel appeared a fifth time on the hill where the plates were deposited. (1832, 1838) (C, P, LS)

He saw the glory of God and Satan & his hosts.	(C)
Joseph saw the plates and Urim and Thummim. They were in a stone box buried in the hill.	(1835, 1838) (C, P) (1838) (C, P)
Joseph was not permitted to take the plates.	(1832, 1835, 1838) (C, P)
Joseph was told to return to the hill each year to receive additional instructions.	(1835, 1838) (LS)

Selections From
REV. JOHN A. CLARK'S
DESCRIPTIONS OF THE
RISE OF MORMONISM*

It was early in the autumn of 1827 that Martin Harris called at my house in Palmyra, one morning about sunrise. His whole appearance indicted more than usual excitement, and he had scarcely passed the threshold of my dwelling, before he inquired whether he could see me alone, remarking that he had a matter to communicate that he wished to be strictly confidential. Previous to this, I had but very slight acquaintance with Mr. Harris. He had occasionally attended divine service in our church. I had heard him spoken of as a farmer in comfortable circumstances, residing in the country a short distance from the village, and distinguished by certain peculiarities of character. He had been, if I mistake not, at one period, a member of the Methodist Church, and subsequently had identified himself with the Universalists. At this time, however, in his religious views he seemed to be floating upon the sea of uncertainty. He had evidently quite an extensive knowledge of the Scriputres, and possessed a manifest disputatious turn of mind. As I subsequently learned, Mr. Harris had always been a firm believer in dreams, and visions, and supernatural appearances, such as apparitions

*[Based upon conversations with Martin Harris during the autumn of 1827 and early 1828, as published in Gleanings By the Way (Philadelphia: W.J. and J.K. Simon, 1842), pp. 222-31].

and ghosts, and therefore was a fit subject for such men as Smith and his colleagues to operate upon. On the occasion just referred to, I invited him to accompany me to my study, where, after having closed the door, he began to draw a package out of his pocket with great and manifest caution. Suddenly, however, he stopped, and wished to know if there was any possibility of our being interrupted or overheard? When answered in the negative, he proceeded to remark, that he reposed great confidence in me as a minister of Jesus Christ, and that what he had now to communicate he wished me to regard as strictly confidential. He said he verily believed that an important epoch had arrived—that a great flood of light was about to burst upon the world, and that the scene of divine manifestation was to be immediately around us. In explanation of what he meant, he then proceeded to remark that a GOLDEN BIBLE had recently been dug from the earth, where it had been deposited for thousands of years, and that this would be found to contain such disclosures as would settle all religious controversies and speedily bring on the glorious millennium. That this mysterious book, which no human eye of the present generation has yet seen, was in the possession of Joseph Smith, jr., ordinarily known in the neighbourhood under the more familiar designation of *Jo Smith*; that there had been a revelation made to him by which he had discovered this sacred deposit, and two transparent stones, through which, as a sort of spectacles, he could read the Bible, although the box or ark that contained it, had not yet book opened; and that by looking through those mysterious stones he had transcribed from one of the leaves of this book, the characters which Harris had so carefully wrapped in the package which he was drawing from his pocket. The whole thing appeared to me so ludicrous and puerile, that I could not refrain from telling Mr. Harris, that I believed it a mere hoax got up to practice upon his credulity, or an artifice to extort from him money; for I had already, in the course of the conversation, learned that he had advanced some twenty-five dollars to Jo Smith as a sort of premium for sharing with him in the glories and profits of this new revelation. For at this time, his mind seemed to be quite as intent upon the pecuniary advantage that would arise from the possession of the plates of solid gold of which this book was composed, as upon the spiritual light it would diffuse over the world. My intimations to him, in reference to the possible imposition that was being practiced upon him, however, were indignantly repelled. He then went on to relate the particulars in regard to the discovery and possession of this marvellous book. As far as I can now recollect, the following was an outline of the narrative which he then communicated to me, and subsequently to scores of people in the village, from some of whom in my late visit to Palmyra, I have been able to recall several particulars that had quite glided from my memory.

Before I proceed to Martin's narrative, however, I would remark in passing, that Jo Smith, who has since been the chief prophet of the Mormons, and was one of the most prominent ostensible actors in the first scenes of this drama, belonged to a very shiftless family near Palmyra. They lived a sort of vagrant life, and were principally known as *money-diggers*. Jo from a boy appeared dull and utterly destitute of genius; but his father claimed for him a sort of second sight, a power to look into the depths of the earth, and discover where its precious treasures were hid. Consequently long before the idea of a GOLDEN BIBLE entered their minds, in their excursions for money-digging, which I believe usually occurred in the night, that they might conceal from others the knowledge of the place, where they struck their treasures, Jo used to be usually their guide, putting into a hat a peculiar stone he had through which he looked to decide where they should begin to dig.

According to Martin Harris, it was after one of these night excursions, that Jo, while he lay upon his bed, had a remarkable dream. An angel of God seemed to approach him, clad in celestial splendor. This divine messenger assured him, that he, Joseph Smith, was chosen of the Lord to be a prophet of the Most High God, and to bring to light hidden things, that would prove of unspeakable benefit to the world. He then disclosed to him the existence of this golden Bible, and the place where it was deposited—but at the same time told him that he must follow implicitly the divine direction, or he would draw down upon him the wrath of heaven. This book, which was contained in a chest, or ark, and which consisted of metallic plates covered with characters embossed in gold, he must not presume to look into, under three years . . . . After his marriage and return from Pennsylvania, he became so awfully impressed with the high destiny that awaited him, that he communicated the secret to his father and family. The money-digging propensity of the old man operated so powerfully, that he insisted upon it that they should go and dig and see if the chest was there—not with any view to remove it till the appointed time, but merely to satisfy themselves. Accordingly they went forth in the stillness of the night with their spades and mattcocks to the spot where slumbered this sacred deposit. They had proceeded but a little while in the work of excavation, before the mysterious chest appeared; but lo! instantly it moved and glided along out of their sight. Directed, however, by the *clairvoyance* of Jo, they again penetrated to the spot where it stood, and succeeded in gaining a partial view of its dimensions. But while they were pressing forward to gaze at it, the thunder of the Almighty shook the spot, and made the earth to tremble—a sheet of vivid lightning swept along over the side of the hill, and burnt terribly around the place where the excavation was going on, and again with a rumbling noise, the chest moved off out of their sight. They were all terrified and fled towards their home. Jo took his course silently along by himself. On his way homeward, being alone and in the woods, the angel of the Lord met him, clad in terror and wrath. He spoke in a voice of thunder: forked lightnings shot through the trees, and ran along upon the ground. The terror which the appearance of the divine messenger awakened, instantly struck Smith to the earth, and he felt his whole frame convulsed with agony, as though he were stamped upon by the iron hoofs of death himself. In language most terrific did the angel upbraid him for his disobedience, and then disappeared. Smith went home trembling and full of terror. Soon, however, his mind became more composed. Another divine communication was made to him, authorizing him to go along by himself and bring the chest and deposit it secretly under the hearth of his dwelling, but by no means to attempt to look into it. The reason assigned by the angel for this removal, was that some report in relation to the place where this sacred book was deposited had gone forth, and there was danger of its being disturbed. According to Harris, Smith now scrupulously followed the divine directions. He was already in possession of the two transparent stones laid up with the GOLDEN BIBLE, by looking through which he was enabled to read the golden letters on the plates in the box. How he obtained these spectacles without opening the chest, Harris could not tell. But still he had them; and by means of them he could read all the book contained. The book itself was not to be disclosed until Smith's child had attained a certain age. Then it might be published to the world. In the interim, Smith was to prepare the way for the conversion of the world to a new system of faith, by transcribing the characters from the plates and giving translations of the same. This was the substance of Martin Harris' communication to me upon our first interview. He then carefully unfolded a slip of paper, which contained three or four lines of characters, as unlike letters of hieroglyphics of any sort, as well could be produced were one to shut up his eyes and play off the most antic movements with his pen upon paper. The only thing that bore the slightest resemblance to the letter of any language that I had ever seen, was two uprights marked joined by a horizontal line, that might have been taken for the Hebrew character ח. My ignorance of the characters in which the pretended ancient record was written, was to Martin Harris new proof that Smith's whole account of the divine revelation made to him was entirely to be relied on.

[Journey to New York]

He was so much in earnest on this subject, that he immediately started off with some of the manuscripts that Smith furnished him on a journey to New York and Washington to consult some learned men to ascertain the nature of the language in which this record was engraven. After his return he came to see me again, and told me that, among others, he had consulted Professor Anthon, who thought the characters in which the book was written very remarkable, but he could not decide exactly what language they belonged to. Martin had now become a perfect believer. He said he had no more doubt of Smith's commission, than of the divine commission of the apostles. The very fact that Smith was an obscure and illiterate man, showed that he must be acting under divine impulses:—"God had chosen the foolish things of the world to confound the wise, and the weak things to confound the mighty; and base things of the world, and things which are despised—yea, and things that are not to bring to nought—things that are—that no flesh should glory in his pre-sense:" that he was willing to "take of the spoiling of his goods" to sustain Smith in carrying on this work of the Lord; and that he was determined that the book should be published, though it consumed all his worldly substance. It was in vain I endeavoured to expostulate. I was an unbe-liever, and could not see afar off. As for him he must follow the light which the Lord had given him . . . . The way that Smith made his trans-cripts and translations for Harris was the following. Although in the same room, a thick curtain or blanket was suspended between them, and Smith concealed behind the blanket, pretended to look through his spectacles, or transparent stones, and would then write down or repeat what he saw, which, when repeated aloud, was written down by Harris, who sat on the other side of the suspended blanket. Harris was told that it would arouse the most terrible divine displeasure, if he should attempt to draw near the sacred chest, or look at Smith while engaged in the work of decyphering the mysterious characters. This was Harris's own account of the matter to me. What other measures they afterwards took to transcribe or translate from these metallic plates, I cannot say, as I very soon after this removed to another field of labour where I heard no more of this matter till I learned the BOOK OF MORMON was about being published . . . . This book, which professed to be a translation of the golden Bible brought to light by Joseph Smith, was published in 1830—to accomplish which Martin Harris actually mortagaged his farm.

LETTERS OF CHARLES ANTHON

The first of these letters describing Martin Harris' conversation with Charles Anthon was published in E. D. Howe's *Mormonism Unvailed* (1834), pp. 270-72 and the second in John A. Clark's *Gleanings by the Way* (1842), pp. 233, 237-38. These letters are reproduced in this appendix in parallel columns to aid the reader in identifying their similarities and differences. Contradictory statements have been placed in italics.

Anthon's Letter to E. D. Howe February 17, 1834	Anthon's Letter to Rev. T. W. Coit April 3, 1841
Dear Sir: *I receive this morning your favor of the 9th instant, and lose no time in making a reply.* The whole story about my having pronounced the Mormonite inscription to be "reformed Egyptian hieroglyphics" is perfectly false.	Rev. and Dear Sir: I have often heard that the Mormons claimed me for an auxiliary, but as *no one, until the present time has ever requested from me a statement in writing,* I hve not deemed it worthwhile to say anything publicly on the subject. What I do know of the sect relates to some of the early movements; and as the facts may amuse you, while they will furnish a satisfactory answer to the charge of my being a Mormon

proselyte, I proceed to lay them before you in detail.

Some years ago, a plain, and apparently simple-hearted farmer, called upon me with a note from Dr. Mitchell of our city, now deceased, requesting me to decypher, if possible, a paper, which the farmer would hand me, and which Dr. M. confessed he had been unable to understand. Upon examining the paper in question, I soon came to the conclusion that it was all a trick, perhaps a hoax.

Many years ago, the precise date I do not now recollect, a plain looking countryman called upon me with a letter from Dr. Samuel L. Mitchell requesting me to examine, and give my opinion upon, a certain paper, marked with various characters which the Doctor confessed he could not decypher, and which the bearer of the note was very anxious to have explained. A very brief examination of the paper convinced me that it was a mere hoax, and a very clumsy one, too. The characters were arranged in colunmns, like the Chinese mode of writing, and presented the most singular medley that I ever beheld. Greek, Hebrew, and all sorts of letters, more or less distorted, either through unskillfullness or from actual design, were intermingled with sundry delineations of half moons, stars, and other natural objects, and the whole ended in a rude representation of the Mexican zodiac. The conclusion was irresistible, that some cunning fellow had prepared the paper in question, for the purpose of imposing upon he who brought it, and I told the man so without any hesitation. He then proceeded to give me a history of the whole affair, which convinced me that he had fallen into the hands of some sharper, while it left me in great astonishment at his own simplicity.

When I asked the person, who brought it, how he obtained the writing, he gave me, as far as I can now recollect, the following account:

A "gold book," consisting of a number of plates of gold, fastened together in the shape of a book by wires of the same metal, had been dug up in the northern part of the state of New York,

The countryman told me that a gold book had been recently dug up in the western or northern part (I forget which), of our state and he described this book as consisting of many gold plates, like leaves, secured by a gold wire passing through the edge of each, just as the leaves of a book are sewed together, and presented in this way the appearance of a volume. Each plate, according to him, was inscribed with unknown characters, and the paper which he handed me, a transcript of one of these pages. On my asking him by whom the copy was made, he gravely stated, that along with the golden book there had been dug up a very large pair of spectacles! so large in fact that if a man were to hold them in front of his face, his two eyes would the remaining part of the spectacles would project a considerable distance sideways! These spectacles possessed, it seems a very valuable property, of enabling any one who looked through them, (or rather through one of the lenses,) not only to decypher the characters on the plates, but also to comprehend their exact meaning, and be able to translate them! My informant assured me that this curious property of the spectacles had been actually tested, and found to be true.

and along with the book an enormous pair of "gold spectacles"! These spectacles were so large, that, if a person attempted to look through them, his two eyes would have to be turned towards one of the glasses merely, the spectacles in question being altogether too large for the breadth of the human face. Whoever examined the plates through the spectacles, was enabled not only to read them but to fully understand their meaning.

All this knowledge, however, was confined at that time to a young man, who had the trunk containing the book and spectacles in his sole possession. This young man was placed behind a curtain, in the garret of a farm house, and, being thus concealed from view, put on the spectacles occasionally, or rather, looked through one of the glasses, decyphered the characters in the book, and, having committed some of them to paper, handed copies from behind the curtain, to those who stood on the outside. Not a word, however, was said about the plates having been decyphered "by the gift of God." Every thing, in this way, was effected by the large pair of spectacles.

The farmer added, that he had been requested to contribute a sum of money towards the publication of the "golden book," the contents of which would, as he had been assured, produce an entire change in the world and save it from ruin. So urgent had been these solicitations, that he intended selling his farm and handing over the amount received to those who wished to publish the plates.

A young man, it seems, had been placed in the garret of a farm-house, with a curtain before him, and having fastened the spectacles to his head had read several pages in the golden book, and communicated their contents in writing to certain persons stationed on the outside of the curtain.

He had also copied off one page of the book in the original character, which he had in like manner handed over to those who were separated from him by the curtain, and this copy was the paper which the countryman had brought with him. As the golden book was said to contain very great truths, and most important revelations of a religious nature, a strong desire had been expressed by several persons in the countryman's neighborhood, to have the whole work translated and published. A proposition had accordingly been made to my informant, to sell his farm, and apply the proceeds to the printing of the golden book, and the golden plates were to be left with him as a security until he should be reimbursed by the sale of the work. To convince him more clearly that there was no risk what-

As a last precautionary step, however, he had resolved to come to New York, and obtain the opinion of the learned about the meaning of the paper which he brought with him, and which had been given him as a part of the contents of the book,

ever in the matter, and that the work was actually what it claimed to be, he was told to take the paper which purported to be a copy of one of the pages of the book, to the city of New York, and submit it to the learned in that quarter, who would soon dispel all his doubts, and satisfy him as to the perfect safety of the investment.

although no translation had been furnished at that time by the young man with the spectacles.

As Dr. Mitchell was our "Magnus Apollo" in those days, the man called first upon him: but the Doctor, evidently suspecting some trick, declined giving any opinion about the matter, and sent the countryman down to the college, to see, in all probability, what the "learned pundits" in that place would make of the affair.

On hearing this odd story, I changed my opinion about the paper, and, instead of viewing it any longer as a hoax upon the learned, I began to regard it as part of a scheme to cheat the farmer of his money, and I communicated my suspicions to him, warning him to beware of rogues. *He requested an opinion from me in writing, which of course I declined giving,*

On my telling the bearer of the paper that an attempt had been made to impose on him, and defraud him of his property,

he requested me to give him my opinion in writing about the paper which he had shown to me. I did so without any hesitation, partly for the man's sake, and partly to let the individual "behind the curtain" see that his trick was discovered. The import of what I wrote was, as far as I can now recollect, simply this, that the marks in the

and he then took his leave carrying the paper with him.

paper appeared to be merely an imitation of various alphabetical characters, and had, in my opinion, no meaning at all connected with them.

The countrman then took his leave, with many thanks, and with the express declaration that he would in no shape part with his farm or embark in the speculation of printing the golden book.

This paper was in fact a singular scrawl. It consisted of all kinds of crooked characters disposed in columns, and had evidently been prepared by some person who had before him at the time a book containing various alphabets. Greek and Hebrew letters, crosses and flourishes, Roman letters inverted or placed side-ways, were arranged in perpendicular columns, and the whole ended in a rude delineation of a circle divided into various compartments, decked with various strange marks, and evidently copied after the Mexican Calendar given by Humboldt, but copied in such a way as not to betray the source whence it was derived. I am thus particular as to the contents of the paper, inasmuch as I have frequently conversed with my friends on the subject, since the Mormonite excitement began, and well remember that the paper contained anything else but "Egyptian hieroglyphics."

The matter rested here for a considerable time, until one day, when

I had ceased entirely to think of the countryman and his paper, this

Some time after, the same farmer paid me a second visit. He brought with him the golden book in print, and offered it to me for sale. I declined purchasing.

same individual, to my great surprise, paid me a second visit. He now brought with him a duodecimo volume, which he said was a translation into English of the "Golden Bible." He also stated, that notwithstanding his original determination not to sell his farm, he had been induced eventually to do so, and apply the money to the publication of the book, and had received the golden plates as a security for repayment. He begged my

He then asked permission to leave the book with me for examination.

acceptance of the volume, assuring me that it would be found to be extremely interesting, and that it was already "making a great noise" in the upper part of the state. Suspecting now that some serious trick was on foot, and that my plain looking visitor might be in fact a

I declined receiving it,

very cunning fellow I declined his present, and merely contended myself with a slight examination of the volume while he stood by. The

although his manner became strangely urgent.

more I declined receiving it however, the more urgent the man became in offering the book, until at last I told him plainly, that if he left the volume, as he said he intended to do, I should most assuredly throw it after him as he departed.

I adverted once more to the roguery which had been in my opinion practiced upon him, and asked him what had become of the plates.

I then asked him how he could be so foolish as to sell his farm and engage in this affair; and requested him to tell me if the plates were really of gold. In answer to this latter inquiry, he said that he had never seen the plates themselves,

He informed me that they were in a

which were carefully locked up in a

trunk with the large pair of spectacles.

I advised him to go to a magistrate and have the trunk examined.

He said the "curse of God" would come upon him should he do this. On my pressing him, however, to pursue the course which I had recommended, he told me that he would open the trunk if I would take the "curse of God" upon myself. I replied that I would do so with the greatest willingness, and would incur every risk of that nature, provided I could only extricate him from the grasp of rogues. He then left me.

I have thus given you a full statement of all that I know respecting the origin of Mormonism,

trunk, but that he had the trunk in his possession.

I advised him by all means to open the trunk and examine its contents, and if the plates proved to be of gold, which I did not believe at all, to sell them immediately. His reply was, that if he opened the trunk, the "curse of heaven would descend upon him and his children." "However," added he, "I will agree to open it, provided you will take the 'curse of Heaven' upon yourself for having advised me to the step." I told him I was perfectly willing to do so, and begged he would hasten home and examine the trunk, for he would find he had been cheated. He promised to do as I recommended, and left me, taking his book with him. I have never seen him since.

Such is a plain statement of all that I know respecting the Mormons. My impression now is, that the plain-looking countryman was none other than the prophet Smith himself, who assumed an appearance of great simplicity in order to entrap me, if possible, into some recommendation of his book. That the prophet aided me by his inspirtion, in interpreting the volume, is only of the many amusing falsehoods which the Mormonites utter relative to my participation in their doctrines. Of these doctrines I know nothing whatever, nor have I ever heard a single discourse from any of their preachers, although I have often felt a strong curiosity to become an auditor, since my friends tell me that they frequently name me in their sermons, and even go so far to say that I am alluded to in the prophecies of Scripture!

and must beg of you, as a personal favor, to publish this letter immediately, should you find my name mentioned again by these wretched fanatics.

If what I have written shall prove of any service in opening the eyes of some of their deluded followers to the real designs of those who profess to be the apostles of Mormonism, it will afford me satifisation, equalled, I have no doubt only by that which yourself will feel on this subject.

Yours respectfully,

I remain very respectfully and truly your friend,

Signed CHAS. ANTHON

Signed CHAS. ANTHON

AN INTERVIEW WITH MARTIN HARRIS

Published in the *Iowa State Register* (Des Moines), August 16, 1870

(While Martin Harris was traveling from Kirtland, Ohio, to Salt Lake City, Utah, in 1870 with Edward Stevenson, he was interviewed by a non-Mormon reporter. Although this testimony which was printed in the Sunday morning edition of the *Iowa State Register* is similar to many other statements made by this witness, it is the only known statement by one of the elelven witnesses in which an estimate is given of the weight of the plates from which the Book of Mormon was translated.)

A witness to the Book of Mormon.—The main facts, or the fiction, as the case may be, relative to the discovery of the golden plates from which was translated the present, Book of Mormon, are doubtless as familiar to many of our readers as to ourselves. None of us can claim to have been an eye witness, and few have heard the incidents connected therewith related by those who claimed to have been there, to have seen and handled the tablets of gold, and afterwards, under the divine commission, to have assisted in the translation of the mystic characters inscribed upon them.

A few days since we acknowledged a call at our sanctum, from Martin Harris, who was on his way from Ohio to take up his residence at Salt Lake City, to spend the remainder of his days with the "chosen people." Mr. Harris was now in his 88th year, though still quite vigorous and sprightly, and he is Mormon, soul and body. He, as he claims, and as Mormons claim, together with two others, Oliver Cowdry deceased, and David Whitmer, now an apostate living in Missouri, were the divinely appointed witnesses to the Book of Mormon. The old gentleman evidently loves to relate the incidents with which he was personally connected, and he does it with wonderful enthusiasm.

In September, 1828, as the story goes, Joseph Smith, directed by an angel, proceeded to a spot about 4 miles from Palmyra, New York, and upon the point of a hill, extending northward, dug up a very solid stone chest within which were the tablets of gold, inscribed with the characters which no man could read. Joseph Smith was the first to handle the tablets, and Martin Harris, one of the appointed witnesses, the second. Mr. Harris describes the plates as being of thin leaves of gold, measuring seven by eight inches, and weighing altogether, from forty to sixty lbs. There was also found in the chest, the urim and thummim, by means of which the writing upon the plates was translated, but not until after the most learned men had exhausted their knowledge of letters in the vain effort to decipher the characters.

It had been revealed to Joseph Smith that the writing upon the tablets contained a history of the aborigines of this country down to the time of Columbus' discovery, and after, all human means had failed to secure a translation, Smith was commissioned to undertake the task. By means of the urim and thummim "a pair of large spectacles," as Mr. Harris termed them, the translation was made, and Mr. Harris claims to have written, of the translations as they were given by Smith, "116 solid pages of cap." The remainder was written by others.

Soon after the finding of these plates of gold, Mr. Harris sold his farm, of which he owned a large one, and consecrated himself to the new religion, to which he has adhered himself tenaciously throughout a long life, and still adheres to its tenets and advocates its genuineness with all the earnestness of an enthusiast. he believes in visitation of angels in bodily form, he has seen and conversed with them, as he thinks and is satisfied.

The old gentleman related some incidents, which, could one feel that they were verities, would be interesting, but as they seem largely imaginative they lose interest.

AN INTERVIEW WITH DAVID WHITMER

In 1881 David Whitmer was interviewed by a reporter of the *Kansas City Journal*. After an article was published in that paper, based on this interview, David Whitmer identified what he considered to be the major errors in the article and his corrections were published in a subsequent issue. In a letter written by Whitmer on November 18, 1881, Whitmer asserted that the article with the corrections was "substantially correct." The following are excerpts from that article as it was published on June 5, 1881. Corrections that appeared on June 19, 1981, and those noted in his letter of November 18 have been inserted in brackets. The importance of this selection, therefore, is that it was written by a competent non-Mormon reporter; and after David Whitmer had an opportunity to correct the major mistakes in the article, he verified the general accuracy of the report. See *Kansas City Journal*, June 5 1881; David Whitmer to S. T. Mouch, November 18, 1881, Whitmer Papers, typescript, RLDS Church Library Archives; *MS* (1881):421-23, 437-39.

MORMONISM.
Authentic Account of the Origin of This
Sect from One of the Patriarchs.

Discovery of the Plates,

And the Translation of the Book of Mormon—

I first heard of what is now termed Mormonism in the year 1828. I made a business trip to Palmyra, N. Y., and while there stopped with one Oliver Cowdery. A great many people in the neighborhood were talking about the finding of certain golden plates by one Joseph Smith, jr., a young man of that neighborhood. Cowdery and I, as well as others, talked about the matter, but at that time I paid but little attention to it, supposing it to be only the idle gossip of the neighborhood. Cowdery said he was acquainted with the Smith family, and he believed that there must be some truth in the story of the plates, and that he intended to investigate the matter. I had conversations with several young men who said that Joseph Smith had certainly golden plates and that before he attained them he had promised to share with them, but had not done so and they were very much incensed with him. Said I, 'how do you know that Joe Smith has the plates?' They replied, 'we saw the plates in the hill that he took them out of just as he described it to us before he obtained them.' [place (not the plates) from which the plates were taken just as he described them to us before he obtained them.] These parties were so positive in their statements that I began to believe there must be some foundation for the stories then in circulation all over that part of the country. I had never seen any of the Smith family up to that time, and I began to inquire of the people in regard to them, and learned that one night during the year 1827 Joseph Smith, jr., had a vision, and an angel of God appeared to him and told him where certain plates were to be found, and pointed out the spot to him, and that shortly afterward he went to that piece and found the plates which were still in his possession. After thinking over the matter for a long time, and talking with Cowdery, who also gave me a history of the finding of the plates, I went home, and after several months Cowdery told me he was going to Harmony, Pa.—whither Joseph Smith had gone with the plates on account of persecutions of his neighbors—and see him about the matter. He did go and on his way stopped at my father's house and told me that as soon as he found out anything either

TRUTH OR UNTRUTH

he would let me know. After he got there he became acquainted with Joseph Smith, and shortly after, wrote to me telling me that he was convinced that Smith had the records and that he (Smith) had told him that it was the will of heaven that he (Cowdery) should be his scribe to assist in the translation of the plates. He went on and Joseph translated from the plates and he wrote it down. Shortly after this Cowdery wrote me another letter in which he gave me a few lines of what they had translated, and he assured me that he knew of a certainty that he had a record of a people that inhabited this continent, and that the plates they were translating gave a complete history of these people. When Cowdery wrote me these things and told me that he had revealed knowledge concerning the truth of them I showed these letters to my parents, and brothers and sisters. Soon after I received another letter from Cowdery, telling me to come down to Pennsylvania and bring him and Joseph to my father's house, giving me a reason therefore that they had received a commandment from God to that effect. I went down to Harmony, and found everything just as they [Cowdery] had written me. The next day after I got there they packed up the plates [did not say "packed up the plates"] and we proceeded on our journey to my father's house where we arrived in due time, and the day after we [he, Smith] commenced upon the translation of the remainder of the plates. I, as well as all of my father's family, Smith's wife, Oliver Cowdery, and Martin Harris were present during the translation. [I did not wish to be understood as saying that those referred to as being present were all the time in the immediate presence of the translator, but were at the place and saw how the translation was conducted.][1] . . .

When Joseph first received the plates he translated 116 pages of the book of 'Lehi,' with Martin Harris as scribe. When this had been completed they rested for a time, and Harris wanted to take the manuscript home with him to show to his family and friends. To this Joseph demurred, but finally

ASKED THE LORD

if Harris might be allowed to take it. The answer was 'no.' Harris teased Joseph for a long time and finally persuaded him to ask the Lord a second time, pledging himself to be responsible for its safe keeping. To this second inquiry the Lord told Joseph Harris he might take the manuscript,

---

[1] It is difficult to know what David Whitmer meant when he said that he and others saw how the translation was conducted. Probably David Whitmer did not actually see Joseph Smith translate but was near the Prophet during the translation of part of the Book of Mormon. I have retained in this selection David Whitmer's opinion concerning the method or possibly a method (if different methods were used) of the translation.

which he did, showing it to a great many people, but through some carelessness allowed it to be stolen from him. This incurred the Lord's displeasure, and he sent an angel to Joseph demanding the plates, and until Joseph had thoroughly repented of his transgressions would not allow him to have the use of them again. When Joseph was again allowed to resume the translation the plates were taken care of by a messenger of God, and when Joseph wanted to see the plates this messenger was always at hand. The 116 pages of the book of 'Lehi' which were stolen were never recovered nor would the Lord permit Joseph to make a second translation of it.

[It is my understanding that the seer stone referred to was furnished when he commenced translating again after losing the 116 pages. My statement was and now is that in translating he put the seer stone in his hat and putting his face in his hat so as to exclude the light and that then the light and characters appeared in the hat together with the interpretation which he uttered and was written by, the scribe and which was tested at the time as stated.]

"A few months after the translation was completed, that is, in the spring of 1830, Joseph had the book published and this (showing a well worn volume) is a copy of the first edition which I have had in my possession ever since it was printed."

"When did you see the plates?"

"It was in the latter part of June, 1829. Joseph, Oliver Cowdery and myself were together, and the angel showed them to us. We not only saw the plates of the book of Mormon, but he also showed us the brass plates of the book of Ether and many others. They were shown to us in this way. Joseph and Oliver and I were

SITTING ON A LOG

when we were overshadowed by a light more glorious than that of the sun. In the midst of this light but a few feet from us appeared a table upon which were many golden plates, also the sword of Laban and the directors. I saw them as plain as I see you now, and distinctly heard the voice of the Lord declaiming that the records of the plates of the Book of Mormon were translated by the gift and the power of God."

"Who else saw the plates at this time?"

"No one. Martin Harris, the other witness, saw them the same day and the eight witnesses, Christian Whitmer, Hiram Page, Jacob Whitmer, Joseph Smith, sr., Peter Whitmer, jr., Hyram Smith, Jno. Whitmer and Samuel H. Smith saw them next day."

"Did you see the angel?"

"Yes, he stood before us. Our testimony as recorded in the Book of Mormon is absolutely true, just as it is written there."

"Can you describe the plates?"

"They appeared to be of gold, about six by nine iches in size, about as thick as parchment, a great many in number and bound together like the leaves of a book by massive rings passing through the back edges. The engraving upon them was very plain and of very curious appearance. Smith made facsimilies of some of the plates, and sent them by Martin Harris to Profs. Anson and Mitchell, of New York city, for examination. They pronounced the characters reformed Egyptian, but were unable to read them."

"Did Joseph Smith ever relate to you the circumstances of his

FINDING THE PLATES?"

"Yes; he told me that he first found the plates in the early spring of 1828; that during the fall of 1827 he had a vision,[2] an angel appearing to him three times in one night and telling him that there was a record of an ancient people deposited in a hill near his fathers house called by the ancients 'Cumorah,' situated in the township of Manchester, Ontario county N. Y. The angel pointed out the exact spot and some time after he went and found the records or plates deposited in a stone box in the hill just as had been described to him by the angel. It was some little time, however, before the angel would allow Smith to remove the plates from their place of deposit."

"When was the church first established?"

"We had preaching during the time the book was being translated but our church was not regularly organized until after the book was printed in the winter of 1829-30. The first organization was in Seneca county, New York, under the name of 'The Church of Christ.' The first elders were Joseph Smith, Oliver Cowdery, Martin Harris, Hyrum Smith, Jno. Whitmer, Peter Whitmer and myself. On the 6th of April, 1830 the church was called together and the elders acknowledged according to the laws of New York. Our instructions from the Lord were to teach nothing

---

[2]David Whitmer erred regarding the date of Moroni's first appearance and neglected to correct the date in his revisions. When the article was reprinted in the *Millennial Star* the account was corrected to read "He [Joseph Smith] first found the plates in the year 1823; that during the fall of 1823 he had a vision, an angel appearing to him three times in one night." *MS* 43 (1881):437.

except the old and new testaments and the Book of Mormon. From that time the church spread abroad and multiplied very rapidly . . . .

The reported copied the following certificate of the standing of Mr. Whitmer in the community, among his papers, and obtained his permission to use it. It shows the character of the man, and adds to the value of his statement given above.

We, the undersigned citizens of Richmond, Ray county, Mo, where David Whitmer, sr. has resided since the year A. D. 1838, certify tht we have been long and intimately acquainted with him, and know him to be a man of the highest integrity, and of undoubted truth and veracity.

Given at Richmond, Mo, this March 19, A. D. 1881.

A. W. Doniphan

Geo. W. Dunn, judge of the Fifth Judicial circuit.

T. D. Woodson, president of Ray County Savings bank.

J. T. Child, editor of *Conservator*.

H. C. Garner, cashier of Ray County Savings bank.

W. A. Holman, county treasurer.

J. S. Hughes, banker, Richmond.

James Hughes, banker, Richmond.

D. P. Whitmer, attorney at law.

Jas. W. Black, attorney at law.

L. C. Cantwell, postmaster, Richmond.

Geo. I. Wasson, mayor.

Jas. A. Davis, county collector.

C. J. Hughes, probated judge and presiding justice of Ray county court.

Geo. W. Trigg, county clerk.

W. W. Mosby, M. D.

Thos. McGinnis, ex-sheriff Ray county.

J. P. Quensenberry, merchant.

W. R. Holman, furniture merchant.

Lewish Slaughter, recorder of deeds.

Geo. W. Buchanan, M. D.

A. K. Reyburn.

This ended the interview and after bidding the old man adieu and thanking him for his kindness the writer took his leave.

Index

Methodist church, 23, 27
Methuselah, 34
Missouri, 141, 142, 162
Mitchill, Samuel Latham, 60, 67, 80, 82
Moredock, Esquire, 13
Mormon, 34, 41, 61
Morning Courier and Enquirer (New York), 68
Moroni, 33, 34, 35, 38-50, 55, 68, 82, 114, 115, 126, 166, 178
Moses, 34, 113
Murdock, Samuel, 146

Nauvoo, Ill., 2, 35, 142, 143
Nebuchadnezzar, 89
Neibaur, Alexander, 19
New England, 142
New York, 1, 8, 13, 17, 69, 142, 199
New York City, N.Y., 58, 59, 61, 66, 67, 79, 80, 81, 82
New York *Spectator*, 19
New Hampshire, 2
Noah, 34
Norwich, Vt., 11, 13

Ohio, 142, 143
Ontario County, N.Y., 12, 47

Painesville, Ohio, 65
Page, Hiram, alienated from Church, 135; examines plates, 160; testimony of, by others, 161, 164
Palmyra, N.Y., 1, 11, 13, 15, 16, 22, 47, 58, 64, 66, 72, 77, 80, 83, 86, 125, 145, 170, 171, 176, 177, 178, 184, 185
Palmyra *Reflector*, 173, 174, 176
Parker, Dr., 7
Partridge Edward, 129
Paul, Apostle, 28
Peck, Electa, 193, 194
Pennsylvania, 66, 78, 79, 83, 89, 92, 182, 183
Perkins, Cyrus, Dr., 7
Peter, James, and John, 56, 110, 111, 113-15, 131
Philadelphia, Pa., 58
Pierce, Willard, 14

Pratt, Orson, 3, 19, 35, 68; on Joseph's visions, 30-32, 41, 55-56, 82-83; on Joseph's education, 30; on Joseph's move to Pennsylvania, 78-79; on Book of Mormon witnesses, 166-68; on testimony, 199-200
Pratt, Parley P., 98, 99, 141
Presbyterian church, 22, 23, 24, 27, 134, 145, 195

Reorganized Church of Jesus Christ of Latter Day Saints, 172
Reformed church, 195
Rich, Charles C., 198, 199
Rich, Minerva, 199
Richmond Democrat, 147
Richmond, Mo., 135, 147, 163
Rigdon, John Wickliffe, 99
Rigdon, Sidney, 98, 99, 127n, 129
Rochester, N.Y., 72, 170
Rockwell, Orrin Porter, 189
Rosetta, Egypt, 61
Rosetta Stone, 61, 64
Royalton, Vt., 7, 14

Salem, Mass., 142
Salisbury, Katherine Smith, 12, 53, 70, 137n, 197
Salt Lake City, Ut., 140
Sharon, Vt., 1, 6
Satan, 25, 26, 45, 75, 92, 190-92, 194
Seer Stone, 84
Seneca County, N.Y., 121, 125, 129
Seymour, Mr., 193
Smith, Alvin, 12, 13, 53
Smith, Don Carlos, 12, 75, 76, 141, 161
Smith, Emma Hale, 57, 71, 79, 85, 86, 92, 93, 118, 121, 124, 172; marriage of, 54, 55; scribe, 94, 102, 117, 126; testimony of plates, 107; testimony of Book of Mormon, 126, 127
Smith, Ephraim, 7
Smith, Hyrum, 12, 15, 69, 75, 76, 102, 121, 185, 193; character of, 9; membership in Presbyterian church, 24, 134; persecution of, 133, 144; testimony of, by others, 139; church